I NEVER LEFT HOME

MARGARE

Poet, Feminist,
Revolutionary

I NEVER
LEFT
HOME

a memoir of time & place

RANDALL

Duke University Press
Durham and London
2020

Printed in the United States of America
on acid-free paper ∞
Designed by Aimee C. Harrison
Typeset in Garamond Premier Pro and Avenir by
Westchester Publishing Services

Library of Congress Cataloging-in-Publication Data
Names: Randall, Margaret, [date] author.
Title: I never left home : poet, feminist,
    revolutionary / Margaret Randall.
Description: Durham : Duke University Press, 2020. |
    Includes index.
Identifiers: LCCN 2019032709 (print)
LCCN 2019032710 (ebook)
ISBN 9781478006183 (hardcover)
ISBN 9781478007616 (ebook)
Subjects: LCSH: Randall, Margaret, 1936– | Authors,
    American—20th century—Biography. | Women
    political activists—Biography. | Women college
    teachers—Biography. | Jewish women authors—
    Biography.
Classification: LCC PS3535. A56277 Z465 2020
    (print)
LCC PS3535.A56277 (ebook) | DDC 818/.5403
    [B]—dc23
LC record available at https://lccn.loc.
    gov/2019032709
LC ebook record available at https://lccn.loc.gov/
    2019032710

Cover art: Photograph by Bud Schultz.

For my
great-grandchildren,
Guillermo Manuel Martín
and Emma Nahuí;
grandchildren,
Lía Margarita, Martín,
Daniel Pablo, Ricardo Sergio,
Sebastián, Juan, Luis Rodrigo,
Mariana, Eli, and Tolo;
children, **Gregory,**
Sarah, Ximena, and Ana;
and wife, Barbara.

THIS IS
WHAT I
REMEMBER.

CONTENTS

TO THOSE BORN LATER

You who will emerge from the flood
In which we have gone under
Bring to mind
When you speak of our failings
Bring to mind also the dark times
That you have escaped.

Changing countries more often than our shoes
We went through the class wars, despairing
When there was only injustice, no outrage.

And yet we realized:
Hatred, even of meanness
Contorts the features.
Anger, even against injustice
Makes the voice hoarse. O,
We who wanted to prepare the ground for friendship
Could not ourselves be friendly.

But you, when the time comes at last
When man is helper to man
Think of us
With forbearance.

—BERTOLT BRECHT

We have never been what we are,
the faces of our lives are not our own,
the voices that you hear, the voices that
   have spoken so loudly above the storm
are not our own,
nothing you have seen is true,
nothing we have done is true,
we are entirely different.

—VICTOR SERGE

Those who do not move, do not notice their chains.

—ROSA LUXEMBURG

Chapter One

HOW THIS
BOOK
CAME TO BE

For those coming into adulthood long after the events that shaped my life, let me begin by saying that I was born in 1936. My parents moved my siblings and me from a suburb of New York City to New Mexico in 1947, where I began falling in love with the high desert landscape. From an early age I knew I wanted to be a writer. McCarthyism cast a pall on my consciousness, although I was too young to understand that or how. Despairing of college, which I found dull in mid-twentieth-century America, I returned to New York to seek out communities of other creative people. As a young single mother with a son, I traveled to Mexico, then Cuba and Nicaragua, places where social change exploded with exuberant promise. I lived in Latin America for twenty-three years, participating in and witnessing great political upheavals. I moved in and out of other relationships and gave birth to three more children. In 1984 I came home.

Back in the land of my birth, I waged a successful five-year battle against deportation, recognized my lesbian identity, and retrieved a long-buried memory of incest at the hands of my maternal grandparents. What I endured personally and when and where I lived allowed me to make important connections between the private and public spheres: the invasion of a child's body by someone with power shared important similarities with the invasion of a small country by a more powerful one; even the victims' responses are comparable. Propelled by civil rights, the American war in Vietnam, and eventually a feminism that helped me develop a gender analysis of society, I have worked for social justice wherever I've been. And I did become a writer—I think of myself first and foremost as a poet, essayist, oral historian, and translator—having published more than one hundred books in those genres (I include a list in an appendix at the end of this memoir).

The idea of a memoir is complicated. We may be moved to publish one too early in life. Emphasize the wrong things. Say too much or too little. Or wait so long that memory itself begins to fray. We may give in to another's plea for censorship or censor ourselves, include what is better left unsaid or omit what is most important, bore our readers and embarrass some of them.

This time around, I started by writing about my years among the abstract expressionist painters in New York City. I'd long thought of the 1960s as an era that has been misunderstood or misrepresented: depoliticized, trivialized, reduced to drugs and scandal. Within that context and compared with the earlier exponents of social realism, most historians have portrayed the abstract expressionists as apolitical. I hoped to be able to create a memoir in which time and place were the central protagonists and, in so doing, return cultural and political identity to the time about which I was writing.

At eighty-three, my memory is diminished. I've forgotten people and events or the order in which some events took place. After writing an advanced draft of my time in New York City, I continued with the decade in Mexico, including my clandestine escape to Cuba. Chronologically, that Caribbean country came next. I'd already written a memoir of my life on the island, though, and wondered what I might add. As my current assessment superimposed itself on the previous book, I realized I did have more to say.

After Cuba came Nicaragua, and that's where I hit a wall of posttraumatic stress. Increasing anxiety as the Contra war heated up seems to have erased many of the details of my years among the Sandinistas. I also may retain some residual guilt about having left my comrades in a situation of intensifying war. It was difficult for me to get more than a general outline of that chapter on paper. I kept returning to my storyline though and, to my relief, when on a reading trip to New York and staying at my daughter Ana's house, I was able to break through the writer's block and the experience began flowing back. Ana and I didn't talk about Nicaragua on that visit, but she was the child who accompanied me there, so perhaps some osmosis was involved.

While Nicaragua was on hold, I'd moved farther back again. I'd begun thinking about what it had been like to be a young woman in a provincial southwestern US city during the suffocating 1950s. Toward the end of the twenty-first century's second decade, women in this country and others have developed new forms of resistance, and #MeToo has enjoyed some dramatic successes as well as dangerous backlash. We would be wrong to think we've dealt with patriarchy, although we have made an important breakthrough. But during my adolescence and young adulthood, we were imprisoned by a cruel conditioning. Individual girls and women broke free from time to time, but collective consciousness and movement was still a long way off.

The Brett Kavanaugh congressional confirmation hearings showed how frightened the power structure continues to be of anything resembling gender equality.[1] It was dispiriting to observe the similarities between the treatment of Dr. Christine Blasey Ford and that of Anita Hill three decades earlier. I wanted to write about my experiences coming of age in the 1950s because I don't believe any woman not old enough to have lived through that time can imagine the spirit-killing degradation. From my high school years, I continued going back in time as far as memory and family lore allowed.

In the midst of extending what started out as an essay about my time in New York City to a memoir covering my life to this point, a fortuitous event changed everything. I'd been telling a dear friend, Robert Schweitzer, about my project. He reminded me that twenty years earlier I'd sent him a 607-page memoir. In manuscript form, it had never found a publisher. "You must have a copy," he said. I didn't. What's more, I had no memory of having written such a manuscript. I still don't. Robert lives in Italy and offered to send me his copy via the postal service. I didn't want to trust what may have been the only existent text to the mail, so my friend scanned every one of those 607 pages and sent them to me digitally, in batches of forty to sixty. I downloaded and printed each JPEG image. When we were done, I had a very thick loose-leaf binder filled with an enormous book written twenty years before and containing details I could not have accessed without Robert's generosity. In the memoir you are reading, I've preferred to go with today's version of my life—the places I've lived, people I've known, events I've been part of, and how I remember each—but that earlier text helped me fill in some of the blanks.

In almost every instance I've decided to use people's real names rather than disguise them with pseudonyms. I want to pay tribute to those who walked briefly in my life as well as to those who have enriched it significantly. Each was important in weaving the whole. Naming them is part of making their story one that belongs to us all. I hope they will feel well represented, or at least not misrepresented, and I thank them for our relationships, short-lived or enduring.

Poems and quotes from others are springboards to the book as a whole and to these chapters. Throughout, I've also inserted poems of my own, particularly when they reflect a moment about which I'm writing; I still include some of these in my public readings. And I've reproduced photographs that often speak louder than words.

I want to express my deepest gratitude to Greg Smith for urging me to write about New York; to my wife, Barbara, and my friend V. B. Price for listening to chapters or parts of chapters and making valuable suggestions; to John Randall, Sabra Moore, and Rita Pomade for important input; and to my son, Gregory, who read the entire book and offered a critical view that saved me from what would have been some embarrassing omissions and errors. My editor, Gisela Fosado, took to the project with her usual enthusiasm. Many other professionals at the publishing house worked hard to make this a better book. Duke's two blind reviewers also made comments that helped me produce a more coherent narrative. Thanks to all.

The foregoing explains the mechanics of this memoir. A need to explore feelings and historical periods explains the texture. I am fortunate to have lived at a time, been in places, and taken the risks that shaped me. I am privileged to have interacted with people central to that history.

Chapter Two

WHERE IT ALL STARTED

Before My Birth
and the Early Years,
1936–1947

All grown-ups were once children . . .
but only few of them remember it.
—ANTOINE DE SAINT-EXUPERY, *THE LITTLE PRINCE*

Coming from somewhere, discovering destination as I move. This has been my modus operandi, the way I've constructed my life.

I go back now, bringing up moments, images, faces, a hazy scene or isolated gesture. What the temperature of a room felt like. How a person or place smelled. The modulation of seasons. At eighty-three, I am certain of where I've been. But the connective tissue, while more meaningful, is beginning to thin. It stretches and fragments as time passes, leaving islands of experience— too often devoid of continuity. Before memory fades completely, I have a few things I want to say.

I want to do more than showcase a singular journey. None of us are separate. I hope in these pages to reproduce the meaning and feelings of a particular era, what its cultures, politics, and textures were. How our time and place embraced or failed to embrace us. How we embraced them and with what expectations, desires, hopes.

What of all that was passed on to me was I able to use? If I had absorbed it in a different way, would I more easily have recognized the signs, more deliberately crafted my ideas and actions? What mistakes did I make and why? Who was I among my contemporaries, and why did we as a group make the choices we did? What did we believe in? What do I believe in still?

I remember someone who entered my life, stayed a while, then receded. I try to recapture how important he seemed at the time. I begin to write about him and the next day come across his obituary. I grapple with another scene, a visit from someone else. I search for a way to render her in the fullness of then and have a chance encounter with her daughter. I have not seen mother or daughter in forty years. I learn the mother is still alive but failing. The baton has been passed. New knowledge layers upon old. Each turning enriches memory, which burns like sun.

....

A few decades back a woman's face began appearing in my dreams. Her dress and demeanor situated her in the late nineteenth century. I felt a great affinity for this woman, knew she was an ancestral sister, wondered about her life. I did not yet know her name but felt an intensity of kinship that suggested two-way recognition: not only me of her but also her of me, as if she'd been waiting for me to show up. As if a greater dream was dreaming us both. This woman seemed to be asking me something, hoping I might explore with her the questions left unanswered while she lived. She fought her way into several of my poems.

In the early 1990s I read one of those poems at Trinity College, where I was teaching in Hartford, Connecticut. A distant cousin on my mother's side attended the reading. This whole branch of our family had been a recent discovery for me; when I was ten, my family moved west, effecting an abrupt cutoff from our relatives in the east. My parents kept contact only with our grandparents and one uncle. Who provoked that separation? Did my parents break with the family members they'd left behind, or had those family members discarded my parents? And, if so, why?

I am still searching for answers to these questions and for the people who can provide them. In Hartford, toward the end of my nine-year visiting professorship at Trinity, I discovered Tony Keller, Andrea Miller-Keller, and their family. That included elderly Charles Keller, still a card-carrying member of the US Communist Party: quite a surprise to find him in my mother's otherwise conservative clan. Through these people I met others. That night, after the aforementioned reading, the distant cousin approached: "I know who the

Hannah Pollack, author's great-great-aunt (photo taken in 1897 at a professional studio, precise attribution unknown).

woman in your dream is," she said, "and I must tell you there's a striking resemblance. Your ancestor's name was Hannah Pollack."

A few days later Jane Keller-Herzog brought me a photograph taken a hundred years earlier. October 19, 1897. In the studio portrait Hannah looks to be in her forties or early fifties. Faint lines at the outer edges of her eyes betray an otherwise youthful complexion. Her hair is parted in the middle over an unusually broad forehead and pulled back into what must have been a bun or twist, revealing large but delicate ears. She has heavy brows, like mine, which threaten to merge in an unbroken line. Her eyes are expressive, her nose large and aquiline, her lips thin—the top one slightly crooked as is my own.

Hannah is dressed in a plain but representative garment of the era: high collar, puffed shoulders, shirred bodice. Hannah Pollack, sister of Aaron Davidson, might have been my twin, so physically alike are we. Aaron Davidson was my maternal grandfather's father. Hannah Pollack was his sister, my great-great aunt.

....

MY LOPSIDED GRIMACE

You were surprised when I said she lies beside me
in this bed we share.
You'd never noticed
and I hadn't thought to introduce her

but you must know
she is with me
from before I learned her name and since.

Her photograph my hologram
on this generational journey,
her face my connection to ancestors,
Hannah Pollack, lost and found,
proud chin over high-collared shirtwaist
center-parted hair
pulled back from expansive brow.

Clear eyes side-stepping the camera's lens
full cheeks
and large straight nose
above thin lips
where I recognize my lopsided grimace
born of this arduous attempt
at normalcy.

Flying below the radar yet soaring
on our terms:
we women out of sync
with the sordid demands
of those who would prune our branches
to Bonsai trim
or erase us entirely.

She in her pre-equality time, me in my now,
how we clamor
to make it to the end,
scaling the shoulders
of sisters who lift and pull,
sucking wisdom from their marrow
as we go.

....

Both my parents were from families where money spoke. In my father's it spoke the complicated language of the self-made immigrant Jew. Dad's father came to New York from somewhere near Munich in southern Germany, long before the desperate waves of those fleeing mid-twentieth-century European fascism. Albert Reinthaler arrived with $16 in his pocket and shortly after his arrival shortened his surname to Reinthal. This, at least, is the story handed down from generation to generation and repeated throughout my childhood. My paternal grandfather made a fortune from co-ownership of a factory that reproduced Currier & Ives prints, Maxfield Parrish's whimsical maidens on swings, fanciful images popular in that era. They became greeting cards, calendar art, the covers of expensive candy boxes. He died before I was born.

My father's family fortune was real wealth. It defined those grandparents' circumstances, which were also shaped by the fact that they were Jewish and so unable to rise to their adopted country's inner circles of social or political power. Albert Reinthal died of a heart attack in his fifties. It was said that the market crash of 1929 did him in. Family lore says he "lost everything." I don't believe the crash was solely to blame for his death, though, or that he really lost everything.

My father spoke of his father as a man of great rigidity, unable to talk to his sons, someone for whom a ten-dollar bill beneath a child's pillow often took the place of praise or a hug. No one alive today can tell me what my grandfather's childhood was like. The phrase "he lost everything" didn't really seem to apply, because they still lived well. Which is why I judge him to have produced a fortune of some sort. I remember a large armchair in my grandmother's apartment. A broad satin ribbon crossed it diagonally. In deference to his memory, no one was to sit there.

The full-floor apartment on Park Avenue exuded a musty elegance. Leather-bound first editions lined dark wooden shelves along one living room wall, their gold-embossed spines arranged not according to subject matter or author but size. These were Book of the Month Club selections, purchased for show. My grandmother Nana Daisy's reading of choice was *Reader's Digest*. Her little square bedside table always held a few copies.

In that apartment, tapestries hung like thick padding against the outside world. Satin sachets were tucked in clothes closets and nestled in underwear drawers, exuding a scent that still evokes my paternal grandmother for me. A heavy oil painting, portrait of a stern matriarch from an earlier generation, leaned slightly forward on the wall above the dining room table. Its angle seemed threatening to the child me. There, at Wednesday night dinners I was quietly instructed not to drink from the finger bowls.

That apartment's kitchen is the room I would most like to revisit. I remember it as dull cream and pale green with glass-doored cabinets and a waxed linoleum floor. It was the domain of Agnes, Nana Daisy's Irish Catholic maid. Did she cook kosher? I recall vague allusions, but also know that this family was not especially religious and that Daisy frequented New York's impressive Temple Emanuel only on high holidays. In her later years not even then. I can't imagine that Agnes separated meat from dairy.

Daisy's Jewishness was inherited, a point of reference, more cultural than faith-based. Agnes once secretly hustled me off to her own church, St. Ignatius Loyola, where I marveled at the saint's thighbone encased in a small glass box. Later Agnes was suddenly forced from my grandmother's employ when, after years of faithful service, she dared sit one morning on the edge of the old lady's bed instead of on the little stool placed beside it for that purpose. She was taking dictation for the day's marketing list. My Nana Daisy fired her for disrespect.

Although a reputation for ostentation and vague ignorance defined her, my own memories of Nana Daisy are linked to the joys of childhood. She took me to my first Broadway shows, musicals such as *Peter Pan*, *Guys and Dolls*, *West Side Story*, and *The King and I*. She invited me to New York the Christmas following my fifteenth birthday, which coincided with a great blizzard and thousands of troops coming home from Korea for the holidays.

Planes were grounded from Chicago east. I had to switch to a train, where I shared salami sandwiches with friendly soldiers on leave who must have found my pseudosophistication amusing. I arrived in the city thirty hours late, to the immense relief of my grandmother, who was beside herself with worry. That was the only time I saw my Nana Daisy without her hairpiece, a marcel wave she wore to hide a bald spot from temple to temple.

When I was a bit older, sixteen or seventeen, I received a mouton coat from that grandmother. My parents thought it inappropriate, but I was captivated by its elegance. Eventually I must have sold that coat, as I later sold the single strand of oriental pearls and small gold brooch she left me when she died. I do remember walking into Tiffany's—the store name embossed on the narrow oblong box that held those pearls—uncomfortable and out of place in my bohemian attire. I was shocked when a clerk, grabbing the opportunity, offered me $18 for both the necklace and small cameo of a woman's face etched on ivory in a setting that included ruby and sapphire chips in dulled gold. This would have been at the end of the 1950s. I took the money and spent it on food.

....

Albert Reinthal Sr. and his wife, my Patrician-looking, pampered, enormously heavy, and lavender-scented grandmother, Daisy Heavenrich, had three sons. The oldest, Edward, followed his father into business. I think he had a knife factory. My parents spoke disparagingly of Edward and his wife, Mabel; they weren't intellectual enough for Mother. Still, Mom and Dad left me at their home in Larchmont, New York, for a week or two when they traveled to Mexico in the mid-1940s. I remember being fascinated by a laundry chute in their upstairs bathroom. Down and out of sight and mind slid my badly soiled panties after I'd ingeniously rid myself of the huge turd they'd contained behind some bushes in Edward and Mabel's yard.

Albert Jr., the middle son, was always spoken of as "different." The word and tone of voice implied "not quite right." During his college years he'd come down with encephalitis, popularly known as sleeping sickness back then. He never again held a job or did anything very specific. When I knew him, Albert lived with his mother and every Sunday rode his beloved horse, Dusty Boy, in Central Park.

I was eighteen when Nana Daisy died. A few weeks after the funeral, family members and friends received small engraved cards: Albert announced his marriage to Jean, his devoted riding partner of twenty years. No one had been aware of Jean's existence. It may have been that Albert didn't mention her because she wasn't Jewish, nor of the social status so important to his mother. Jean worked as a secretary. The fact that a middle-aged man would delay his happiness so as not to incur his mother's disapproval shows how deeply engrained those values were. The newlyweds were in their fifties. They held hands, looked lovingly into one another's eyes, and made a shared life until his death in 1983. We stopped hearing from Jean some years later.

During my years in New York, Albert and Jean were my only relatives who befriended me. They weren't put off by my lifestyle. I visited them at their sunny apartment on Madison Avenue, a startling contrast to my grandmother's large mahogany-paneled and heavily draped Park Avenue place. Once Albert and Jean even came down to my Lower East Side walkup to babysit my son.

....

I remember another relative whose life was even more devastatingly shaped by our family's class snobbery and lack of compassion. She was Marjorie, an aunt or cousin on my mother's side. When her name was mentioned, it was invariably paired with the label "nymphomaniac." The onus was on her. My elders whispered that she seduced doormen, taxi drivers, guys she met on the street, whoever would have her.

There was never any talk about what caused Marjorie to seek such liaisons. Even as a teenager, I wondered what had happened to cause those proclivities. What had her childhood been like? Could some person or event have caused her to be the way she was? Now I ask what male entitlement went unmentioned and unpunished while she paid the price of its pain? In and out of mental institutions, Marjorie nonetheless seemed a lovely woman. During my young adulthood and until she died, we occasionally corresponded. Her letters, with their careful penmanship on monogrammed stationery, displayed a wide range of interests.

....

My father, born in 1906, was the youngest of his siblings. After two boys, his parents hoped for a girl. And so, they simply pretended, pretense being typical of those families. I have photographs of Dad at age six, wearing an elaborate white dress, his long blond curls fastened with a large satin bow. Whatever the reasons—it was never easy for my father to talk about his childhood; it seemed elusive even to him—his preschool representation was clearly female. I don't think he wanted to remember. Of his parents he generously said: "They did the best they knew how."

What I know is that my father grew up loving music and sports. He struggled through the University of Pennsylvania's Wharton School of Business because that was where his father sent him and expected him to excel. My grandfather's monied influence carried him through graduation and beyond.

Sixty years later, not long before he succumbed to Alzheimer's, Dad grappled with words that wouldn't come: "Pass . . ." he said, over and over. My brother and I leaned over his nursing-home bed, eager to understand what he was trying to tell us. "Made me . . . pass." A long silence, and there they were again: the word *made*, the word *pass*. Just before we gave up, Johnny and I finally got it. Our father was gratefully remembering that long-ago moment when someone—it must have been his father—had arranged it so that he would be able to get a college degree. Perhaps he saw that as having been his ticket to a happy life.

At the University of Pennsylvania, Dad was part of a sculling crew. He swam and boxed. And he played the cello. None of those loves were deemed appropriate as career choices, though. Not in a family in which a German Jewish immigrant past had been Americanized through successful business careers. I try to imagine those family's longings, the measure by which success or even happiness was gauged, at a time when quotas prevented Jews from attending the better universities and supporting his family was a man's first responsibility. Making it through the Wharton School must have been considered key to the next generation's assimilation.

Dad tried one small retail venture after another, always failing, inevitably having to be bailed out by his concerned parents. He had no head for numbers and genuinely cared about his customers, qualities that proved an impediment to success. When I was six or seven, he had a tiny pipe and tobacco shop in the Wall Street district of Lower Manhattan. Sometimes he would take me there on Saturdays. We would ride the commuter train into the city and I would help him with one thing or another, ingratiate myself with his customers, feel very grown up and deeply loved. That was the thing about Dad: his children absolutely knew he loved us.

For lunch he would crumble saltines into a bowl of Campbell's alphabet soup, which we shared. On the train home we would talk about all sorts of things. I asked questions I would remember for a lifetime: why a green light stops pedestrians but sends automobiles on their way, what makes water freeze, why a feather doesn't fall as fast as a rubber ball. My father would circle my shoulder with his arm as he explained those answers he knew. Or he would say he wasn't sure, but we would find out together. He was my protector, teacher, encouragement, support. I owe him what self-confidence I have. Somehow a man who was a misfit in his family of origin—passive, timid, deeply afraid of authority, and unsatisfied in many areas of his own life—managed to give his children a solid store of love and emotional support.

Long after the pipe shop closed, my parents kept using its huge roll of ugly green and white holiday gift-wrapping paper each time Christmas came around. Mother and Dad rarely threw anything away. They carefully removed, folded, and saved the wrapping paper from others' gifts, paper clips and rubber bands, restaurant napkins, string. You never know when it will come in handy, they said.

Dad had other jobs in those early years, each as dissatisfying as its predecessor. One was at Lord & Taylor, where he worked in the men's department. By this time, he was a simple salesman, a position in which he would at least not lose money although he couldn't have earned very much. His mother continued to provide some inherited income.

....

I must also talk about my grandparents on my mother's side. Knowing what I know now makes it difficult for me to evoke them as I perceived them in my childhood. Will the pain keep me from minimal objectivity? Will it make me say too much? Or can there be such a thing as objectivity when attempting to move back through layers of shredded consciousness? My maternal grandparents were complicated. Perverse is the word that comes to mind, and their perversions would have a lasting effect on me.

Where money spoke the language of cultural but only casually religious Judaism on my father's side of the family, on my mother's its vocabulary was narrower, more deceitful, often insidious. It would take a book to explore the Davidsons' smug rhetoric and dark secrets, the proper exterior hiding an abuse I still struggle to unravel. If our class and culture allow it, we all construct the way we present ourselves to the world; to varying degrees we choose who we want to be. It wasn't unusual in the early decades of the past century for American Jews to try to divest themselves of an uncomfortable, perhaps dangerous, identity. That pretense never resonated with me, though. I preferred looking reality in the face and standing with the oppressed.

My grandfather DeWitt A. Davidson was Jewish but spent a lifetime trying to escape that heritage. I think the self-hating anti-Semitism that would become such a shadowy presence in our lives must have begun with him. He married Josephine Lehman, a niece in the Isaac Sanger clan. The Sangers were also Jewish and also had emigrated from Germany in the late nineteenth century. Each of several brothers worked to bring over the next in age. They eventually settled in Dallas, Texas, where Sanger Brothers department store brought wealth to successive generations.

DeWitt and Josephine stayed in New York. My grandfather was the iconic ladies' man. He was tall and good-looking in a dandy but refined sort of way, elegant of manner, soft-spoken. Self-absorption passed as wisdom. He wore three-piece suits, got regular manicures, shopped at Abercrombie & Fitch, and collected cameras, socks, wrenches, and screwdrivers, most of which he never removed from their wrappers. Hundreds of these unopened items were found among his things when he died.

As a young man DeWitt was said to have traveled the country, working for a time as a ranger in one of the newly designated national parks. Guns were a part of his story, and large thoroughbred dogs. Later he continued traveling, selling precious gems and jewelry settings. I'm not sure if he designed those settings or retailed them from a wholesaler. His frequent trips undoubtedly allowed him to keep the proverbial woman in every port.

My maternal grandfather married a woman who coped with her considerable frustration through a cultivated attitude of self-indulgent martyrdom. Mother told me that she had played the violin as a young woman but gave it up when she married. They were quite a pair, those grandparents, each vying for the other's—and the world's—attention. He had patriarchy on his side, a beguiling manner and position as head of household, his deals and perversions obscured by class, gender, and cultural privilege. While he easily assumed his male freedom, she was reduced to whining and rolling her eyes.

No one seems quite sure how DeWitt Davidson made his money. Some say at least part of it came from other family members he convinced to lend him large sums and who, for propriety's sake, never pursued his failure to pay them back. The Sangers also left what may have been a modest fortune to my mother, which her father simply claimed as his. He must have made something from designing and selling jewelry, but it couldn't have been enough to finance a lifestyle that knew few limits. When my mother confronted her father about having spent her Sanger inheritance, he began paying her back at the rate of $100 a month. He never came close to erasing that debt.

How DeWitt Davidson spent his money is a matter of easier record. He always had the latest gadgets. His personal tastes were impeccable. When I was a child, he took me to an oyster bar; I always wondered how he imagined that a youngster of six or seven might enjoy sucking raw oysters from the half shell. Sometimes he took me to visit the Metropolitan Museum of Art, where we'd stop at the milk bar after viewing parts of its vast collection. I enjoyed those visits more.

My mother grew up in a mansion in Sea Cliff on Long Island, New York. There was shoreline and a greenhouse, a little boat landing, a gardener, and acres of trees. Once, she remembered, her father bought one thousand small firs. Josephine, or Nana Jo as we called her, was forced to put up with her husband's wild extravagances, infidelities, flights of corruption, and obsessive desire. But she was also deviant. One family story has her having to sell eggs door-to-door to augment their domestic economy. They had a butler, chauffeur, and several other servants at the time, and I imagined her with her basket of eggs being driven around in the family Daimler-Benz.

Years later, when my mother was in her early eighties, my brother, sister, and I took her east to visit her childhood home. She'd talked about wanting to see it once more before she died. The most recent among the families who'd lived there since hers was that of William Casey, and the ex-CIA director's widow was still in residence. Sophia Casey was gracious and sweet, welcoming us into those rooms where our mother had spent such a memorable part of her youth. Mother recalled sliding down the long hall banister as a child. The design of the marble floors brought back a flood of stories. A sapling she remembered helping to plant now towered at the back of the house. I imagined her memory superimposing childhood scenes on each room as it looked now.

The Caseys had replaced whatever the Davidsons' decorating scheme may have been with Irish Catholic Baroque: pink shrines, ornate mirrors, carved crucifixes. My brother was fascinated by the books in Casey's enormous personal library: not a single novel or book of poetry, but history from the upper-class white male perspective and lots of titles on counterinsurgency. My sister photographed our mother making her way from room to room. I fought off asthma that day, images of Casey and his life's work layered upon images of my grandfather and what by then I knew he'd done to me. Terror all but closed my throat as Mother accepted the widow's invitation to stay for lunch.

After he lost or sold the Sea Cliff mansion, my maternal grandfather took his family into Manhattan. Legend describes this as a downward move, one of those "after he lost everything" stories. Not true, because the apartment they lived in at the Belnord, 225 West 86th Street, was ample and expensive. My mother's younger brother, also named DeWitt and eight years her junior, was born there.

Young DeWitt was named after his father. The only difference was that the older man was DeWitt A (for Aaron), the younger DeWitt S (for Stetson). A severe inner ear infection during the son's first months of life required a mastoid operation and the subsequent services of a convalescent nurse. That nurse led the family in an unexpected direction. She was a devout Christian Scientist. From then on and throughout my childhood, DeWitt Davidson the traveling salesman became DeWitt Davidson the Christian Science practitioner and finally DeWitt Davidson the Reader at New York's Second Church of Christ, Scientist. His new identity positioned him ever more confidently beyond his Jewish past.

Christian Science was made for someone like my grandfather. It appealed to his strange notions of cause and effect and provided a quasi-spiritual arena in which he was able to exercise control. Dreamy-eyed, he stopped drinking, even coffee and tea, but justified the beer he kept in his refrigerator by calling it *beah*. Now the women with whom he surrounded himself were his adoring patients, wealthy and grateful. And Christian Science allowed him to distance himself from any vestige of Jewishness.

Nana Jo, by virtue of her husband's new identity, also acquired another context in which to exercise her will. She could look up to him, important in his church, while continuing to whine and moan about his failures—not the least of which was that he never paid enough attention to her. Still, she was deeply hypochondriac and must have found it at least a little bit difficult to accept a philosophy that judged physical ills unreal. As a young woman, Josephine Lehman had been in a bad automobile accident, leaving her with chronic pain. She also complained, in whatever circumstance and to anyone who would listen, that her husband ignored her sexual needs. My Nana Jo had a habit of mentioning something of which she disapproved, then looking around the room to seek sympathy one by one in the eyes of each of those present. She invented new levels of petulance and nurtured self-importance and cruelty as if they were art forms.

I have memories of my grandfather reciting passages from Mary Baker Eddy's *Science and Health with Key to the Scriptures*. Or from the large black leather-bound St. James version of the Bible he always had at hand. During our years in the east, Grandpa would come to see us, his face flushed as he announced some miracle cure that he claimed to have wrought through prayer. Mother told me that when her father was dying, and she went to be with him in his last days, she offered to read to him from *Science and Health*. She thought it might give him comfort. Unable to speak, he angrily pushed the book away. She asked him then if he still believed. Weakly, he shook his head no. Had he ever believed? Who can say? More than philosophical certainty, in Christian Science he may have found a vehicle through which to wield power over others.

By the time I knew them, these grandparents lived in Tudor City, in a small midtown Manhattan apartment near the United Nations. The constipated neighborhood had a park for adults, another for children, and one just for dogs. DeWitt, the unmarried adult son, now lived a block away. Near enough so he could look in on his mother every day. He was devoted to her, even as she continued to destroy any sense of self he might have developed. My Uncle DeWitt worked as a travel agent, handling advertising accounts for several large steamship lines. He journeyed all over the world and drank excessively. No one back then talked about alcoholism. He once proudly told my mother that he was "gay but had never given into it."

This uncle and I never liked one another. I have vague memories of him touching me inappropriately as a child. Later he found my book about incest unacceptable, claiming I was ruining a good man's name.[1] When I recognized my lesbian identity, it made my uncle even more uncomfortable, perhaps because he had kept his own sexuality hidden and that had made him so unhappy. Of course, those were different times, when externalizing an alternative sexual identity was much more difficult. Somehow, toward the end of his life my uncle and I managed to make a truce of sorts. By then he had married a widower, the mother of my brother's first wife, and they'd moved to Albuquerque.

Nana Jo volunteered to sell greeting cards at the UNESCO shop in the lobby of the UN. She did this for years, while her husband prayed for the miracle healings of bodies, which he claimed were not composed of matter but only will and submission. When she retired as a volunteer, Mother told me her coworkers honored her at a dinner her husband refused to attend. He was too busy with that world of faith-healing in which he was the star. In my family we called my grandfather the Saint.

My grandmother was obsessed with enemas. I remember frequent stories in which they'd suddenly appear without any apparent connection to context. I try to remember how my mother reacted to this obsession but can't. I have no childhood recollection of my grandmother forcing enemas on me, but I know I was terrified of them by the time I was hospitalized to have my tonsils out, aged six or seven. This may simply have been an acceptable practice of the times, but my cellular memory tells me it was one of Nana Jo's numerous control mechanisms. She related to others best through manipulation.

And then there was the bedrock foreboding that always surrounded her. If you spilled something on a dress or sweater, Nana Jo's immediate and satisfied response was "You know, that will never come out!" I echo the phrase in similar situations to this day, but jokingly. My maternal grandmother was preoccupied with cleanliness and order. She would empty ashtrays before the smoker finished a cigarette and take advantage of a guest momentarily getting up from his or her seat to puff up the sofa cushions before that person sat down again.

Furniture played an interesting role in the dynamics between my parents and these grandparents. When we moved to New Mexico and they visited, I remember repeated scenes in which Nana Jo simply moved a couch or table, beaming at "how much better it looks over here." My mother or father, furious, would move it back. Those furniture wars may have started in the east, but I was too young to notice them there. Mother would complain, "I wish she'd leave my furniture alone," and Dad would second her: "She damn well better."

My maternal grandmother judged everything by how it affected her. When later, as a young woman living in New York City, I paid my grandparents a courtesy call without thinking to telephone first, it was reported to my parents as an intentional attempt to shock and frighten her. My vibrant blue-green eye shadow and black mesh stockings were clearly meant to insult her sensibilities. I could do no right in my grandparents' eyes, and soon stopped trying.

Yet not every memory involving my maternal grandparents is a bad one. There were the museum visits when I was a child, especially to the Metropolitan and to the Museum of Natural History. My first contact with the great cultures of Egypt and Greece, Rome and Ethiopia, date from those visits: I in my impeccable navy-blue coat with the little white Peter Pan collar holding tight to my grandfather's hand. At the Met, the Cellini cup made a deep impression, almost as great as Tutankhamen's gold funeral mask. I wrote my first story, at age six or seven, about stealing that cup from the museum. I laboriously hand-penciled it in several copies that I distributed around our Scarsdale neighborhood, pretending it was a newspaper.

I don't remember real newspapers being terribly important in my childhood home. Still, Nana Jo admired Eleanor Roosevelt and never failed to read her column "My Day."[2] My grandmother considered Mrs. Roosevelt a model of breeding and wisdom. I've often wondered what she might have thought of her idol had she known the full range of Eleanor's life and interests, her ability to set prejudice aside and the courage of her changing values, her work for justice beyond what her husband was able or willing to accomplish, her long-term intimate relationship with another woman. She might have continued to admire her, or at least claim she did. Nana Jo was at her best when applauding someone she would like to have emulated had she been endowed with a fraction of the other's integrity.

Not unlike my father's family of origin, my maternal grandparents' singular quality was their classism. I once heard Nana Jo mock a maid who only painted her thumbnails because the others remained unseen beneath the serving platter. Bad taste was offensive, imperfect diction or pronunciation something to be ridiculed, uncouthness a failing worse than almost any crime. Appearances counted far more than substance. Hypocrisy was intricately crafted.

I no longer remember whether it was my grandmother or mother who first told me, "You talk like a Brooklyn shop girl." This wasn't about bad grammar but code for a noticeable New York (Jewish) accent. In response, I am to this day the only member of my family to have retained the speech patterns of my youth. Perhaps an unconscious rejection of prejudice.

These, then, were my parents' parents. As with each new generation, Mother and Dad did their best to move beyond those strictures that inhibited them. And in their defense, I must say that they consistently defended me from my maternal grandparents' criticisms.

．．．

MOTHER AND THE MAC TRUCK

Mother sat erect, her hands firmly
grasping ten and two
and always drove
a good twenty miles slower
than the speed limit,

which is why in my dream
I was surprised
she was speeding
and swerving all over the road,
even onto its broken shoulder.

I tried to grab the wheel but she was
determined to make it
to the yellow stucco hospital—
a building like the old French ones
I saw in Hanoi, 1974.

She needed medication. I held
a lab envelope that may have
contained her shit
in the hand not concerned
with steadying the wheel.

She really confused me, though,
when she briefly became
a teenage delinquent male
I was trying to hide
from the police.

I smoothed his hair, tucked him
into bed and promised
I wouldn't let them get him.
He smiled gratefully, begging
over and over *please keep me safe.*

All I knew about the boy was
he'd stolen a Mac truck.
Then it was Mother
who'd stolen the truck
and the kid had a plan

to give it back. I woke thinking
my mother's shit shouldn't
have been too heavy for me to carry,
and Law and Order wreaks terror
everywhere in this New World Order.

....

I was born at Manhattan's Lenox Hill Hospital on December 6, 1936. The name on my birth certificate was Margaret Jo Reinthal, later changed to Randall. The Jo was for my maternal grandmother, Josephine, unfortunately a woman I disliked and feared. The attending physician was Mother's Uncle Harry Davidson, my grandfather's brother, whom I was told was the hospital's head of obstetrics.

Less than a year before, Mother had given birth to a daughter who died a few hours later. She always said it was as if she had been pregnant with me for eighteen months. Stories about this older sister changed over time. For years Mother said she too had been named Margaret, something about which I remember feeling uneasy—as if I had usurped another's name or identity. Later she changed her story. "No, of course not. How did you get that idea? You come up with the craziest things! Your sister didn't live long enough to have a name." That sort of shift was a constant in my family of origin. Some piece of information upon which I had come to depend would take a sudden turn or vaporize on Mother's lips.

In 1936, the year of my birth, the lynching of black men in the southern United States—and even in the North—was a common occurrence. It was only the most visible atrocity in a pattern of entrenched Jim Crow, affecting every black person and, whether or not they were conscious of it, the humanity of every white. A few whites were beginning to understand that they had to take a stand. The same year, the Association of Southern Women for the Prevention of Lynching had been endorsed by 35,000 southern white women. The 1930s saw an upsurge in people's struggles for equality, including interracial political organizations against anti-miscegenation laws and officialized

Author, 1941 (family snapshot, attribution unknown).

violence. The US Communist Party was legal and active. The Wobblies rode freight trains, spreading the doctrine of One Big Union and selling poetry pamphlets for a penny.

When I was young, I remember my father's pride in donating money to negro causes, as they were called back then. He contributed to the NAACP and United Negro College Fund, and frequently spoke to us about racial prejudice and how wrong it was. This was a moral question for my father, shared by my mother at least theoretically. Neither was able to internalize the struggle against racism, though, or work for antiracist causes. They had no friends who were nonwhite.

Anti-Semitism still kept Jews out of many US colleges and country clubs. This hit closer to home. My parents' response was to distance themselves from their Jewishness rather than identify with the oppressed. As I grew up, I acquired some consciousness about the issue and began to question them about the name change. They always began their response by pointing out the difference between race and religion. Judaism was a religion, they said, and since they didn't subscribe to it, they weren't Jews. I remember asking if Davidson, my maternal grandparents' surname, wasn't Jewish: son of David. My mother told me it was Scotch. "Your ancestors even have their own plaid," she said, as if to reinforce her argument. I'd ask if there were no Jews in Scotland and she would fall silent.

Others—Native Americans, Hispanics or Chicanos, Italians, Eastern Europeans, even the ethnically Irish—were absent from my childhood because "we just don't know any." Our neighborhoods were segregated, which meant our schools were as well. Race, economic status, and culture kept us apart. My parents' contact with people different from themselves was limited to those with whom they might come in contact in service jobs, and to the compartmentalization that even well-intentioned tolerance exudes. Much later, when we moved to New Mexico, Mother asked a Mexican American waitress whose face she thought exotic to pose for a clay bust.

As for gender or sexual politics, we were years away from articulating them. My mother didn't participate in the cheerful housewifely activities of her time, but her rejection of them was compelled by her always frustrated quest for satisfaction, translated into a self-centeredness and need for approval from others rather than any sort of gender consciousness. My father was not a dominant or domineering man. His innate kindness and generosity of spirit dictated he do more than his share of work around the house. I remember him washing dishes, running the washing machine, and vacuuming when no one else's father engaged in those tasks. Long before it was fashionable to speak of male/female roles, he was a model in this respect. But Dad never really questioned the traditional family structure. He had a salaried job; Mother stayed home.

Many years later, when Dad's children's children were born, he gifted the male grandchildren with insurance policies worth twice those he gave to the girls. The boys would have to take care of their wives, he explained; the girls would be taken care of by their husbands. As his daughter, I grew up feeling he encouraged me, while the model he provided aspired to solid all-American, upper-class, male-centered family values. Image contradicted words, providing one of the many mixed messages so endemic to our culture.

Homosexuality? Not a whisper to indicate it existed or might be an option. My Aunt Janet lived in Santa Fe with her lifelong partner, Phyllis. My parents were close to them both, but their lesbianism was never mentioned. When I finally asked, long after they were gone, Mother's response was "Well, we don't really know they were lesbians. They never said they were." Sexually I had no model but the traditional man/woman paradigm. My parents' marriage was painfully unhappy. On the outside, it was as close to perfection as they could make it look. On the inside, a soap opera of Mother's thinly veiled affairs and Dad's patient misery consumed us all.

....

My childhood spanned the Spanish Civil War, an uneasy prelude to World War II, and our country's postwar retreat into isolationism and paranoia. I didn't know about Spain's war; the conservative politics of both Mother's and Father's families kept that cause distant, suspect, exotic at best. The war in central Europe was more present in our lives. We were good Americans supporting our boys at the front. Dad genuinely felt the antifascist cause as his own. I have a dim memory of him opening a letter and reading about a distant relative annihilated in one of the Nazi concentration camps. He refolded the letter, returned it to its envelope, and sobbed. My father didn't cry often, but when he did it was open and unashamed.

I remember Franklin Roosevelt's death. It was a Saturday morning and I was glued to the radio listening to *Let's Pretend*, one of my favorite weekly shows. Suddenly classical music replaced the episode. A woman's voice said the president was dead. Mother, who was upstairs washing her hair, came to the railing of the small balcony overlooking our living room, parted the heavy muslin drapes, and looked down on me. I hold an image of a white towel fallen crookedly to my mother's shoulders, her strands of wet hair dripping, her tears. I was sad too. It seemed my favorite show would be cancelled for the week.

My childhood was pre-TV. Radio was a defining aspect of the culture. It marked those my age as the last generation challenged to develop our own imaginations about the characters we loved and what they looked like. We conjured visual images of radio protagonists, invented landscapes and interiors, were forced to engage our creativity in order to bring the events and relationships into focus. Radio is so much closer to reading than television is; it was as if we were being read to in voices. But imagination was needed to flesh out the experience. Today so much is flashed in readymade images, emoticons standing in for self-expression, brief texted messages or Twitter comments replacing the need to express oneself in one's own words.

In my family, after Roosevelt's death there was a lot of talk about the possible presidency of New York's governor, John Dewey. Dad said he'd done a great job "cleaning up New York." Truman might have been too working-class, too common for my parents. Their relationship to politics was like that. It depended largely on image, and on the repetition of an opinion uttered by someone else—the "they say" or "you know" of those who believe what they hear from people in authoritative positions and don't think to ask questions.

....

ABOUT LITTLE CHARLIE LINDBERGH

The truth about little Charlie Lindbergh's murder?
A hero's dark love of eugenics.
President Kennedy's lone killer,
or the Tonkin Gulf incident:
ghosts that still haunt us
pushing fantasy as fact
or fact as fantasy.

A year before I was born, Mother
gave birth to her first daughter,
named Margaret
and dead within hours.
I too am Margaret.
She always said she was pregnant
with me eighteen months.

Throughout her long life
she repeated
that other Margaret's name
and the story of her death
until once, toward the end,
she turned to me in mock surprise
and asked
How could you think such a thing?
You have the wildest imagination!

Gesture here, comment there,
years of disparate clues
slipped between my anxious fingers
or lodged themselves in doubt.
The twin name unraveled.
The mysterious death remained.

Facts erased in a moment,
then reinforced:
Mother's fear of illness—
the common cold
but also quieter hidden ills,
unseen and menacing.

Pressing my brother
not to date
the college sweetheart
whose sister was rumored
to be mentally ill.
Fear of the raucous gene
compounding a shadowy blight.

I'd point out the mental illness
rife in our family as in many.
For Mother,
if no one saw
it wasn't there.

Grandfather just a dreamy old man.
Grandma's biting petulance,
her lies.
Uncle took a drink too many
but wasn't an alcoholic.
Never giving in to his gay identity:
choice, not tragedy.

No wooden ladder remains standing
against the open second-story window
of a New Jersey mansion
in my family history.

No grassy knoll
obscures another script.
No fabricated strike
authorized a war
that would claim two million lives
and usher in the right to first attack.

My family secrets were humbler,
easier to hide.
They shaped individual
rather than collective lies.
They only made me crazy
and didn't seed posttraumatic stress
among nations.

As I got older, I often heard Mother say that she came from a Republican family and only became a Democrat after she married. I can't imagine that my father's family had anything resembling liberal politics, though, so that comment perplexes me. My parents' instincts were decent, but they were heavily invested in being accepted by their peers. They eventually became liberals who believed campaign promises and rarely had more than a summary grasp of the issues. They bought the American dream. Political discussion was superficial. And when issues such as poverty, race, patriotism, or war emerged, I was gradually startled to learn that their loudly touted values of equality, honesty, and generosity of spirit were mediated by "what the neighbors might think."

Dad, especially, was genuinely kind and concerned about the plight of those less fortunate. We took baskets of Christmas foods to families in poor neighborhoods, and on Thanksgiving Dad might go so far as to invite someone he'd just met, who had nowhere to be, to share our holiday meal with us—something that made my mother extremely uncomfortable. Invariably she would later find a way to make him pay.

Dad genuinely loved people and was happy when giving—money, energy, time. But he cowered before authority and ended up following his wife's lead. This tension between the values my parents articulated to their children and their fear of standing up for those values caused me to grow up wondering what their beliefs really were. The bottom line always seemed to be don't make waves, don't do anything to disrupt or affect the upper middle-class life they'd so carefully constructed.

In the more intimate realm, a perceived modernity gave the illusion of openness—my parents often walked around the house naked and spoke readily about bodily functions and the mechanics of sexuality. We were raised to feel we could ask questions and receive honest answers. I remember no few conversations between my parents and my friends, conversations they might not have been able to have in their own homes.

As I grew into adolescence, I understood that I could bring boys home and, later, that I could have sex with them—"better to do it in a safe place," Mother said, "than somewhere out there." She herself took me to be fitted for a diaphragm when I was still a teenager. The apparent ease with which she approached the subject was ahead of its time but confusing to me. I didn't use the diaphragm, had no desire to. Looking back, I don't think my mother was capable of conveying the profundity of intimacy; she herself rarely enjoyed it. And my parents' incompatibility in that area made it impossible for them to broach those deeper regions with their children.

....

To my parents, inherited as opposed to earned income always seemed to be a source of embarrassment or shame. We were coached not to talk about the fact that we had money beyond what our father brought home. Dad earned a very modest salary and, wherever we lived, our lifestyle was the least ostentatious of those around us. The family car was secondhand. We acquired a television set years after our neighbors did. We children wore hand-me-downs and Mother made an elaborate show of saving on bloody eggs, fifty-pound drums of powdered milk, and ground horsemeat instead of beef. "I challenge you to taste the difference," she would say. Family lies supported the idea that they spent less on everything than they really did.

During her marriage, our mother never worked at a salaried job. She had earned an impressive $125 a week while still in her teens, fashioning the first department store mannequins and stylized cocktail-party pretzel holders. But after a couple of months her parents left for their yearly vacation in Maine and she saw no reason not to go with them. When she returned at the end of that summer, someone else had her job.

As my brother, sister, and I grew up, our parents consistently described the family as hard up, or barely making it: absurd by any measure. And yet in later years, when Dad taught school and had his summers off, we would go on lavish family trips. Mother insisted the money for those trips came from what they saved buying powdered milk and bloody eggs, second-hand clothing, and other bargains. And we children believed her stories, even repeating them to others until we were old enough to realize how foolish they sounded. Money secrets were rivaled only by our changed surname. Or by Mother's cancer. These were issues about which fabricated stories were repeated until they became truth—at least to the one spinning the tale.

Mother was in her forties when she was diagnosed with breast cancer. I was fifteen. The mastectomy was a double whammy for my mother. To begin with, the first time he saw her scarred chest, my father couldn't dissimulate his queasiness. He recapacitated quickly, but his first impression had already widened the physical gulf between him and his wife. From then on, they had separate bedrooms and I'm not sure they ever slept together again. The larger problem was the shame the cancer itself produced in Mother. Women didn't yet speak openly about having the disease back then. It was as if doing so would have made it their fault. Like mental illness, a terrible secrecy surrounded the subject.

In the midst of this craziness, there were also islands of sanity. Even about money. Our parents taught us a work ethic, to earn our own way, organize what we had, and save. I was given a clothes allowance from the time I was twelve, and I remember great rigor and seriousness around decisions about managing it. If I bought a winter coat or new pair of shoes, for example, I wouldn't have anything left for that longed-for cashmere sweater set or billowing crinoline. My siblings and I shared a sense that the rules were more strictly enforced with me, the eldest. By the time they came along, our parents may have been less sure of their strategies, more relaxed, or simply tired. Then too my brother was the youngest and a boy; they always indulged him more.

We moved from Manhattan to White Plains, then Hartsdale and finally Scarsdale, Westchester County towns and villages, increasingly "good" addresses where the suburban elite migrated from a crowded, unsafe city to houses with yards on placid, quiet streets. But life, especially in the upscale village of Scarsdale, had its own rules. One was expected to conform to the snobbish aspirations of one's neighbors. Mother once told me that in Scarsdale, the community's young wives got together to decide the appropriate age for a daughter to begin wearing lipstick.

I was my parents' oldest child. I lived in a magical bubble that involved the privilege of age, the pride of accomplishment, and the excitement of being first. To that combination I added my own profound sense of justice, adventurous spirit, and proclivity to risk. Despite the incest I would remember much later in my life, I grew up with the idea that I could do almost anything I desired.

....

Mother quit school, which she said she always hated, in the middle of junior high. She told me about being chased on the playground by other students chanting "Dirty Jew, dirty Jew"—which may have accounted for some of her self-hatred and for urging our father to change our surname from Reinthal to Randall. Toward the end of her life she admitted she had wanted to protect us from the discrimination she experienced. But for years she responded to my insistent questions about the name change with "Oh, it was easier to spell." It was just before Dad's death that she began talking about the real motivation for the act, adding that I couldn't imagine how horrible it was to be hated like that. "I didn't want you to have to suffer like I did," she said. She also confessed that it was she who insisted on the name change: "Dad went along, like he did with everything I wanted."

After leaving school, Mother enrolled in New York's Art Students League, where she studied for five years, becoming a monitor in the sculpture studio. She always said those were among the best years of her life. When I was a child she still sculpted, although her talent for making complex molds was greater than her artistry. "I wasn't original enough" was the strangely superficial way she sometimes explained having given up her early vocation.

My father was an eligible bachelor: athletically handsome, likable, kind, and from a family with money that wasn't constantly threatening to disappear as it had in Mother's. My brother, sister, and I often asked our parents why they married. Or why they stayed married. Although they provided a loving home—and Dad especially was a wonderful parent—they were so obviously mismatched. Bickering and arguments were the norm as we grew up: frustrated sarcasm from Mother followed by that look around the room in search of agreement and sympathy, which she had inherited from her mother. Passive endurance was infrequently punctuated by a sudden angry outburst from our father. Dad would say he loved our mother. We didn't doubt that was true. But we wondered at the humiliation he bore. Mother sometimes told us that she did love our father at first. At other times she admitted to having married him for his money.

Central to their staying together for sixty-two years was Mother's fear of being alone, of having to fend for herself. Being cared for, supported, was important. It was what she was educated to expect. And then there was Dad's devotion to family. To family and to the idea of family. In his worldview, you nurtured and provided for your own. No matter what happened, what personal sacrifice was required, you held your family together, preserving it against all odds.

When, after nineteen years of marriage, my brother left his first wife, both our parents took it hard. It wasn't only that they loved Joanna, although that was part of it. It was also and deeply the idea of family per se. "You just can't do this," our father told my brother. "Your mother and I haven't been that happy, but you don't see me leaving her, do you?" Interestingly, neither parent responded to my sister's two or my three divorces in the way they did to my brother's one. They expected something different from their boy than what they tolerated from their girls.

....

Memories of my childhood in the east grow dimmer and fragment as time passes. The order in which events took place is no longer always clear. One memory may fail to connect with another. Still, I easily transport myself to third grade. I was standing on my school playground, surrounded by other kids. Our music teacher, Mrs. Benfield, demanded I sing a scale in front of my classmates. She must have noticed that I only moved my lips when asked to sing in class. My parents had told me I was tone deaf, and I believed them to the point that I was unable to utter a sound if I thought anyone was listening. There on that playground I refused to sing. My teacher insisted, and I continued to refuse. Then, in ultimate fear and defiance, I wet myself. I felt the warm urine running down my leg. I burst into tears and made a dash for home, which was just across the street.

There are sweeter grade-school memories, those involving my first- and second-grade teacher, Miss Peek. She was a large woman with pale red hair and clearly thought I was special. I loved decorating my written lessons for her, making elaborate borders for the stories I was so enthusiastic about writing: stylized vines and birds from whose beaks sprang musical notes. I loved to draw as much as I loved to write. My parents encouraged both, and I remember a series of Saturday sketching classes in which we were taken to a nearby stream and challenged to render it in watercolor.

And there are also darker, more frightening memories. Like the school picnic at Saxon Woods, where I strayed from my group and then couldn't get back to it, frozen as I was at the sight of what I remember as an immense and terrifying toadstool in my path. My phobia of mushrooms, which it would take me years to deconstruct, dates to my earliest memories. It made me dread summer camp. With the approach of each new season I begged my parents not to send me, but they always did. Once there, I became adept at inventing reasons why I couldn't venture among the trees. There was always the possibility that, once they discovered my vulnerability, the other children would use it against me. Which, of course, they did.

One moment from those suburban New York years that stands apart from all others is the one around the pocket knife. I must have been seven or eight. I had seen a green mother-of-pearl Girl Scout knife at our local Woolworth's and coveted it. Mother wouldn't give in to my pleading. She might have planned on giving it to me for Christmas or perhaps she thought me too young for a knife. Whatever her reason, I was determined. I stole the knife from the store, then fabricated an elaborate tale in which I announced that my Brownie troop leader had given it to me for excelling at the skills we were expected to master.

Scarsdale was a village back then. In a matter of days, Mother ran into the troop leader on the street and expressed her pride in my accomplishment. The other woman stared back at her, blankly. Quickly, my story fell apart. I was forced to confess, and Mother insisted I return the knife to the store manager, explaining in detail my crime and promising I would never do such a thing again. As I recall, she herself dragged me, resisting and in tears, and stood beside me while I recited what I had done. The incident remains an indelible lesson in truth. Or at least in more foolproof lying.

Images from World War II are vivid: the double sets of window shades. The silly air-raid drills during which we put our heads down on our school desks or hid beneath them. The blue denim bag with "Bundles for Britain" machine-embroidered in red and white. The exhortation, at every meal, to clean our plates. Didn't we know the children of Europe were starving? Ever the pragmatist, I wanted to know if the food we left uneaten would be given to those starving children, and how. I did my child's part in the war effort by taking a vigorous fork to large square blocks of pasty white margarine and mixing the orange powdered colorant until the spread turned a uniform yellow that tasted something like soap.

The war hit me hardest the day after my fifth birthday. December 7, 1941: Pearl Harbor. Mother, Dad, and I were driving across the George Washington Bridge on our way to the birthday party of a little boy in Jersey who celebrated the day after me. Mother and Dad rode in front. I sat on the edge of the back seat, in the middle and as far forward as possible, eager to be included in my parents' conversation. They had the car radio on—a modern and novel acquisition at the time—and news of the attack suddenly pierced the calm of our family outing.

Dad was visibly upset. Mother began to cry. I remember her asking: "Do you think Albert will have to go?" Go where? I had no idea. Dad must have tried to reassure her. In their panic they ignored me. I asked, and then asked again, what was going on? What did it mean that we were going to war? Unable to get either parent to respond, I retreated to the comforting companionship of my four imaginary friends. Mr. Beeuf, Miss Level, Camp, and Girlie could be counted on in such situations. When one of them assured me that wars were nothing to worry about, I hastened to tell my father the good news. I needed to make things right.

That was the only time I can remember my father slapping me. He turned around amid heavy bridge traffic and flung his open palm across my face. Then he burst into tears. The gesture surprised and offended me, but it devastated him. For weeks he begged my forgiveness. Physical violence was not in my father's nature, especially not with his children. The advent of war had upset him beyond his control.

Then Dad himself went to war. Although he was over the draft age and had children, our father wanted to do his part in the fight against fascism. He and Mother also may have needed a break. Dad enlisted in World War II and made it as far as basic training at Fort Knox, Kentucky. His goal was Officer Candidate School, but he wasn't judged apt. He left home in his smart uniform and, for a year or so, was away for months at a time. I remember him coming into my bedroom late one night to tell me he was going off again. He took his envelope-like serge cap off and placed it on my peach-colored blanket. I touched its fabric as we murmured in sad, low tones. I loved my father and wanted him to be there, always.

After Dad's honorable discharge, he came home and went to work on the assembly line at a local aircraft plant. One night he returned from that factory with a long burn the length of his forearm. It may not have been as serious as it seems in memory, for I recall his pain—again, legitimate tears—but no subsequent scar. Still, those were times that continued to speak of sacrifice, communal effort, the worthy fight.

In a later image I might be six. A fir tree, so tall and its branches so lavish it exemplifies the species, fills my vision. My mother and I are standing in the driveway to one side of our Scarsdale house. She looks willowy in a smart print dress as she shows the family car to a strange man with dark, wavy, slicked-back hair. It must have been 1942. My father is at Fort Knox. Mother is selling the car because, as I hear her tell this stranger, "My husband is in the Army. He may not be coming back." I shrink against the bark of the great tree, feeling orphaned and alone.

My imaginary friends consoled me, then and later. I would huddle with them in a small storage space beneath the stairs that led to our home's second floor. Mr. Beeuf was a factory worker; like my father when he worked on the aircraft assembly line, he carried a black metal lunchbox each day. Miss Level was a nurse, with her starched white uniform and winged cap circled by a narrow black band. They were the two adults in my secret coterie. Camp was an adolescent who rode a motorcycle; Girlie, his girlfriend. Invented stories, of one sort or another, were always places for me to hide.

Dad too told stories. His were about Pufti and Mike, two characters he created and about whom he spun intricate tales in many installments. Now I remember only fragments of a single one of them in which Pufti unpacked a picnic for Mike and the two of them sat beneath a tree, gnawing on drumsticks and tossing the bones.

Storytime with Dad also meant learning to read. The skill had not come easily to me in first grade, as it seemed to for my classmates. My teacher must have told my parents I needed extra help, and Dad took the challenge. All that summer between first and second grades I would sit on his lap each night and read to him from a book with a dark red cover. I cannot remember its name, only the slant of black letters across red pasteboard. With his patient help I learned to read better and faster than anyone I knew. A whole other world opened to me.

An incident that happened in first or second grade at Edgewood Elementary—right across the street from our house—would leave a deep impression. Although I have no memory of studying ballet, I appeared in an end-of-year recital to which my parents came. I performed with my typical enthusiasm but later overheard my father telling Mother, "Our daughter is like a bull in a china shop!" My sense of myself as awkward and lacking in grace, a feeling I struggled with for years, may have had its roots at least partially in that comment he couldn't have imagined I overheard.

I was a child who wet my bed years longer than expected. Once in a while I would wet my panties as well, unable to control the urge that suddenly overtook me. Sometimes I felt faint, nauseous. Those days I didn't want to go to school. As parents often do, mine first approached the problem as if it were willful rebellion. If I would just try a little harder, make sure I went to the bathroom before it was too late. But when the problem persisted, they took me to the family doctor. He recommended we see a urologist. Before I knew it, I was in the hospital about to undergo an exploratory procedure to determine what was wrong.

That hospital experience lasted ten days or so. On the eve of my being admitted, Mother made me a little rag pig, a simple stuffed toy I hugged to my breast throughout the ordeal. It was a predecessor to Heather, my favorite childhood doll. She too was of the pliable rag variety. I can't remember if

Mother made her or if I got her from someone else. Mother's creativity showed itself in all sorts of ways and often resulted in delights for us all.

The urologist was a man notably lacking in anything resembling charm. His name was Dr. LePaste. I dubbed him Mucilage, after a popular brand of glue, and drew an uncomplimentary but recognizable portrait. The hospital housed a ward of Norwegian sailors—can this be true?—who were there because they'd suffered wartime wounds to their arms or legs. I remember that several moved around with a wrist fixed to a thigh, waiting out the adherence of the skin graft that promised to return them to some semblance of what they'd been before the war. I became a mascot to those men, giving them some of the drawings I did on reams of x-ray paper provided by a friendly nurse.

I was asleep for the exploration and woke without pain but touched a strange oiliness about my vaginal lips. Mother explained that the doctors had entered me with a tiny camera on the end of a wire; the photographs obtained would tell them what was wrong. What they discovered was that my urethra had a malformation, a kink that impeded the normal flow of urine. In a second procedure I was "unkinked." My vivid imagination produced all sorts of images: a camera the size of a pea, a bodily passageway doing flip-flops until it landed right-side up and ready for action. A nurse told grumpy Dr. LePaste about my rendering of him, name and all. I never again wet my bed or pants.

The end of the war also shines in my memory. Nineteen forty-five. The long-anticipated news came over radios late one evening. Children ran out into the suburban streets. We were wearing our pajamas, banging on pots and pans. Later we saw images of the famous Times Square celebration and they replaced our own experiences of what the war's end looked like. Much later came those other images, from the concentration camps: piles of skeletal bodies, the dead and those who had somehow survived. After another decade, when I had access to better information, I would struggle with the issue of national responsibility in a more multilayered way.

....

That war had seemed uncomplicated. It was the glorious fight against fascism. When it was over, life might have settled into a drearier pattern. This is the feeling I have, so many years later. But two events, at least, were central to our family during those war and postwar years. My sister, Ann, was born at the end of 1939. War was on the horizon but the sense, at least among middle-class Americans, must have been that we would not be seriously affected. And in

November of 1944 I had a baby brother, John. We called him Johnny Boy to distinguish him from my father.

I write their arrivals in this way—my sister was born, and I had a baby brother—because this is how I experienced each event. My mother gave birth to Ann, three years younger than I, and my sister altered our family dynamic irrevocably. I was no longer the only child, unique. I could still be the oldest, even the smartest and cleverest. But never again the only.

I loved my sister, cherished her as little girls tend to embrace special human dolls. I suffered her intrusion upon my terrain, was proud of her accomplishments, protected her and hated sharing our parents' attention, or my bedroom—our fate for years. But Ann had it worse. At school she was frequently judged against my previous showing and I undoubtedly encouraged such a comparison, secretly gloating when I emerged as the more intelligent or creative. As youngsters we were dressed alike, especially by our grandmothers who delighted in buying us identical plaids and dresses with little shirred bib fronts and starched white collars. My hair grew thick and was soon braided into long plaits that Mother wound about my head. Ann's was thin during her first years; I remember our mother giving her a boy's cut in the hope it would come in thicker. I don't remember my sister's humiliation, although I learned of it later.

I was extroverted; Ann, introverted. She listened, quietly, and internalized more than a few admonitions meant for me as if they were directed at her. Mother used to tell me to keep my teeth apart and lips together. This would make my nose appear shorter, she said. "When you're old enough, eighteen or nineteen," Mother promised, "we can get you a nose job." She assumed I wanted one. Her insistence did give me pause, adding to the overall insecurity I felt about my body. But I had no intention of letting a surgeon near my nose.

Ann took Mother's admonitions to heart. Her nose was much smaller than mine and looked just fine on her face. But one summer when she was in her late teens and our parents were traveling, she took it upon herself to have it "fixed." The surgeon botched the first operation and she had to repeat the ordeal. My sister also internalized Mother's ethnic self-hatred; for years after she'd moved to California, become a teacher, and married her first husband, Ann hid her Jewish heritage. This would have tragic consequences. Had she told her doctor about her ethnicity, the intestinal problem that almost killed her might have been more accurately diagnosed. She suffered from Crohn's Disease, common among Jews and a condition responsive to medication, rather than ileitis, which was addressed by operating.

Our mother's prejudice that affected me most deeply throughout my own life was her disgust at overweight people, coupled with an eating disorder of her own. She would sit at the table with me, talk about how delicious a particular dish looked, then say that although she desperately wanted it, she wasn't going to indulge. She was proud of her willpower and hoped some of it would rub off on me. Looking back and trying to dissect Mother's relationship to food, several contradictory attitudes stand out. She didn't really enjoy cooking. The kitchen, as it does for many women, must have evoked household slavery. She was known for a couple of frequently repeated dishes—"Elli Randall Spaghetti" and later, in New Mexico, her version of chile con carne: both made with canned products, overcooked and bland, although we thought them delicious.

Mother was small and slim, occasionally dropping below 100 pounds. In contrast, I've suffered a lifetime of being overweight. She tried to convince me it was all about will. She would urge me to control my eating, then tempt me with dessert. Her concern for my body shape always revolved around food; she never suggested exercise or seemed to enjoy it herself, although she did swim and walk for a while later in life. But I had the sense those activities were chores, not pleasures. Eventually I got to the point where I found it more and more uncomfortable to eat in front of my mother.

For years my sister and I sparred in sibling rivalry and frustration. The damage to a potential relationship was too much for either of us to overcome. Even when we could understand how completely our unhealthy competition had been caused by others—our parents, teachers, society at large—it took a long time for us to come to an easier place with one another. We both tried but the truth is that we never really got there. Or got there only partially. My sister died in 2017. Despite a genuine desire on both our parts, we hadn't managed to become friends.

Ann escaped our parents' home by moving permanently to California. There she became a remedial English teacher, married, had a son, and adopted twin daughters. She eventually divorced her first husband and married again, but that marriage too ended in divorce. One of her daughters died of breast cancer in her thirties. Ann eventually began taking photographs of abstract details of flowers and other natural designs. She also photographed the places and people she visited, and those were the images of hers that resonated most with me.

John's arrival was very different. It was our mother who conceived her third child, carried him for nine months, and delivered him to the world. But

I always felt as if my baby brother belonged to me. Mom had a difficult time with my brother's birth; part of the placenta remained inside and resulted in a serious infection. Several hours after giving birth, our mother had to undergo an operation to have it removed. And for months she remained delicate. At the age of eight, I attended to many of the new baby's needs.

I'm sure our parents also had professional help at that time. I'm sure I didn't take over completely. But that is the way it feels in memory. And from feeding, bathing, and diapering to encouraging Johnny's first steps and teaching him to skate, ride a bike, or swim, wasn't much of a leap. My sister's very existence fades as I think back to those years. My brother became the person in my family to whom I feel the closest. He still is.

John reaped the benefits of being the youngest and only male. Mother, especially, doted on him. She was overprotective, something against which he had to struggle later on. I remember my brother, age ten or eleven, taking money he'd saved to the bank, exchanging it for rolls of pennies or quarters, and carefully examining each coin. He knew which ones were worth something and gradually acquired quite a valuable collection. He did the same with stamps. In adulthood he graduated to books, for a while owned a terrific Albuquerque bookstore,[3] and finally retired to deal in used and rare books online.

....

One memory from the time we lived in the east involves the acquisition of my first typewriter, a black Royal portable with its faintly oiled matte finish, round keys covered by perfect little plastic windows, and a scent that will always evoke writing for me. It's the smell of precomputer life, one that hardly exists anymore, at least in the developed world. By the age of eight or nine I knew I was going to be a writer. And I longed for a machine upon which to practice my craft. This was America, after all; writers had typewriters.

Mother and Dad told me that if I could teach myself to touch-type and earn half the money for that $150 machine, they would put up the other half and allow me to buy it. The touch-typing was easy. I got a mail-order course and with earnest discipline repeated J-U-G jug, J-U-G jug and other simple three-letter combinations to a ditty about a syncopated clock. Before long I had mastered sixty words a minute. But how could a young girl of my age earn enough for a typewriter? I sold boxes of candy door-to-door, got my first babysitting jobs, even had a short-lived newspaper route, neatly rolling and tying each paper, stacking them in the canvas bag that straddled the rear fender of my red Mohawk bike, and aiming carefully at each well-kept Scarsdale stoop. Reaching $75 was one of the proudest days of my young life. My parents were proud too. They immediately took me to the store where the typewriter became mine.

Girls with paper routes were not favorably looked upon in the Scarsdale of that era. Social rules remained unspoken but were rigorously observed. Between the community's cultural stuffiness and their own families' class snobbery, our parents grew restless. Mother invariably led the charge when it came to new ideas or big life changes. Dad followed her loyally.

....

My mother and father despised the confines of their upwardly mobile eastern life: the Wednesday night dinners with his mother, occasional weekends with her parents, the petty values, desperate aspirations, vapid expectations, and, yes, the boredom of thoroughly assimilated, vaguely Christianized Jews. Or Jews who believed themselves to be assimilated. I'm speaking mostly of my mother's family. One of the more surprising characteristics of my family of origin was the extent to which my parents believed the image they presented was taken by others at face value. Their last name was Randall now, so they weren't Jewish. They skimped to save so weren't wealthy. After my mother's mastectomy her left arm became swollen and she had to keep it bandaged for the rest of her long life; the story she repeated was that she had wrenched it while driving. It didn't seem to occur to her that she was telling people she wrenched it while driving every time they asked—for years.

Johnny wasn't quite three, Ann almost seven, and I just shy of eleven when our parents decided they were suffocating in the east. They piled us all into their old black Studebaker and headed west. We visited Yellowstone and Jackson Hole, Bryce, Zion, and Grand Canyon. We had adventures I still remember with delight: laughing when my baby brother threw his cap to some cows alongside a Pennsylvania back road, my showing off astride a stocky pony for a young cowboy I fancied might be paying attention, all of us reading out loud the lines of verse on the little red and white Burma Shave signs as we drove from state to state. I thought the peach-colored rock formations at Bryce Canyon too beautiful to be real. And, when there were no other vacancies in an Illinois town, we all endured the wretched dinginess of a third-rate motel and settled in for the night. The place was called Ruby's. For years we referred to it as Ruby Fooey's.

It was on that trip west that I asked the Question: not where babies come from or how they get inside their mothers' tummies, but why does the father's blood affect the RH factor in a newborn? I had heard some radio program about RH and couldn't understand what the father had to do with the baby's blood. Mother took my question as a sign that I was ready to hear the Facts of Life, as they were called back then.

It was quickly decided that I would sleep with her that night, my brother and sister with our father. Mother did the best she knew how. She began with a lengthy prologue about bees and birds and flowers. I waited impatiently for her to get to humans. When she did, I was horrified. Her explanation was purely anatomical and didn't include anything about desire or feeling. That night I decided I would be a nun—the only escape in my young girl's mind from what my mother was telling me lay ahead.

Our parents were running from something as they moved toward something new. In the tradition of my paternal grandfather, Mother and Dad were looking for another place to live. A new start. They found it in New Mexico.

Chapter Three

LANDSCAPE
OF DESIRE

High School and Beyond,

1947–1958

Considering how dangerous everything is,
nothing is really very frightening.
—GERTRUDE STEIN

If you are a woman alive in the United States today, you would have to have
been a young girl in the 1950s to understand the weight of gender repression
in every fiber of your mind and body. Because it was the norm, and almost no
one questioned it: every stifling objectification felt inevitable on our shoulders. Assault, by turns aggressive or passive, could be a festering wound or numb
us into acquiescence—or both. Those were the years immediately following
World War II, when our commodity culture was enticing women back into
domesticity with gleaming home appliances and promises of a satisfied husband and cared-for life. Society was clearing the way for men returning from
the front, and women were the collateral damage.

 If you are a man alive today, there is no way you can understand how that
cruel era of gender repression shaped and still shapes women's lives.

 In the preceding decade the United States had joined the allies in the
great war against fascism, and the country's participation undoubtedly helped

turn the tide of that war. When the details of the enemy's mass murder machine revealed themselves in photographs and testimonies of survivors, the world was shocked. The Nazi genocide of European Jews strained credulity.[1] We thought of our nation as heroic, saviors of humankind. The popular mantra was that such atrocity must never be allowed to happen again. Yet we've suffered many genocides since, no few of them instigated or supported by the United States. This is the political context in which I came of age. The gender tension we experienced, in a time and place that cast make-believe as reality, mirrored that larger sociopolitical dichotomy.

The omissions, lies, and half-truths are legion. It would be years before we learned about the allied bombing of Dresden in February of 1945. It has been estimated that 350,000 civilians died in that attack on a purely civilian target. Neither were we told about the MS *St. Louis*, a German ocean liner on her maiden voyage in 1939. Her captain, a good man named Gustav Schröder, was desperately trying to find homes for more than nine hundred Jewish refugees. Cuba, Canada, and the United States refused to allow the ship to dock. The endangered men, women, and children were forced to return to Europe where approximately a quarter of them perished in the death camps. These are but two of many events, unreported or underreported at the time, that tarnish our country's otherwise heroic involvement in that war.

We didn't know, back then, that the fire-bombing of Tokyo or the atomic bombs the United States dropped on the Japanese cities of Hiroshima and Nagasaki, killing and maiming hundreds of thousands, weren't necessary to end the war; Japan had already agreed to surrender. Our school books didn't tell us those stories. Many of our history books continue to distort them. We also had no knowledge of the Japanese internment camps that dotted this country. Exaggerated patriotism has always been a one-way street, a reason not to ask questions, a safeguard against critical thought. The United States was already on its way to becoming a national security state.

The armistice gave way to the long period of the Cold War. McCarthy's witch hunts swept the country with their menacing broom. Ethel and Julius Rosenberg were executed in 1953. Their supposed crime was having given the secret of the atom bomb to the Soviets. The ridiculous evidence would not have stood up in any US court of law except during that period of anti-Communist hysteria. And, as has been true in so many crisis situations since—Bosnia, Rwanda, and others—special torture was reserved for women. In those later wars, rape was the weapon. In the Rosenberg case, the government knew that by sending Ethel to the electric chair it was murdering an innocent. It tried unsuccessfully, until minutes before putting her to death, to get her to save herself by turning state's witness against her husband: a particularly egregious example of a government manipulating a mother based on traditional concepts of familial loyalty.

In the United States throughout the early to mid-1950s, holding a progressive point of view or even voicing an opinion that differed from government policy could mean losing your job, being blackballed in your profession, going to prison, or finding yourself forced into exile. Among the actors, directors, and screenwriters called to the House Un-American Activities Committee (HUAC) hearings, men made up the original list of the Hollywood Ten and their stories are better known to this day. But that repression affected women in particularly painful ways. While men are considered stars well into their later years, women lose their appeal as they age. Some of the female stars caught in that web never acted again.[2]

I was in high school at the time. Although I was not aware of these political events, my generation of young women was being thoroughly schooled in the subservience and shame that would make us complicit in our own gender repression. There was one place where I experienced that repression in all its brutality, although I could not have articulated it verbally. That place was my yearning teenage body.

....

A SADNESS OF PLYWOOD

We didn't know De Anza as a surname of Conquest,
just another set of unfamiliar syllables
in this new place:
"de anza to a tourist's prayer"
my mother joked.

The motel shone on the city's main street, Route 66
once rode the country going west,
Central Avenue as it passed through Albuquerque
its Pachucos and Indians
stoking my adolescent fear.

Our Anglo family of five enjoyed a few nights
of De Anza luxury
before moving to shabbier rooms with kitchenette

Fourth Street's bar-studded thirst
then on to the safety of our uptown home.

For years De Anza stood: beckoning invitation,
signpost
in our arrival script,
bridge to our family's break
with East Coast propriety.

Older, I remember dark nights, midnight pranks
with friends
who climbed its pumice wall
slipped naked and gleeful
into its private swimming pool.

We had to stop when one guy's outraged wife
discovered I'd shown my naked body
to her man,
spewed venom across our Fifties threshold
demanded I stay away.

Shame held me mute before her screams
and other neighbors' faces
floating in other doorways,
condemnation that would fester
in me for years.

Today De Anza is boarded up,
its smog-stained windows
hidden behind a sadness of plywood.
Today the dead motel is one more ruin
along a strip of empty structures

where summer nights tough women
approach a crawl of low riders,
crack costs a few dirty bills
and the homeless lady walks, brown blanket
pulled about her shoulders.

Once the best promise of a western city,
the old motel's demise

careens near where I turn
to enter today's map,
home that finally feels like home.

....

NOTHING WAS WHAT IT PRETENDED

Words I'd never heard took up residence
in my mouth.
Montaño, even if city signage
refused to put the tilde over the n,

names like *De Vargas, Cabeza de Vaca*
or Juan Tabó,
shepherds and assassins enshrined on street corners
unquestioned and mispronounced.

Indian words like *Acoma, Navajo*—now *Diné*—
or place-names like *Canyon de Chelly*
the conquerors left us with
when they couldn't speak what they couldn't hear.

Names imposed: *Oñate, Coronado, Santa Fe.*
Another's holy faith bringing death
and leaving division, delighting
those who arrive on private planes.

Common words like *tijeras* and *frijoles*,
scissors and beans
began to quiver on my tongue,
stood easily in later years.

I too came from somewhere else,
a childhood far away,
with other sounds in my ears,
other familiars in my mouth.

The new words tested teeth, stretched lips
and exercised my landscape
until language caught meaning in its net
and I knew nothing was what it pretended.

I lived the tension between desire and what was socially acceptable. I had grown up with that tension; my parents—like others of their class and culture—reproduced it in all areas of their lives. They maintained an appropriate public face while keeping the secrets that would have revealed anything suspect, unacceptable, or even different. Yet Mother also cultivated a sort of difference. She liked hanging out with artists and thought of herself as an intellectual. While pretending a social acceptability, she also found a shock value in straying from it. My parents kept their secrets so well that they themselves believed them. From Mother especially I learned that secrets and lies were acceptable strands in the social fabric.

When I was fifteen and sixteen one of my delights was taking the family's secondhand Studebaker to a spot along the highway going north, parking it and beginning to walk. I'd follow the rises and dips on a Geological Survey map past where discarded beer cans and bottle caps revealed evidence of modern-day life. I'd find a remote spot on the desert, take off all my clothes, and sleep the night. As I closed my eyes and gave myself to darkness, I'd imagine I was a woman on that land before Conquest claimed it. But I didn't feel I could be honest with my parents about where I went or what I did. I'd tell them I was spending the night at a girlfriend's house, and the girlfriend that I was with a boy. My girlfriend lied for me as easily as I did for myself. Deceit was a social disease.

This particular pleasure, which a decade or two later would have been an invitation to rape or worse, was typical of the sort of activity I engaged in back then. I sought the most conservative model of social conformity on the one hand, a rebel nonconformity on the other. And I didn't question the contradiction, even to myself.

But throughout my adolescence, my relationship to the space and light of New Mexico wasn't limited to those nights of desert fantasy. The land itself took me into her arms. That landscape continues to have a central presence in my consciousness and poetry. My love affair was initiated by my parents' fascination with the state, their early weekend trips north and south, east and west—to Jémez, White Sands, Carlsbad, and Taos: mesas and canyons, vast hills of gypsum we rolled down as kids, mysterious caves with their stalagmites and stalactites, and impoverished but exoticized Indian pueblos. Weekend after weekend we explored our new home.

In line with the custom of those times, Mother and Dad sometimes took bundles of old clothes to an Indian reservation to trade for silver and turquoise jewelry. Mother soon had a beautiful collection of bracelets, a sandcast belt buckle, and a traditional squash-blossom necklace. I know I got my love of that jewelry from her. But it didn't take long for the nature of that exchange to make me uncomfortable. Charity's ugly face was writ large in a practice through which secondhand rags were traded for valuable heirlooms.

I wanted to get to know the Indian peoples of New Mexico in a context more conducive to legitimate friendship. Having emigrated from the upscale, mostly white New York suburb of Scarsdale, I was awkward at first with New Mexico's diversity. I remember crossing a downtown street during my first months in our new home and experiencing something between confusion and fear as I looked at the brown faces so absent from my Scarsdale life. I would have to move away, live in Latin America, and come home years later before I was able to relate on more comfortable terms.

If my racist conditioning made it difficult for me to know the native inhabitants, I touched the land itself more easily. When I was a very young child, my father had given me a series of picture books about different peoples and the places they inhabited. Those books were beautifully produced, almost square in format and with evocative illustrations. I remember one about the Pennsylvania Dutch. But the one that impressed me most was about the Indians of the American Southwest. Images of blue sage, bright green rabbit brush, and purple mountains took up residence in my eyes. Dancers with bear and deer headdresses and small bells at their ankles moved across them as if animating a film strip. I dreamed of those colors and people, what I imagined early morning dew on cactus arms must smell like, the endless blue of those huge skies. When I finally saw that land, I felt I had come home.

In some deep way I could not have expressed back then, that landscape introduced me to desire. It put me in touch with my own body, its rhythms and needs, the feelings it would invite me to experience when I knew enough to meet it on its terms.

....

In high school, though, the land was still a mystery, so different from the crowded suburban map I'd grown up on in the east. Here there were deep slot canyons and pinyon-dotted hills, bright sunlight 360 days a year, almost no rain, and ferocious spring sandstorms biting our calves as we walked to and from school in our regulation below-the-knee skirts and saddle shoes. Mostly, there was space. A vastness that might have given me a feeling of freedom, had the repression aimed at young girls not imprisoned me.

I wanted desperately to fit in. And I knew that to do so I had to play the game my class and culture presented as survival. In junior high I joined the Episcopal church for a while and became a member of Job's Daughters, the young girl's division of Masonry. I became a majorette, twirled a glittering baton. In high school I longed to be one of the popular girls: a member of the "in" crowd, a cheerleader or homecoming queen. Eventually, all those activities bored me. Back then, although I never achieved those goals, I felt acting my prescribed role was my only option. I raged inside yet was too thoroughly conditioned or shy to externalize dissatisfaction or discomfort.

We owed this conditioning, at least in part, to Sigmund Freud (1856–1939), who was so influential in shaping our modern ideas about women and power. I hadn't yet read Freud, but his teachings permeated the culture in which I lived. The father of psychoanalysis had developed a theory of seduction that went a long way toward explaining how male entitlement affects women's lives. He'd initially believed his female patients' stories of childhood sexual abuse, concluding that such abuse was responsible for many of their neuroses. But he would soon abandon that theory. In subsequent writings he explained that it would have required accepting that all fathers, including his own, were perverse, and that couldn't be true. This about-face led to his theory of female hysteria, so damaging to women since. Freud's failure to believe his female patients mirrored society's refusal to believe what girls and women experience.

Gender discrimination wasn't only psychological or emotional. It was economic, manifest in the labor force in a variety of ways. In the 1950s women earned 64 cents for every dollar earned by men.[3] They weren't hired if pregnant and were fired or penalized if they became pregnant while working. They were expected to put up with sexual harassment without complaint. A perfect storm of discriminatory practices prevented women from achieving management positions. The "glass ceiling" seemed unbreakable. In fact, gender discrimination was apparent in every area of life: personal relationships, education, advertising, civil law, health care, the military—the list goes on.

In my adolescence, when it came to relations between the sexes—male and female, the only two genders acknowledged at the time—it was the girl's responsibility to preserve her reputation. Only "bad" girls let boys "go all the way." "Good" girls were expected to resist letting boys do more than give us a goodnight kiss or engage in what we called mild necking or petting. Expressions such as allowing a boy "to get to first, second, or third base" employed the male sports metaphors that permeate our culture. Honest discussion of female desire or need wasn't part of our experience.

Meanwhile, "boys would be boys."

The logical prelude to "men will be men."

Those limitations extended to our minds as well. When I was in high school, girls weren't required or even expected to take math or science courses. We were taught homemaking—pretentiously called Home Economics—while boys learned skills considered more appropriate to their gender, such as mechanics or carpentry. We were taught to type so we'd have something to fall back on as we waited for a husband, or in case we never found one. The word "spinster" carried an aura of failure, while "bachelor" evoked eligibility.

My biology teacher Carl V'Cella and his wife rented a couple of rooms off my parents' garage. That may have been why he passed me with a D rather than give me the failing grade I deserved when all I could draw after staring into the microscope were curved black lines: my own lashes. It wasn't until 1957, when the Soviets launched Sputnik, that female students in the United States were encouraged to take the courses it was hoped would help the country catch up, or even put it ahead in the race to conquer space.

Miss Shannon was my high school drama coach. I was attracted to theater, auditioned for the lead role in my junior-year play and got it. I can't remember the name of that play or my character. I do remember that she was a bride, tragically murdered on her wedding day. Miss Shannon lent me her own wedding gown for the part. She said she'd been married for a few days many years before. No further explanation was forthcoming, and I didn't ask. Looking back, I realize she was a lesbian, deep in the closet. The stench of whiskey she exuded undoubtedly had something to do with how fearful she must have been that her sexual identity might be discovered.

....

Tom Erhard was the faculty sponsor of our yearbook, student newspaper, and literary magazine. I worked on the latter two, writing a fashion column for the first and several romantic stories for the second. Although poetry still eluded me, I already knew I wanted to be a writer. I sought mentorship where I could find it. Erhard was easygoing, gregarious, and encouraging. A group of literary-minded students often hung out after school at his house where the conversation was stimulating, and Tom's wife always had a platter of freshly baked cookies.

On one of those afternoons my teacher got me alone and calmly began describing the physical attributes of his penis, hoping to spark my enthusiasm.

"It's thin but long," he said, searching my startled face for signs of interest. I was embarrassed, then horrified, and quickly changed the subject.

From then on, I avoided being alone with Erhard, but continued to frequent his group of would-be writers. The one-sided conversation about his penis had simply been one in a series of aggressive moves against women and girls that characterized that place and time. I could neither bring myself to challenge the inappropriate remark nor report it to anyone. Who would have believed me? Many years later I wrote to Erhard. By then I was able to verbalize my anger. He vehemently denied my accusation. I heard that his first wife had left him, and he'd married an ex-student, a woman one-third his age.

As long as patriarchy has existed, men have felt entitled to abuse women, most often using sex as their weapon. We call it sexual abuse, but it is really about power. The thing about the sort of proposition I experienced from my writing teacher was its inevitability. Like background noise, it was so routine it wasn't worth mentioning. "Your skirt must have been too short," was the counter-accusation leveled at a woman who dared report such an assault, shifting the blame to her.

In my generation, incest and rape were considered taboos. The acts themselves were far from taboo; they crossed all class and cultural lines and were much more pandemic than we knew. It was talking about them that was unacceptable. No public discussion, no campaigns to let us know our rights, no trained specialists at police precincts, no rape kits preserved in connection with the attacks, and few adults who would have believed a girl or woman brave enough to accuse a man of such behavior. Over the course of my life we've moved from that suffocating silence through travesties such as the congressional hearing at which Anita Hill was forced to face an all-male panel of disrespectful senators,[4] and finally to the empowering contemporary movement called #MeToo. I came up in a world in which #MeToo was unimaginable.

....

In junior high we didn't date one-on-one but went out in groups to the local community center where western tunes screamed from an old record player until a respectable hour, and girls and boys congregated on opposite sides of the room. Sometimes I spent an entire evening without being asked to dance. Invariably I was one of the last girls left standing. I tried to act as if I didn't care. A relentless hope kept me returning week after week. I remember sleeping with the photograph of a boy I liked beneath my pillow.

FRIDAY NIGHT AT THE COMMUNITY CENTER

The street is *Buena Vista*, Good View,
but the corner building
sheds its peeling stucco
of fake adobe,
scuffed walls sweat the used-up sound
of old 78s.

Friday night at the community center
our fathers shuttled us there
to stand and yearn:
stuffed bras, cinched waists,
shifting
from foot to foot.

I always stood against the wall
where girls no one asked to dance
watched our popular classmates
stomp across the wooden floor
obedient eyes lost in strains
of repetitious sound.

Crinolines. Circle skirts.
Diminishing hope
then home to bed
with a photo of the basketball team
pressed against future promise
of breasts.

Kissing his face in that picture
was the closest I got to junior high romance
until an older dropout asked me out
and I gagged on his tongue
pumping machine-gun fire
down my throat.

I don't know when the community center
closed its doors,

its western music beat gone still,
ferocity of spring winds
whipping sharp nettle of tumbleweed
across a cracked patio.

I turn a corner. The old building
greets me:
hungry, mocking,
vomiting memory
too sad and hapless to forget,
too smoldering in pain.

If only we could do it over again. If we
could do it over
with what we know now:
a different music,
other rules or no rules
but pure rhythm of the human heart.

On one of those Friday nights I had begged my mother to let me wear a heishi of hers, a single strand of turquoise beads I loved. My father drove a couple of my girlfriends and me to the community center. Riding in the back seat of our family station wagon, I leaned against a door that suddenly gave way. We weren't going fast, but I landed on the street, the precious beads scattering across the intersection. When Dad carried me into the house, Mother's first question was about the heishi. She swore she was most concerned about me, but that's not what it felt like.

Still, Mother's creative mind continued to delight us. When the city removed a regulation blue postbox from the corner of our lot, she replaced it with a miniature replica two inches tall she'd purchased at our local Five & Dime. She invited us outside to contemplate the altered landscape. "Look," she said, "at how the mail box has shrunk!" This was typical of the pranks for which our mother was famous—with friends as well as family. The intricately rhymed poems she wrote for our birthdays were also clever, funny, often moving. In them she was able to express emotions she couldn't manage in more casual everyday exchanges.

Unacknowledged abuse in her own childhood must have made it difficult for Mother to express vulnerability as an adult; perhaps this was the reason she had such a hard time opening up to those she loved most. This inability must have been as painful for her as it was to us. Her close friends definitely saw a different side of her. We sometimes had trouble recognizing the expressive, compassionate woman they knew.

....

Most boys I dated in high school took me out for the proverbial movie and milk shake, engaged in the expected half hour of truncated foreplay, then brought me home. I knew that afterward some of them would go down to Saint Mary's, the city's Catholic high school, where the girls could repent of their "sins" in confession and were therefore more relaxed about sex—or so rumor had it.

There were exceptions, though. Dave was painfully shy and only dared touch his tightly clenched lips to my eager ones after we'd been dating for months. Following his graduation from high school, he made a lifelong career of portraying the role of a cowboy hero, offering what he called good values to generations of young boys. Many years later, after my return to Albuquerque, we met once for coffee. I hoped we might be able to talk about how each of us had felt back in high school. Instead, he presented me with a glossy 8 × 10 that he signed "Sincerely, Red Ryder." He died the following year.

Larry's first-generation Italian parents lavished me with expensive gifts. They hoped we would marry one day. He too was reluctant to engage in physical intimacy. I didn't know why and assumed it was my fault. A few years after graduation Larry and I reconnected in New York and he was able to admit he was gay. By that time—at least in the big city—the tough shell of rigidly contrived gender roles had begun to crack. For girls like me, its damage took years to unravel.

And then there was Sam, son of a Baptist minister whose dream was to follow in his father's footsteps. Sam was also interested in writing; my senior year we were coeditors of the school paper. It might have been by default that he asked me to be his date for senior prom. I feel a slight shudder of repulsion now, as I recall Sam's pudgy body, stale odor, and total commitment to Christ His Savior. I remember my dress with some delight though; I'd chosen a deep red velvet bodice and matching long tulle skirt, decidedly different from the pastel formals popular with my friends. But what remains most indelibly from that night was what we did after the dance ended. While our contemporaries found places to make out, Sam and I drove up into the Jémez Mountains, accommodated ourselves in full prom regalia atop a large flat rock, and argued about the existence of God. Neither of us convinced the other.

One high school night I went out with a boy I hardly knew, a fellow student but older and from a rougher, tougher culture. He grabbed me hard and stuck his tongue down my throat, gagging me. I had never experienced this before and was shaken. His was not a tentative or exploratory tongue but one that bored hard, choked, intended conquest. As I pushed him away, he laughed and began talking about war, machine guns, bayonets.

My most memorable date during those years was with the captain of the football team at Albuquerque High. This was the other public high school, the one with a reputation for "bad" kids. I was surprised when Freddy asked me out, surprised and excited. I couldn't have anticipated how the evening would end.

It was a double date and I didn't know the other couple. Freddy and I sat in the back seat. After the requisite movie and snack, we drove into the foothills of the Sandias, those mountains to the east of the city that I would one day hike and come to love. I grew increasingly anxious but was afraid to say anything. The driver eventually pulled onto a narrow dirt side road and parked the car.

As if on cue, Freddy grabbed me. His hands were everywhere, tearing at my blouse, pushing beneath my skirt, shoving his rough fingers inside my panties. I was terrified. In a voice so weak and hoarse I hardly recognized it as my own, I begged him to stop and cried for help from the girl in the front seat. Fully involved with her date, she ignored me.

Then I remembered something my father had told me: If a boy or man ever attacked me like this, I should try bringing my knee up into his groin, hard. How I managed to do this then, I can't remember. Freddy recoiled in pain. I opened the car door, fell out, picked myself up and began to run. After a few hundred yards I looked back and was relieved to see no one was following me. The car had disappeared in shadows. I ran and ran, sobbing and eventually wetting myself. We had parked a few miles outside the city, and it took me several hours to get home—enveloped in darkness for a while, then stumbling along streets weakly illuminated by city lights. I think it was four or five a.m. by the time I stood at my front door.

My mother heard my key in the lock. I may still have been crying. She got up and asked what had happened. I told her, and her only question was "Did he penetrate you?" When I said he hadn't, she breathed a deep sigh of relief. "Okay," she said, "so no harm done. Get some sleep and you'll feel better in the morning." For my mother, if you could pretend an event away, there was nothing to worry about.

The story about the volcano is an Albuquerque legend. I was older by then, in my last year of high school. Perhaps my friendships with best friends Lucy Ann and Carol had begun to wear thin. I became friendly with two boys who were definite outsiders, both of them gay but unaware or already adept at hiding their sexuality: safely unsexed in their relationships with me.

One was Clarence, a complete misfit who would later become a kleptomaniac, graduate to breaking and entering, then get help and settle down in a small antique shop in the village of Bernalillo. Once, long after I'd moved away and returned for a visit, I went to see him there, discovered a little statuette he'd stolen from me, picked up a Navajo bracelet I coveted, and told him I'd take it in trade. He smiled. Much later I heard that Clarence had died in his fifties, victim of a rare heart disorder.

The other outsider was James. In appearance he was the perfect ladies' man—tall, good-looking, with elegant manners. On the inside who knew what torments hid. We were an unlikely threesome but inseparable for a time. Our peers perceived Clarence, James, and me as strange. Occasionally a female friend—her name may have been Dee or Dinah—joined us, completing a foursome that may have fooled some.

I can't remember whose idea it was to drive out to the volcanoes west of the city. Who borrowed the pickup truck. Who gathered the old tires and cans of gasoline. It was dark, maybe midnight or one a.m. Clarence, James, and I were squeezed together on the truck's only seat. Our awkward load thudded and shifted as we made our way along the winding dirt road.

The line of extinct volcanoes cut a barely discernible silhouette on the horizon. A rarely traveled road led to the largest crater. We pulled up to the rim, got out, and walked to the edge of the dark hollow. Wordlessly, as I remember, we unloaded the tires and tossed them into the void. Then we emptied our cans of gas. Before we scrambled back into the pickup, we'd set a confident fire. And it was back down that dirt road once more. Clarence and James dropped me at my house and then made their own ways home. Before separating, we'd stopped for a few minutes, pricked our fingers, mixed our blood and promised each other "never to tell." I would keep that promise for more than thirty years.

Within an hour an agitated radio announcer was spewing instructions: "One of the volcanoes is showing unexpected activity . . . citizenry must leave town in an orderly manner . . . take only what is absolutely necessary."

Road to the volcano west of Albuquerque, 2009 (photo by Margaret Randall).

When my parents routed me from bed, I feigned surprise. But before we could actually evacuate, we and the rest of Albuquerque were informed that the plume of black smoke had been a prank. No need for alarm. Everyone should remain calm.

We weren't found out. We never spoke, even with one another, about what we had done. No gleeful "got away with it, huh?" No retracing our steps or going back, even in conversation, to that night. An act carried out for its own sake.

As the years passed, I've stumbled upon missing pieces of my friends' lives. At my fortieth high school reunion, James put in an appearance. He was living in London, still closeted—at least at that event—and seemed to want to avoid being seen with Barbara (my wife) and me. Pieces of Clarence's life overtook me as I learned that mutual friends had known him after he and I lost touch. One remembered they'd studied anthropology together at the University of New Mexico. Then, just as I was writing these lines, someone else told me that when it became possible to live an alternative sexual identity my old friend began living his to the full. He had a large Virgin of Guadalupe tattooed across his chest and ran with a gay Mexican biker gang.[5] Had he died of a heart condition or of AIDS? The man with whom I was reminiscing wasn't sure, though he'd always assumed the latter.

....

PERSONAL CARTOGRAPHY

I couldn't stay away, not forever, although
spring winds parched my throat
and tiny cactus needles
pierced the flesh of my breasts.

Three hundred sixty degrees of cloudless sky
spun my head until graying eyes
threatened to jump
orbits unable to rein them in.

Then a furious thunderhead
released its ferocity
of desert storm,
scouring life from canyon walls.

Towering red rock fortresses
pressed in on either side,
wringing awe
from stooped shoulders.

Silky wax of the single bloom
on a defiant Prickly Pear
met my fingertips,
reminding me survival matters.

....

My high school girlfriends and I talked about boys, clothes, and what we hoped our futures might be like. Those future hopes reflected all the assumptions of the era. We never spoke about our deeper feelings or the values each of us was beginning to form. That would have embarrassed us and, besides, we didn't yet know what they were.

Lucy Ann's family was New England proper: her father a Republican member of the New Mexico State House of Representatives, her mother a woman whose excessive weight may have protected her from an intimacy she didn't want. She was very sweet and did her best to pretend away her husband's alcoholism. I remember being impressed when I noticed that the Kleenex and toilet paper in their bathroom always matched: sets of pink or pale yellow or powdery blue. Every family had its secrets, and every family devoted considerable energy to keeping them under wraps.

My other best friend, Carol, lived around the corner. Her family seemed more relaxed and open. Only many years later did she confess that her father had been abusive. I never learned how. I remember being startled one day when Carol told me she'd lied about something or other. She was so casual about it. In my family, lies were elaborate, the effort to hide them determined. I couldn't imagine so freely confessing that one had lied.

We had no language with which to express the wars raging within us. Words such as alcoholism, battery, incest, and shame weren't in our vocabulary. Yet language was the tool that might have helped us articulate the many faces of gender inequality. Our very conditioning—the ways in which we'd been shaped from before birth to please men, take abuse, strangle our own needs, and pretend it was all good—made it impossible for us to know ourselves.

....

From my earliest memory, there was an elephant in the room of my life. I suffered from a terrifying phobia: toadstools, mushrooms, tree fungus. Even turning the page of a magazine or book and seeing a picture of one of these wracked me with sudden nausea. Those cute little red ceramic figurines with white dots struck me as obscene. If I came across the real thing growing out of doors, I froze. Sometimes I fainted. I was terrified by the idea that they could appear from one moment to the next. I imagined them entering me and squeezed shut every one of my body's orifices in defense. For years I had a repeated dream in which I was walking along a country path bordered on both sides by what I most feared. The path got narrower and narrower until I woke in a cold sweat. Forests were places I avoided. Even lawns unsettled me.

My fear was so intense that I refrained from telling anyone about it. In kindergarten a young childhood neighbor I believed to be my best friend chased me with a small toadstool, forcing me to lock myself in a bathroom for hours. In fourth grade a school picnic turned into a nightmare. As I got older, I understood that fickle alliances could not be trusted. Used against me, knowledge of my vulnerability could be a lethal weapon. My immediate family members knew, of course, and were perplexed but protective.

The fear seemed out of sync with my otherwise adventurous risk-taking spirit.

It wasn't the phobia that was the elephant in the room, but what it symbolized. And I would be fifty years old before I remembered what that was. After my return from Latin America I entered psychotherapy. I was fortunate to find a wonderful therapist who followed the teachings of Wilhelm Reich. Through several years of talk and body work, she helped me discover the origin of my trauma.

My maternal grandfather had sexually abused me when I was an infant. It happened before I possessed the use of speech. My maternal grandmother looked on; that passive but twisted interest may have had something to do with the abuse she also suffered at his hands or farther back in her own childhood. I had disassociated completely, erasing the incest from memory when I was unable to do anything to prevent it. The mushroom wasn't a stand-in for my grandfather's penis but for his face or tongue: powdery white and always too close in its menacing invasion of my innocence.

For so many years the elephant in the room was invisible even to me. But it was there, walking beside me, keeping me off-balance and afraid. The produce sections of supermarkets were dangerous. Certain restaurants could be too. As I got older, I developed coping skills and excuses (lies) to help me navigate. By the time I was able to remember the incest, those grandparents were long dead. I have never been able to rid myself of the phobia. It continues to plague me and writing about it feels risky.

Discovering its origin has been helpful, though. It's allowed me to know myself better and care for myself with greater intention. Like so many other women (and some men), the recovery movement of the 1980s offered an embracing community. I chose to try to deal with the memories through my art and produced the small book *This Is about Incest*, in which I used my skills as a poet, essayist, photographer, and oral historian to tell my story. I traveled the country reading from that book. Invariably audience members would approach me afterward and share their own stories of molestation.

....

THE GREEN CLOTHES HAMPER

Rain almost hides my mountains today.
Low clouds snag the rocky skirts, colors
of rain and clouds clean everything.

I speak of the rain, the clouds, the living
colors of this land
because it seems impossible to cut this silence with the words

my grandfather was a sick and evil man
posing as healer.
Now I retrieve his hands and eyes, his penis
filling my tiny infant mouth

as he forced himself into a body, mine,
that still finds reason easier than feeling.
Here is the green Lucite top
of a clothes hamper where rape impaled diapers.

Here is memory catching up with itself,
overtaking asthma, compulsive food, fear
of that which is not itself.
This lost green hamper. My body coming home.

Internalizing my grandparents' incest also enabled me to make important connections between an adult abusing his power by invading a vulnerable body and a country abusing its power by invading a dependent one within its sphere of influence. I noticed that the signs of trauma are the same, whether we are looking at an individual or a nation. This analysis came at the end of a long process of remembering, though, in which the personal and the political showed themselves to be of a piece. Throughout my childhood and adolescence, I continued to feel as if I walked a tightrope strung between two realities: the one woven of the hypocrisy and lies society so carefully crafts and the one I was beginning to intuit in my desire.

High school gave way to college, but I didn't feel engaged with the courses offered in the mid-1950s at my hometown University of New Mexico (UNM). Although supportive of all three of their children, my parents conceived of a university education differently for their son than for their daughters. My brother could have attended any college he chose. It would be important for him to graduate with a career that would make them proud and enable him to support the woman he married. Our parents imagined my sister and I would find men who would take care of us. We might find those men at university, but the quality of our education wasn't of primary importance. Until much later, they considered our career choices to be hobbies.[6]

In high school I had been good at drama and literature. The university offered me a $100 theater scholarship. Back then, this covered in-state tuition, and I continued living at home. I don't remember any discussion about whether I might prefer to go somewhere else. So, I shifted my attention to UNM where I decided to major in drama and minor in philosophy. I found college uninspiring in every way and quit after little more than a year. I wonder now how this may have mirrored my mother having quit school to attend the Art Students League.

The era was plagued with more than patriarchy; racism was also everywhere in our small southwestern city where a minuscule neighborhood of blacks was mostly composed of porters who worked for the Atchison Topeka and Santa Fe Railway. The much larger Indian and Mexican American communities were completely segregated. My high school had one black student and a small number of Hispanics in a graduating class of five hundred.

My parents had always taught us that racism was unacceptable. Their discourse was one of equality, but their actions didn't always measure up. When a university friend of mine, an exchange student from Ghana, faced blatant racism at his dorm and couldn't find a landlord in the city willing to rent to him, I had no doubt my parents would be happy to have him live in the little apartment off their garage.

I was wrong. "It's not us," my mother and father insisted. "It's the neighbors. What if they won't let their children play with your little brother? And think about what could happen to the property values." They hoped I would understand. I didn't. Confused and angry, I stopped speaking to my parents for several months. The contradictions between what they'd taught us was right and their own actions became more and more intolerable to me. Or I was becoming more aware. And I wasn't yet able to situate my mother and father within their generation, grappling with the values, secrets, and lies they'd inherited.

....

Despite the subterfuge, despite their patriarchal assumptions and occasional racist attitudes, my parental home was in many ways open and loving. When they moved our family west in 1947, Mother and Dad were rebelling against their own parents' values. I was ten at the time. They were tired of my maternal grandfather's hypocritical religious piety, my paternal grandmother's ostentation and Wednesday night family dinners replete with finger bowls and three forks to the left of each plate. They fell in love with New Mexico, chose Albuquerque as their new home and moved us there, only informing their families after the fact. It was a decision that would profoundly shape my life and work.

Both my parents were able to reinvent themselves in New Mexico. Given what I suspect of her childhood, Mother was a survivor. As a young woman, she had studied at New York's Art Students League and was a sculptor for a while. She never really excelled in that genre but became a skilled mold-maker. When we came west, she took Spanish classes at the university and became an avid translator. Unhappily married, she had a string of affairs, some of them with her professors. She didn't try to hide them, and they were long a source of sadness to our father and embarrassment to my sister, brother, and me.

Mother translated several novels by Ramón Sender, her professor and one of her lovers. Later she discovered Cuban revolutionary writer José Martí and devoted the rest of her life to translating and retranslating his many books. Throwing herself into that work became a passion. It also enabled her to close herself in her room for hours on end so as not to have to interact as much with Dad or even with her children. Dad returned to the music he loved and hosted informal Friday night chamber-music gatherings at which he played his cello. Artists, writers, and musicians frequented my childhood home. Paintings graced the walls.

As a music teacher in the Albuquerque public schools, my father had three months off each summer, and our family took trips to Europe, Latin America, and Alaska—often on freighters and camping out. Although my mother and father were largely ignorant of the political situations in the countries we visited, and our tourism was only slightly more in-depth than that of the typical upper middle-class traveler, there was something adventurous about those trips and they broadened my horizons in important ways. With my parents, my friends and I also talked about things other parents avoided. We had no curfew and our home was considered an ideal place to hang out.

This apparent openness only made the secrets and lies more difficult to recognize and decipher. The anguish I felt about the pain in my parents' marriage plagued me for years. My father adored my mother and forgave her every transgression. My mother admitted she had never been in love with him, and her frustration was a constant undercurrent in our home. Their pretense at happiness crumbled periodically when my ordinarily gentle father, unable to contain himself, would explode in verbal rage and Mother would promise "to be good." Then things would calm down and the cycle would begin again.

My parents' idealized show marriage with its underbelly of incompatibility was a model that confused me. It played well to the pretense of the times but only made me feel less at home in my own skin. Increasingly, my desire seemed at odds with every social expectation.

....

My home life, loving and supportive as it was, seemed restrictive and shallow. Dishonest. Even fraudulent. School didn't excite me. I knew I wanted to be a writer but didn't believe I needed a formal education to reach that goal. I wanted to leave home, escape the lies. The only way a young woman of my class and culture could achieve a degree of independence was to trade her parental home for one with a husband. I married a troubled young man from Cincinnati when I'd just turned eighteen.

Sam Jacobs and I met on the MS *Queen Elizabeth* headed for Europe in the summer between my last year of high school and first of college. My family and I were traveling in tourist class. He and his family were in first, as befitted the owner of a national department-store chain. Sam took to "slumming" on our deck and sometimes snuck me up to his. I was intrigued by his world and unable to see how troubled he was. We stayed in touch. I visited him at Christmas 1953, and in spring 1954 he came to New Mexico and we married in Ciudad Juárez, just across the Mexican border. I was a virgin before I met Sam, and his demanding and insensitive lovemaking introduced me to that aspect of intimacy in a confusing way. It would put me on a physically dysfunctional path for a very long time.

Although Sam left school and didn't tell his parents his plans, ours wasn't really an elopement. My parents knew what we were doing. My power of persuasion and their liberal attitude caused them to go along. They must have realized I would do what I wanted in any case. Sam's parents weren't so understanding. His father appeared in Albuquerque the day after we returned from Juárez and tried to talk him into an annulment. We were married almost four years, miserable ones for me although ones that did get me out of my parental home. But real independence wouldn't come so easily.

Despite his erratic behavior and our incompatibility, that time with Sam gave me some valuable experiences. A year ahead of me, he too left the university. My privileged young husband came up with the idea of cashing our wedding presents in—the pressure cooker, vacuum cleaner, flatware—and buying a Lambretta motor scooter. With the $400 we had left over, he thought we could make it to India. We rode to New York, heavy Bergen backpacks, old Army surplus sleeping bags, and a tent along with the two of us weighing down the small machine, boarded a Dutch freighter for the ocean crossing, and disembarked in Rotterdam. Then came the real test: days of slow progress down through central Europe, nights in youth hostels, romantic and sometimes not-so-romantic noonday meals of bread, fruit, and cheese.

We crossed the Pyrenees and entered northern Spain. Among the few visuals I retain is that lonely and powerful landscape: stark hills dotted with olive groves and medieval fortress towns like Toledo, which in the 1950s conserved considerably more of its authenticity than it does today. When we arrived in Madrid, we were almost out of money. Sam's master scheme included our making an advantageous exchange for Indian rupees in what was then the free port of Tangiers. Meanwhile the time had come to look for work. For what seems in retrospect to have been weeks—though it must have been more like days—we lived on Madrid's streets, sleeping in the shelter of metro entrances, eating how and where we could.

I remember going behind upscale apartment buildings and rummaging through garbage cans, compelled more by hunger than revulsion. I remember Sam urging me to sell my body to the men who hung around the same places we did, and my refusal—out of a healthy mix of pride and fear. Still, I felt I was failing him. Our salvation was meeting Enriqueta, who ran a student boarding house in a working-class section of the capital. She lived with her much older husband, Eraclio; their young son, Cholo; and Queta's eager American lover, Gar. The passionate couple feared discovery by her husband and the consequences of his jealous rage. Sam's and my arrival couldn't have been more propitious: for Queta and Gar or for us. We offered understanding ears, even some concrete aid in a desperate situation. Queta's boarding house provided us with shelter and food.

I cleaned bathrooms, scrubbed the boarders' wash in a stone tub, helped with the shopping and cooking. Sam used our motor scooter to run errands. Each night we slept on a thin mattress rolled out on a grease-coated cot we'd set up in the kitchen after the last of the dinner dishes were done. My Spanish was what I had learned from Mrs. Velásquez in fifth grade: "¿Cómo está usted? . . . ¿Dónde está la estación de trenes?" Indicative of the times? Perhaps today's students learn to ask for the airport instead of the train station. Despite his professed proficiency at almost everything, Sam knew no Spanish at all.

I learned my first useful street Spanish from the women who lived next door. Queta's boarding house occupied half of one floor in a shabby building; the other half was a brothel where a group of sad, low-paid prostitutes went out each night in search of clients. During the day they slept, groomed one another, cared for their children, and ran the sorts of errands common to us all. One of those women, Juana, took me in hand. She would invite me to go with her to a large market, where she'd patiently point out papas, lechuga, frijoles. We became friends. Then one day Juana disappeared. She had been picked up the night before by the local police during a routine raid of a nearby bar. I went to see her in jail. Her head was shaved, her beautiful black hair gone, making her face seem very small. Her deep-set eyes looked larger and empty, expressionless. Days later, fine paid, she was out and back on the street. A few months after that she was dead. Her friend who gave me the news explained that Juana was old: "Twenty-eight," she said. "She's with our Heavenly Father now."

Sam and I got ourselves together and continued on our way. We traveled south to Algeciras, crossed the Strait of Gibraltar to Tangiers and found that free port curiously devoid of rupees. Back in southern Spain our scooter hit an oil slick and took off sideways. She flipped a few times before landing in a ditch at the side of an isolated country road. We were thrown free and, except for a few bruises, managed to emerge unhurt. But the Lambretta couldn't be made to run.

That accident meant a further dent in our diminishing resources. We had to take the scooter to its native Italy to be fixed and spent one long week in Genoa sitting in a garage, trying to stretch our poor Spanish into some semblance of Italian so as to be able to communicate with the mechanic on duty. I remember student restaurants, rich ice cream, and faded buildings of striped black and white marble. Back in Spain, Sam heard about a job on a US Army base near Seville. They were hiring civilians to oversee the building of an oil pipeline. He got hired, and our fortunes went from zero to exuberant overnight.

We rented a rooftop apartment in Seville's old Santa Cruz neighborhood. Orange trees lined the streets and the scent of their blossoms turned the air pungent and sweet. Soon we were sharing the place with three other travelers, all men. A Swede, an Englishman, and an adventurer from New Jersey. I cooked for us all. Once again, I could be the successful wife/hostess/woman of the house. I learned to prepare the food of southern Spain. We always had a 16-liter jug of cheap white table wine standing beside the round table where we ate. Under the thick felt that covered that table was a small pan with live coals where we could warm our feet in winter. One morning, after Sam went off to work, I crawled into the Englishman's bed. I quickly retreated, though, before we made love. I yearned for pleasure but remained fearful of that unforgivable option called unfaithfulness.

One of the most vibrant memories I have of that time is our association with a group of young Flamenco dancers at a club called Patio Andaluz. They traded us beginning dance lessons for English classes. Sam's undisputed musical talent made it fairly easy for him to master a bit of Flamenco guitar. I got good enough with the castanets and special pumps to join the backup dancers in several of the place's nightly numbers. For the club owner we must have been a novelty, perhaps a drawing card: a couple of fresh-faced youngsters from the United States. For us the experience was glamorous, exciting.

In Seville I embarked upon my first overtly political mission. One day a pharmacist with socialist and feminist ideals—although he wouldn't have used the latter term—asked if I'd be willing to help him bring diaphragms into the country. Franco was in power, birth control was outlawed, and the sale or use of any device limiting procreation was punishable by death. Wealthy Spanish women crossed the border into France to buy what they needed. The vast majority of poor Spanish women had a baby a year. This pharmacist, who we met quite by chance, knew he could purchase diaphragms in the free port of Tangiers. The problem was bringing them into the country without being caught.

As would be my response to many future invitations to risk, I immediately agreed that I, an innocent-looking woman from the United States, would have no trouble doing the job. And I would do it, repeatedly, over a period of several months. I traveled to Algeciras, boarded the ferry to Tangiers, bought the diaphragms, and returned with them hidden beneath a false lining in an old Samsonite suitcase the pharmacist lent me. Finally, a customs official may have recognized my too-familiar face. He searched my bags with particular zeal, perhaps expecting to find drugs or money or gems. I don't believe he thought of diaphragms. I wasn't caught but stopped the runs.

Then Sam and I came home. And home meant facing, once again, the problems in our relationship. I remember a brief vacation with Sam's parents to the Red River Valley in northern New Mexico. Sam's mother took me aside and asked how the marriage was. "What kind of a husband is he?" she asked, perhaps amazed that he could be a husband at all. "Wonderful," I lied.

With the money we'd saved and sent home from Sam's job at the base, we bought a tiny house: nothing more than a box in a poor neighborhood

Author in Flamenco dress, Seville, Spain, 1956 (family snapshot, attribution unknown).

near the New Mexico State Fairgrounds. A living room, bedroom, kitchen, and bath surrounded by a listless yard enclosed by a gray pumice-block wall. And we got a dog, a young boxer that Sam named Bouchi after a childhood pet. During the day, when both of us worked, Bouchi remained tied to a long pulley that ran the length of the backyard. One afternoon I came home to find poor Bouchi hanged. She had jumped the wall and the rope wasn't long enough to allow for her descent to the ground on the other side. I remember being horrified by the sight of her hanging body, already beginning to bloat.

I got a job at Lytle Engineering and Manufacturing Company. It produced technical operation and maintenance manuals for the early missile programs. I was hired as a secretary but quickly began helping to write some of those manuals. I remember being told their comprehension level could not exceed sixth grade, something I later remembered with concern. They continued to pay me a secretary's salary.

Sam went back to school. As the man, it was understood that he would be the one to get an education. One of us had to provide support. That was me, with my secretarial jobs. I must have been relieved to have an acceptable reason to quit school. I no longer remember what disciplines Sam studied, changing whenever one bored him, another demanded too much, or a professor in yet another failed to recognize his genius. He was in music for a while but felt he was too advanced for what the University of New Mexico had to offer in that department.

My health coverage at Lytle included psychiatry, the choice at the time when a person was in emotional turmoil. A number of psychiatric theories were beginning to be in vogue. People I knew talked about Freud, Jung, Adler. I was miserable and decided to take advantage of the opportunity and see a psychiatrist. I retain vivid memories of that young male professional whose office I visited each week. A large plate-glass window framed the beautiful Sandia Mountains. I no longer remember the doctor's name, never knew what school of psychiatry he practiced, and didn't question his authority, although I found the sessions perplexing and frequently tedious.

One afternoon I sat as usual in the armchair across from the doctor and began to talk about the possibility of leaving Sam. I was thinking out loud, testing the idea. The doctor looked straight at me and said something like: "Well, it's about time." I was shocked, couldn't understand why he had allowed me to suffer so long. All I felt at that moment was that this man had sat by while I endured endless agony. Wasn't I paying for his help? I picked up a set of smoothly carved wooden figurines from the psychiatrist's low table and fingered their polished surfaces. Then, in a rage, I threw one after another against that plate-glass window. The doctor simply sat there, wordless, watching. I quit those weekly sessions and was out of the marriage in a matter of days.

Toward the end of our relationship, my young husband burned everything I'd written to that point. In terms of the material itself, it wasn't much of a loss. But his jealous rage convinced me I couldn't stay with him. I contacted Sam's parents and told them I was divorcing their son. He was their responsibility now. And I began relating to people older and wiser than my high school friends or those I had acquired while in that early marriage. People who lived their values, who could articulate creative desire through their life choices as well as verbally.

Before I stop writing about my high school years, though, I want to tell a story that links my time with Sam to my later life.

It was at a poetry reading I gave in Santa Barbara, California, in the 1980s, that I heard about Sam for the first time in many years. As the auditorium emptied out, I noticed one young woman who'd remained in her seat. As I made my way toward the exit, she stopped me: "I'm Sam Jacobs's widow," she said, "and I'd like to talk to you." I was stunned. We sat down together in that otherwise empty hall and she told me her story:

> Sam was in a mental hospital for several years. When he got well, he went back to school and became a geologist. He was married briefly to someone else between his marriage to you and ours. And yes, by the time we got together he was capable of a mature relationship. We had two children and were together until the day I came home and found him dead of a heart attack at forty-two. He was the love of my life.

This woman, whose name I no longer remember, told me that Sam had always regretted the way he'd treated me. She asked if I would have breakfast with her the following morning, before I left town. She wanted to show me some family photograph albums, introduce me to the man who had proved such a bad choice for me but had made her so happy.

I was glad to know that Sam had been able to make a good life for himself and others. Bad choice and all, he'd been a stepping-stone to my emancipation.

....

DREAM ME

I want to believe statehood in 1912
dreamed my 1947 arrival

just as the city's seventeenth-century plaza
dreamed today's cluster of skyscrapers,

or native inhabitants
living along the sinuous Río Grande

knew bearded men with guns and cross
would bring a time of terror and death.

What questions do we ask of our dreams?
What stories do they tell us
in the darkness of night?

From left to right: Connie Fox (then Blair), Jane and Herbie Goldman, Elaine de Kooning, and author, at a bar in Ciudad Juárez, Mexico, 1957 (attribution unknown).

WITHOUT WARNING

At the bus stop and out of the corner of my eye
I see myself waiting,
awkward bundle at my feet.
I am wearing the same sky-blue fleece
though it hangs looser against my body.
My hair, still long and full and brown,
frames the younger me in her oblivion.

I swerve and almost hit the car to my right,
snap my neck
to get one last glimpse of myself
before people I loved
took what wasn't theirs,
a child stopped calling home,
and temperature threatened my planet.

Without warning I make a U-turn
and slow way down
to observe every detail
of my younger self.
I even consider a shouted question
might bring an answer
against all mathematical odds.

She looks straight at me and smiles.
I smile back
and keep on driving,
hoping to keep
my appointment with myself.

Chapter Four

THE PICTURE
PLANE

New York, 1958–1961

Art is art. Everything else is
everything else.
—AD REINHARDT, "25 LINES OF
WORDS ON ART," *IT IS* (SPRING 1958)

I moved from where I grew up in Albuquerque, New Mexico, to where I was born in New York City at the beginning of 1958. It wasn't a simple or straightforward journey out and back; I had escaped my family home—loving but often confusing—by way of that bad and short-lived marriage, and my young husband and I had spent a year and a half in Spain. Back in New Mexico and divorced, I was looking for the next great adventure.

Two years earlier, at a party in the east mountains, an event that had a lasting impact on me was listening to painter Richard Kurman read Allen Ginsberg's "Howl" out loud from beginning to end. I was mesmerized. Every word found resonance in me. From that moment, I knew I wanted to be a poet. Poetry had eluded me throughout my public school education. It had been poorly taught, requiring rote memorization rather than being presented as something I could relate to my own restless life.

Ginsberg's poem wasn't obviously related to my life either. He was a brilliant writer and gay man, with a mentally ill mother burdened by residual PTSD from the Jewish Holocaust. He clearly had a very complete formal education and sought to expand his awareness through experimenting with hallucinatory drugs. I was a provincial young woman bursting at the seams with awkward creativity. My family's contradictions and attempt to construct false masks had long made me feel off-balance.

I may have been most compelled by the way "Howl" railed against the social hypocrisy of the times, a hypocrisy that threatened to shape my female life in ways I felt but could not yet articulate. Because of the lies my family lived, and surely because I had been a victim of childhood incest on the part of my maternal grandfather, I felt a deep need for an honest acknowledgment of experience. "Howl" spoke powerfully to that need.

I have written elsewhere about how I wrote to Ginsberg, care of City Lights, telling him I would meet him in San Francisco at such and such a street corner on such and such a night. I drove eighteen hours in my second-hand Austin. The poet didn't show. Years later, as neighbors on New York City's Lower East Side, we would get to know one another. When I told him my story of having driven to the coast to meet him, he was gentle with my naiveté.

Albuquerque had a coterie of working artists in the 1940s and 1950s, a scene quite different from but related to the more famous Taos and Santa Fe schools that had come to prominence earlier in the century. I was introduced to some of the local artists through my parents, and several became my friends as well. A frustrated sculptor herself, my mother in particular sought such friendships (my father was more comfortable going to basketball games and mingling with more ordinary folk but was always supportive of Mother's needs). Art genuinely moved my mother. But there was also something a bit pretentious about her social relationships. Looking back, I think of them as indicative of a certain class snobbishness. My parents hung out with artists in the way working-class, presumably less cultured, people might play cards or drink beer. An intellectual, art-centered identity was important to Mother's sense of self.

While Mother and Dad bought season tickets to the Civic Symphony, where they could see and be seen, I cannot remember listening to a classical music station in my childhood home. My parents bought art from friends but rarely took us to a local museum or gallery. I was taught to value all the creative genres and was grateful for the immersion. But there was a disconnect between art as something one showed off and art as one's life work.

In 1957 Elaine de Kooning came to the University of New Mexico as a visiting professor. She was perceptive, vivacious, and generous, her lithe dancer's body always ready to go somewhere, try something new. She was the first woman I knew who acknowledged what she wanted and walked around obstacles as if they were minor inconveniences. I was eager to show her parts of my fascinating state and to that end taught her to drive. On several occasions we traveled together to the Mexican border city of Juárez, where we went to the bullfights and she began to paint her well-known bull series. We spent one cold winter night at the Zuni Shalako, a yearly dance for the blessing of new homes. We became inseparable friends and she my first real mentor. When she returned to New York, I followed her home. Its burgeoning mid-twentieth-century art scene became my milieu as well for the next few years, and it was her turn to introduce me to its complex mysteries.

....

The most important thing I can now think of to say about that place and time is that it was the beginning of the 1960s, surely one of the most creative, moral, misunderstood, often purposefully trivialized and poorly analyzed periods in US American history. I have often wondered if such misinterpretation hasn't been out of a fear that the era might repeat itself. We could definitely use some of its empowering clarity and creativity today.

In retrospect, I think of that decade—which in my estimation included the final couple of years of the 1950s as well as the first five of the 1970s—as the last time I remember in which honesty seemed a positive social quality. Honesty and the courage to stand up for what one believed in, even when doing so could be dangerous, sometimes fatal. The civil rights movement in the South claimed many young lives (white as well as black) and changed our nation's understanding of racial equality. Its hard-won victories led to subsequent campaigns for Hispanic, Native American, women's, and gay rights. As the 1970s began, protest by great numbers of conscious citizens actually succeeded in forcing an end to the long, cruel war in Vietnam. This was a period when young people felt that we had a voice and could come together and get things done.

Ordinary people believed we could make social change, and vanguard artists didn't ask themselves if they were painting socially relevant work or poets wonder if their poems were "too political." These attitudes changed after McCarthyism. The witch hunt of the early to mid-1950s had destroyed the lives and careers of many artists, filmmakers, writers, teachers, and others. But we came out of that period aware and fighting. We understood the creative force as vital to human life, and some of us felt moved to make lives with that force at the center.

How did the 1960s happen, not only here in the United States but also across large parts of the world? The wreckage of a world war had exposed unimaginable horror and created new international alignments. Crimes against humanity rooted in a nationalistic ideology ran wild. The Nuremberg Trials and other efforts to bring the perpetrators to justice assuaged the immediate guilt of those who turned their backs and let it happen, but it took decades for a deeper discussion of accountability to take place. It never did take place in the larger public arena.

By and large, US Americans were unable or unwilling to understand the ways in which our government had been complicit. Its rhetoric was too little, too late, and hid behind a veil of political righteousness. In that war we had unleashed our own form of terror on Dresden, Hiroshima, and Nagasaki. After it, we replaced our horror of the Holocaust with an irrational fear of Communism and traded Cold War politics for previous deceptions. McCarthy's witch hunts began to take hold. Artists and writers—creative people generally— were among those most affected by their repressive reach.

Such overwhelming social weight inevitably leads to rebellion. Here in the United States, where we prided ourselves on being a nation of laws, not some "banana republic" where anyone can be the victim of such violence, we began to experience the assassinations of revolutionary leaders Malcolm X, Martin Luther King Jr., Fred Hampton, and hundreds if not thousands of black, brown, Native American, and Puerto Rican youth—as well as more mainstream figures such as John and Robert Kennedy. Governmental commissions tried to convince us their assassins acted alone, and those who questioned that conclusion were labeled conspiracy theorists: extremists on the left. Few who were responsible for killing the poor or people of color were charged, fewer still punished.

The FBI and other US security agencies launched a vast covert war on anyone in this country trying to bring about change, by peaceful as well as more desperate means. The operation was called COINTELPRO; it introduced agents into our movements, set comrades against comrades and divided communities, murdered with impunity and imprisoned leaders, many of whom are still locked away forty or more years later. When I think of that period and of the time we are living in today—2018, with a self-serving thug in the US presidency, the systematic destruction of values we want to believe we hold, and groups of citizens beginning to rise up again—it seems an unbroken line from then to now. We keep hoping one day we won't have to reinvent the wheel. But we always do.

"We must never allow this to happen again" is a vow that rings loud and clear after each devastation. Soon, though, people tend to settle back into familiar patterns of opportunistic complicity and cowardice. Looking at the most formative times in my own life, I realize that most of us don't learn that much from reading history; it isn't what keeps us from repeating past mistakes. We learn more fully from personal experience, and unless we ourselves have been victimized by terror or survived extreme authoritarianism, we too often allow criminal behavior and coverup to creep back into our way of being. Even some who have suffered heinous crimes are capable of victimizing others, as we can see in Israel's treatment of the Palestinians.

Patriarchy has long been a breeding ground for nationalism, racism, and social manipulation. We need only look to the millennia of unpardonable abuse and coverup in the Catholic Church, the genocides we have known just in our lifetimes, and so many other crimes against humanity that are repeated, in one form or another, from generation to generation.

A decade after my time in New York, feminism would teach me about power.

I often wonder about those moments in which the covert becomes overt, acceptable or inevitable to great-enough segments of a population that the evil acquires its own unstoppable momentum. When, exactly, did Apartheid become the law of the land in South Africa? When and how did Nazism take hold in a nation of "good Germans"? How did Jews who had suffered so atrociously under Nazism turn against the Palestinian inhabitants of a land they shared? When did Pol Pot's ideology overtake Cambodia? If we look around us in today's United States, at the ways in which Trump's lies have become official governmental discourse, his policies eroding so many of our cherished values, we may gain a deeper understanding of such moments and the danger they represent. And then, what happens when global warming or other scientific phenomena are added to the equation? Do they hasten that momentum?

....

In the 1960s those who were not dead or traumatized rose up against the state terrorism of the era. From the mid-1950s, throughout the 1960s, and into the 1970s, here in the United States we saw Puerto Rican Independentistas attack the US Congress; a Free Speech Movement explode in Berkeley, California;

civil rights sweep through the South; a monumental protest against America's war in Vietnam; the massive burning of draft cards and other forms of resistance against forced military conscription; and serious protests on university campuses with the involvement of white youth in Students for a Democratic Society and the Weather Underground. Women began living our power. The Black Panther Party and others took community solutions into their own hands. A strong Native American resistance emerged. The Stonewall riots ushered in the movement for gay rights.[1]

But this phenomenon only describes the response here at home. In the context of each country's history and in line with its cultural differences, in Western Europe, Africa, Latin America, and Asia, where equally nationalistic and authoritarian regimes had imposed themselves, similar responses occurred. In Africa we began to see the breakdown of colonialism. In Latin America, guerrilla movements flourished. Paris exploded in the spring of 1968, as did Mexico's Student Movement that same year. As I write, neofascism is once again on the global rise, leading me to wonder if the swing from right to left and back isn't pendular, periods of openness and cooperation threatened by extreme nationalism.

The 1950s everywhere had been an era of constriction, a drawing in and down, spawning policies that propitiated a false patriotism, bestowing honor upon returning troops (mostly men) and renewing subservience for women, many of whom had been called upon to step up when their husbands and brothers were away at war. Now the women were being forced back into domestic servitude. This situation eroded possibility and made it particularly difficult for women who craved creative lives to assert ourselves.

When and how did the 1960s end? In many places it was extinguished by the death squads of a neofascistic ideology. In others it was subverted by more sophisticated foreign "aid" programs such as the Alliance for Progress, and by evangelical religious configurations that, pretending to raise people out of poverty, kept them disempowered and dependent instead. In Latin America, a decade of what came to be known as the era of dirty wars erased whole generations of youth fighting against oppressive governments (all supported by a succession of US administrations). Young people were simply disappeared from their homes and off the streets: thirty thousand in Argentina, forty thousand in Guatemala, significant numbers in other Latin American countries.

Everywhere, while the 1960s endured it showcased extraordinary creativity and courage. In Mexico (1961–1969), Cuba (1969–1980), and Nicaragua (1980–1984), I would participate and grow within the embrace of several of those rebel movements. But first I went to New York City, where I lived among a loosely knit group of artists and writers. It is of them I am thinking now.

....

The New York art world was an exceptional place in which to experience this 1960s consciousness. In retrospect it has been said that the late 1950s were when the center of visual arts in the Western world shifted from Paris to New York, from the old world to the new. Abstract expressionism—or "action painting," as some of its protagonists called it at the time—exploded south of 14th Street. Poverty, familiarity, and the pride of ownership made most of those artists reluctant to travel above that invisible boundary, although almost all longed to be accepted into the uptown galleries and have their work in the major museums.

Painters who in a few short years would show in those uptown galleries and museums and be featured in the pages of LIFE magazine, still lived in cold-water lofts, patched together meager incomes, were adept at tapping into water lines, and routinely turned the needle back on their Con Edison meters so as to pay less for electricity. Knowing Elaine had changed my life, and I didn't hesitate to follow her to New York.

Sixty years later I try to remember exactly what was being felt and said and made by those artists, what I learned from them. It was, in great part, a collective search for identity that refused to cede to hypocrisy, mediocrity, and social pressures. Or, more accurately, a collection of individual searches, each nurtured by the others. The abstract expressionists sought creative truth, freedom of process, the unrestrained gesture. They scorned the Man in the Gray Flannel Suit ideal. Process was more important than rendering objective imagery, although the image was taken seriously—sometimes remaining a onetime experiment, sometimes setting an important trend. Where the work began and ended—the picture plane as it was called—was important. In discussing such aspects of the work, we were talking about our lives.

Abstract expressionism wasn't the only painting being done in New York at the time. Visual artists attracting national and international attention included those whose work was monochromatic or minimalist, impressionist or quasi-cubist, colorist, calligraphic, repetitive, figurative, rooted in landscape or interior design, based in mathematical equations, gestural, purely abstract, or any combination of these. Later, as some artists began moving toward Pop Art, quintessential Americana such as a can of Campbell's soup, the flag, or repeat images of Marilyn Monroe emerged with startling power. Brief directed skits called happenings became popular, taking art from the canvas to the human body and from the permanent to the temporal. I viewed and absorbed all of these styles and others but was most deeply moved by the group of painters whose work abstracted the figure in such a way that one could follow its energy from impulse to gesture. That power of movement leaping decisively from a flat surface into my line of vision spoke to me as visual art had not done before.

As in every important artistic shift, a new language was being invented. What did that language have to do with my own, one that used words as its currency? I am still not entirely sure. Perhaps I was attracted as much as anything by the lifestyle, morality, solidarity, sense of purpose, and exuberance. But I believe it was more than that. In finally attempting to write about that time and place, I hope to be able to unravel some added nuance of deeper meaning.

I landed in an amorphous but also somehow rigidly constructed community that included practitioners of all the artistic genres. Thinking back, I realize that they came from diverse social classes, ethnicities, cultures, gender and sexual identities, even races—although none of those differences were prominent in our discourse or caused friction back then. Artists from a great variety of backgrounds easily accepted one another and reveled in what each contributed to the group. Art brought them together, made them colleagues and friends. We appreciated each individual for who he or she was. This diversity, as I say, was not verbally articulated but surely had an impact on people's lives.

Most of these artists didn't have their eyes on future careers. They weren't working toward prestigious professions. Showing and selling were important to them but didn't determine how they painted. They were living their art day by day, and that life produced its own revelations. They took odd jobs to pay their rent and put food on the table; if they were lucky, they might find something in the art world. But those jobs were generally subsistence level, undependable or short-term. It was a given that the making and doing were central to people's lives. Without being able to articulate it, this was an assumption I shared, and it was an enormous relief to find myself among others who felt the same. No longer did I need to produce flimsy excuses or lie in order to concentrate on what I hoped would become my life's work.

Most visual artists inhabited illegal lofts that had once been small factories or sweatshops. Poorly heated if at all, and lacking the most basic amenities, they traded comfort for space and light. I didn't need the sort of space those lofts provided and could settle into a cold-water flat. By law, New York City apartments weren't required to have steam heat until the end of the 1950s; in the winters we kept warm by lighting the gas ovens in our small kitchen stoves and keeping their doors ajar.

Most of these apartments were walkups. My first find was a tiny second-floor place on Third Avenue in the twenties. The sculptor Mark di Suvero told me about it and was helping me move in when I reached into a kitchen cabinet and pulled out a paper bag. I reached into it and drew back in horror. Its contents looked to be dried mushrooms. In fact, the wrinkled brown bits were peyote buttons, but the experience was enough to make me flee that apartment. I couldn't return.

Instead, I moved into a fourth-floor walkup on Ninth Street between First Avenue and Avenue A. Someone told me an old woman had died there and the place was for rent. In the partially furnished flat, I found albums with faded photographs of immigrants who'd landed years before at New York Harbor. I tried to imagine which face in the crowd belonged to the woman who had lived there before me, how her life had unfolded in the promised land. Had she been happy? Lost? Lonely? Resigned? Frustrated?

The apartment was laid out in typical railroad fashion. A tiny toilet (no sink or shower) hid behind a bedroom barely large enough to accommodate a double-bed mattress placed directly on the floor. Then came the kitchen with its bathtub next to the sink. This was the room where one entered the apartment. And, finally, with two identical windows looking out on Ninth Street, a modest-sized living room. The floorboards had been painted and repainted gunmetal gray and some of the original brickwork could still be seen around a fireplace that no longer worked. My landlord, a kind man from Ukraine who didn't speak English—we communicated through a secretary who may have been his daughter—asked me every month if I was sure I could afford the rent.

A painter of Christian Albanian origin lived directly below me. Her name was Anthe Zacharias and we became good friends. She told me that her father was in business with an Albanian Muslim; they owned a delicatessen together in Queens and, after a visit home, she often brought some old-world delicacy for us to share.

A young sculptor named Eddie Johnson, who had also followed Elaine from Albuquerque to New York and was one of her studio assistants, hung out at my place a lot. He had a serious crush on me but was much too timid to act on it. Eddie was a fine artist in his own right as well as extremely skilled

East Ninth Street, Manhattan (photo by Margaret Randall).

with his hands, and he covered my kitchen tub with a beautiful hinged slab of plywood; when down, I could use it as a countertop and cutting board. Like most people I knew, I finished furnishing that apartment with pieces from one of the city's Salvation Army stores. I remember getting everything I needed for $17.

I lived happily in the Ninth Street apartment until a few months into my pregnancy with my first child, Gregory, when the stairs became too much for me and I splurged on a new apartment in an elevator building on Third Street between Avenues A and B. It was more modern, but never really seemed like home. The superintendent there was racist and mean-spirited. I remember the night a black friend came to visit; she wouldn't let her bring her bicycle into the lobby. That incident was my introduction to the fact that racism was alive in the North as well as the South, even in a city as multicultural and cosmopolitan as New York.

Poor artists and writers had ingenious ways of getting the nourishment we needed. Friendly neighborhood merchants often gave us better cuts of meat or semi-fresh produce for the price of day-old items: not because we were artists but because we were poor. A great deal of solidarity characterized the New York of that era. It crossed class and cultural lines.

Sometimes early in the morning a few of us would make our way down to the old Fulton Fish Market in Lower Manhattan. Precursors to later dumpster divers, we'd come home with prize items: robust heads of lettuce, barely bruised vegetables, a package of hot dogs, or day-old cake. When I was pregnant with Gregory, a number of people at my local market or in the specialty shops along First Avenue took pity on a young woman who was single and pregnant. I'd ask for a few chicken wings or a quarter pound of ground round at Mrs. Schiffer's butcher shop and come home to discover she had slipped a plump breast or expensive cut of steak into my package.

Many of us gathered nightly for dinner at the old Cedar Bar on University Place just north of Eighth Street. The dim lighting turned the atmosphere a relaxing brown. A long counter ran along the right side of a passageway opening out to an assortment of tables beyond. To the left of the entranceway stood an old-fashioned telephone booth. I remember that telephone ringing one night and the person who answered shouting out, "Someone in Japan wants to speak to Franz."[2] Kline's work was beginning to gain international attention. For the artists, the Cedar was a second home, and people knew they would find friends there. After a day of creative work, we'd naturally gravitate to its comfort, ready for a night of passionate talk.

A waiter named Johnny carried tabs a month or more for those of us too poor to pay regularly. My typical evening meal at the time was a thin veal cutlet, a small side of spaghetti, and a single glass of sherry. The sherry, perhaps, because I remembered the glass my mother drank each afternoon when I was growing up. Artists who were beginning to make it financially were also generous with those still struggling; I frequently enjoyed a good meal out with Elaine or another friend, particularly after that person sold a painting.

....

My friendship with Elaine was a ticket to everything exciting going on in the arts and elsewhere in New York. She knew key people in the most dissimilar worlds and kept me informed of what was happening. I would drop by her studio almost every day and spend time talking and listening as she painted. She always welcomed those visits, once stopped what she was doing to make a rapid series of seven portraits of me. One became the frontispiece for an early book of my verse and another, decades later, for my *Selected Poems*.[3] One was included in a posthumous exhibit of Elaine's work at the Smithsonian National Portrait Gallery in Washington.[4] I now own three of the seven and often wonder where the other four ended up.

Elaine appreciated everyone: painters, musicians, dancers, theater people, art dealers, immigrants from every part of the world, and the Bowery "bums" (as they called themselves) who hung out on building stoops drowning their sorrows in cheap wine. She made friends with the young Episcopal minister and his wife at Grace Church on Broadway across the street from her loft and took to attending Sunday services. She was as likely to introduce me to a recovering addict who needed help—urging that I ask him to babysit Gregory during his first months of life in order to help build the man's self-esteem—as to a multi-millionaire art collector or influential promoter of cutting-edge ideas.

Elaine was unusual, in that she wrote brilliantly about art and artists as well as being one herself. And she refused to cater to a single group or style. She was expansive in her appreciation, insightful in her analyses. Her articles in *Art News* and elsewhere paid attention to figurative painters and minimalists, abstract expressionists and colorists. And she was as interested in portraying process as she was in evaluating the finished product. Her series "So and So Paints a Picture" is as profound today as it was innovative back then.

Beyond her intellectual insights, Elaine was also the vivacious center of every conversation and group: the kindest, most inclusive, compassionate, generous, and entertaining. She moved in many overlapping circles. From the moment we met, she showed me the value in taking personal risk. But she was equally conscious of her own needs and protected them as she was able during that pre-feminist time.

Not all the fine artists I knew when I lived in New York achieved the fame they deserved. Many eventually tired of fighting a skewed market and increasingly politicized gallery system and gave up, becoming art professors at universities or high schools or settling into jobs that had nothing to do with their passion. Some retained a connection to the world they loved by becoming smalltime art dealers or expert framers, or they became adept at other skills needed by their more successful colleagues. Some eventually left the demands of the city and returned to whatever part of the country or world they'd come from. These latter retreated to familiarity and safety, but I have to imagine they went home richer for having participated for whatever length of time in the exuberantly vibrant community of that time and place.

I cannot say that those who were successful were necessarily the best, or that some geniuses didn't get lost along the way. As everywhere and throughout history, sheer ambition and a fortunate set of circumstances might lift someone above his or her contemporaries. I can say, though, that I witnessed many great artists bear up under years of hardship before they finally made it. Successful or not by conventional standards, quite a few of them changed my life. They did so through their vision, drive, honesty, courage, approachability, and a certain rawness I find difficult to adequately define in retrospect. Perhaps it was simply their lack of pretense.

Looking back, I believe the art world of the 1950s and 1960s was more transparent than it is today, although whom one knew could make the difference between being noticed or not. The media also played a role, and not always a positive one. *Art News* and other specialized magazines did their best to cover the work of upcoming artists. Some artists themselves managed to produce short-lived publications. I remember especially Philip Pavia's rather slick *It Is: A Magazine for Abstract Art*, which made its appearance in 1958, and Al Leslie's large-format tabloid *The Hasty Papers* (1960).

Evergreen Review and *Kulchur* were among the more professionally put together literary magazines; *Trobar* and *The Floating Bear* were artisanal but published some of the best experimental poetry. My last year in the city I wrote book reviews for *Kulchur*, where I began learning the art of criticism. These were serious endeavors. But with a single one of their feature articles, popular national publications such as *LIFE* and *Look* could catapult an artist to instant fame or burden that artist with an unwanted label. I remember being at the Cedar Bar one night when Elizabeth Taylor and Eddie Fisher dropped in. They were looking for the painters they'd read about in the mass media and who had sparked their curiosity. We returned their curious gaze with our own.

By the end of the 1950s, a number of uptown galleries were beginning to show some of the artists I knew: Sidney Janis, Betty Parsons, Tibor de Nagy, and a few others. But most of the younger artists had to come together and rent cheap downtown spaces where they could exhibit. They chose others with whom they felt an affinity, whitewashed the walls, hauled their own work along crowded sidewalks, and took turns keeping the gallery open during month-long exhibitions.

The Ninth Street Gallery was one such venue. Surprisingly, five women artists had been accepted into its juried premier show in May 1951: Lee Krasner,

Elaine de Kooning, Grace Hartigan, Joan Mitchell, and Helen Frankenthaler. When I got to the city, women were still much less likely to get into the downtown galleries and were almost completely absent from those uptown or the museums. It would take years of protest for them to make minimal inroads and even today they are vastly out-represented by the men.[5]

Elaine's relationship with her husband, Willem de Kooning, was unique. She was an early student of his, considered him the greatest painter of their time, and—as a young Frida Kahlo had prophetically claimed about Diego Rivera a couple of decades earlier—said she knew almost instantly that they would marry. Elaine and Bill seemed a magical couple and had a few good years together. Then they separated but stayed married through a lifetime of open infidelities on both sides. Even when one of Bill's lovers, Nancy Ward, gave birth to a child, Elaine remained a strong presence in little Lisa's life as well. Having a child of her own was a deep desire and probably also a realistic fear. She once told me she'd had a false pregnancy several years before we met. She adored her three nephews (her sister Marjorie's children, Luke, Jon Pierre, and Mike), as well as her brother Conrad's daughter, Maude, and she showered them all with love and opportunity.

Elaine's devotion to her husband often kept her own work in the shadows, and yet being linked to him also helped put her on the map. Those were such patriarchal times that separating the personal from the social would require the sort of detailed retrospective reflection that only came much later and is beyond the scope of these lines. Women artists and writers constantly struggled to realize our own creative needs even as we failed to seriously question the double standard that defined our social roles.[6]

Alcohol was a villain in both Elaine's and Bill's lives and eventually made their staying together impossible for her. She once said he was a mean drunk and that, when he drank too much, she often felt his meanness directed at her. They lived apart for many years. Sometime after she managed to stop drinking, she helped him stop as well. And in the years preceding her death in 1989, when he was already deep into dementia, she went to his house every day and cared for him lovingly. On a visit in the mid-1980s she took me there one evening. Bill pretended to remember me. This was long after the years we'd shared.

Elaine and I frequently walked east to a tiny jazz club whose name I no longer remember. We'd sit elbow-to-elbow with the great Thelonious Monk as he worked his magic on the piano. Other nights we made our way through a standing-room-only crowd at the Five Spot to listen to Ornette Coleman blowing his white plastic sax. Once I accompanied her to Madison Square Garden, where I watched in awe as Russian Valery Brumel and US American John Thomas competed in the high jump and Elaine made rapid sketches of their muscular bodies on the drawing pad she always carried with her.[7]

Portraits made in the studio setting or in her subjects' own surroundings rank among Elaine's strongest and best-known work. Sometimes I would come by when she was working on one of them; neither painter nor model seemed to mind. I watched, fascinated, as with a few sure lines she captured Greek painter Alexander Kaldis's immigrant presence, Harold Rosenberg's imposing spread-legged come-on, or his daughter Hypatia's adolescent depth. Her most famous portrait series was the one she was commissioned to make of President John F. Kennedy in the year before he was murdered. Eddie Johnson was her studio assistant for that exciting job, but by that time I had left the city.

Jazz was a big part of our lives. One night I heard about a party somewhere uptown and made my way there alone. I remember two connected lofts, one above the other. In one, a group of musicians had already been playing for more than a night and a day, alone in their own world. The sound was piped to the other, where groups of listeners came and went, partaking of as much good grass as we wanted and losing ourselves in the first-rate music. I stayed for four or five hours, then decided to walk all the way home along dark back streets. I was too high on music and pot to want to descend into the subway. The city seemed delineated in Georges Rouault's black lines, its shapes and idiosyncrasies screaming to be savored.

Among the many memorable moments Elaine provided was finding myself one evening in one of the bathrooms at textile tycoon and art collector Ben Heller's Central Park residence, sitting on a toilet and staring at an original painting by Arshile Gorky. In that vast apartment's several living rooms, uniformed waiters carried drinks and hors d'oeuvres back and forth against a backdrop of masterpieces by Picasso, Modigliani, Cézanne, and others.

....

I had to make a living, even if only to be able to feed myself and pay my rent ($39 a month when I lived on East Ninth Street). None of us could afford to pay for medical attention, buy insurance of any kind, or acquire the endless gadgets we've since become accustomed to thinking make living easier. Yearly medical checkups weren't on our calendars, and we only saw a dentist if we had a really bad toothache. Life was simple, if precarious.

We were not distracted by consumerism, although good work materials were important. Elaine and I were at an art supply store one day when I expressed one of my periodic desires to try my hand at painting. Her immediate response was to buy me a $50 brush, explaining that beginners need the best tools because they don't yet have the experience that allows them to do well with anything less. That brush was outrageously expensive, even by today's standard, and I don't think I ever used it. It was one of the many spontaneous gifts Elaine bestowed upon her friends.

I remember just after my arrival in the city walking one cold January night and looking through a West Village ground-floor window at a scene of inviting warmth. The place was an art gallery or pretended to be. It was run by a group of people who called themselves aesthetic realists. Their guru was Eli Siegel, one of many self-proclaimed philosophers in that time and place who crafted their ideas into a system that attracted devotees. Aesthetic realism advertised itself as believing in "the aesthetic oneness of opposites." I wandered into the well-lit room and my appearance must have screamed need. The aesthetic realists asked me to join them for a "family" dinner, with the expectation that I would stay afterward to hear Siegel speak. There was an offer of a part-time gallery job, which I declined. I was grateful for the evening's hospitality but knew I was not interested in the group's philosophy and never went back.

Other esoteric belief systems were current in the city at the time. Wilhelm Reich's work was popular, and a number of people I knew regularly sat in orgone boxes or otherwise subscribed to his radical concepts. Books by Reich, such as *The Function of the Orgasm* and *The Sexual Revolution*, were censored. A few clandestine copies were passed from hand to hand; I read both sitting in the New York Public Library's banned books room, gaining important insights. The writer Paul Goodman, whom I knew slightly, was influenced by Reich, as was William Burroughs. I was interested in Reich's early work though never embraced his later ideas, which were either too extreme for my taste or beyond my capacity to understand.[8]

Other ideologies and institutions were prominent. Dorothy Day's Catholic Workers fed and clothed the "bums" who lived along the Bowery and elsewhere on the Lower East Side. The organization published an interesting newspaper with reasonable, if limited, political analysis. Its members sold copies for a penny. All these years later it still arrives punctually in my mailbox; I have no idea how its publishers have followed my frequent moves across time zones and countries.

I came to know a Catholic Worker by the name of Ammon Hennacy. He was an anarchist and anti-government protestor proud to have spent the greater part of his life in prison as a conscientious objector. At anti-war demonstrations he held a sign high above his graying head proclaiming: "I Am Ammon Hennacy. Arrest Me." When I gave birth to Gregory, Ammon came to visit my hospital bed each day bearing a single robust peach. Years later he moved to Salt Lake City, where he opened the Joe Hill House and married a nineteen-year-old. He must have been in his late seventies by then.

Eastern religious thought, so pervasive a decade later, hadn't really taken hold in the New York City I inhabited. The era of Zen, meditation, and mind-altering drugs was still mostly in the future, although Beat poets were reading Buddhist texts and using peyote, hallucinogenic mushrooms, and LSD. Tarot cards were popular, either as serious practice or in the spirit of board-game fun, and most of us were open to ideas from other cultures and times. We were curious and not yet adequately suspicious of the many esoteric efforts at manipulation and control that our society spawns.

Regardless of the religions within which we'd been raised or the customs our families observed, as artists and writers we were primarily devoted to our work. We prioritized it and gave up creature comforts so as to be able to practice it as fully as possible. A loosely held ethos allowed us to steal back what we believed was ours from large commercial enterprises—the subway, electric and telephone companies, big-chain department stores—while respecting the smaller family businesses. We wouldn't have thought of taking anything from a mom-and-pop shop.

Soon after my arrival in the city I did find work at a succession of menial jobs. I waited tables and modeled for artists. Leon Golub, a figurative painter with a beautiful sky-lit studio on Washington Square, employed me for a while, a couple of hours five mornings a week. He had me pose nude but always painted me wearing a modest ballet tutu. As he gave me a $5 bill for the two hours' work, he would hand me a glass of freshly squeezed orange juice. Once, when it was raining, he sent me home wearing galoshes over my only pair of shoes.

An employment agency sent me to a secretarial job, but I'd lied about knowing shorthand and was fired at the end of my first month. I had to hand over my entire paycheck to that agency. For a while I worked at a feather factory in the frantic high-pressure Garment District. We hand-dyed feathers that would eventually adorn woman's hats. For another brief period I addressed envelopes at George Braziller, a publishing house that employed rows of mostly black women from the South who felt fortunate to have landed even such repetitive work. In my growing artistic consciousness, my real focus remained my poetry, incipient and clichéd as it still was.

....

I also started experimenting with genres other than poetry. I suppose most writers attempt a novel at one time or another. My first, written a year or so after arriving in the city, was disastrous—as successive ones would be. I walked a lot in those days, exploring the variety of neighborhoods, their cultures transplanted from one Eastern European country or another. This was decades before the waves of Latin American immigrants: Dominicans, Mexicans, Puerto Ricans (who were American citizens with all the obligations but few of the benefits), later those who were escaping violence in El Salvador, Guatemala, and Honduras, and still later those fleeing Afghanistan, Iraq, and Syria—all countries the United States helped destabilize or destroy and then balked at receiving their refugees. Whole groups of older arrivals never learned English. Those sights and sounds made their way into my book, which I called *The Mongrel Sword*. The title is about all I remember of it now, that and one scene in which I likened a building in demolition to an upright, open egg-crate filled with the remnants of ordinary lives. My characters were wooden and undeveloped, and I had no idea how to construct a storyline.

I was blissfully ignorant of my would-be novel's shortcomings and sent it to an editor at Noonday Press named Robert Dash. He too had lived in Albuquerque, had known my family, and I thought he would be sympathetic. Ever confident, when he called and invited me to meet him for a drink at the Cedar Bar, I was sure it was to discuss the details of publication. I still remember walking eagerly to the Cedar that afternoon, looking in the store windows I passed and imagining being able to purchase this or that coveted item with the advance I was sure would be forthcoming.

My walk back home that day was very different. Dash quickly disabused me of my consumerist dreams. He began as soon as we sat down. The novel was bad. I had no talent. I should return to New Mexico, get married, have kids. That, of course, was the default advice for young women with the temerity to believe we could make it in this lofty new world. I was no novelist, he said. And in that, at least, he was right. Poetry turned out to be my genre, and later oral history, essay, memoir, and translation.

Through Elaine I met other artists: Esteban Vicente, José Bartolí, Michelle Stuart, Marisol, and Conrad Marca-Relli among them. Milton Resnick and his wife, Pat Passlof, became dear friends. We would spend hours sitting around the table in Pat's Tenth Street loft, talking about ideas. This talk was new to me, and immensely important to my early formation, my sense of what I needed to know starting out.

I had been raised in a family with certain intellectual and artistic pretensions, but the ideas my parents embraced were gleaned from the unquestioned discourse of those they admired for one reason or another: "They say that . . ." was the prelude to almost every statement and taken at face value. When I asked my mother who the "they" might be, she had no idea. In New York I learned to ask questions, wasn't shy about admitting I didn't understand a concept or asking for further explanation. The discussions about form, content, meaning, representation, interpretation, and the artist's responsibility to his or her work were necessary to the incipient writer I was then, and to the human being I was becoming. Such in-depth exchange continues to be vital to the way I think, make connections, and write and live my life.

When I've spoken about those years, I've often emphasized that it was then I learned about discipline. How to acquire it and how, without it, inspiration invariably fizzles and dies. It was Resnick who suggested the practical steps I needed to take in order to put discipline at the center of my creative practice. When I complained of writer's block, he told me to sit for a fixed number of hours each day before the paper I rolled into my second-hand Remington Rand, until sheer boredom deposited words on the page. Those words would lead to others, more intentional, meaningful, and indicative of what might eventually be my authentic voice.

I followed his advice and slowly found I had something to say. It would take a while for me to develop my unique style, expressive form. And many later experiences contributed to that: my time in Latin America, involvement with revolutionary movements, socialism and feminism, lovers and children, recognizing my lesbian identity, a return to my desert landscape, lessons learned in the hardest ways. As a writer, though, acquiring discipline was a necessary precursor to it all.

An important question for beginning writers is: What do I need or want to say? We all write most convincingly out of lived experience. What experience did I, a provincial young woman in my early twenties, have back then?

The physical landscape of the American Southwest had been important to me, and in some romantic way also its indigenous and Hispanic cultures. My early family life was interesting, but I was barely beginning to figure it out. I knew an intimate loneliness but couldn't plumb its universality. And I was beginning to concern myself with issues of justice but hadn't yet involved myself in any of the important movements of the day. And so, independent of what I may have wanted to express, I didn't possess the maturity that would allow me to express it with anything approaching originality. Perhaps what I most had going for me was desire and chutzpah. Cliché and banality too often kept my poems mediocre and derivative.

As I've said, I regularly walked through much of the Lower East Side, and many other parts of Manhattan. Anthe and I often hiked all the way up to the Metropolitan Museum, some eighty city blocks. We'd pay the 25-cent minimum admission fee acceptable in those years, spend hours exploring different parts of the museum, and then walk all the way back home, not because we couldn't have taken the subway or bus but because we wanted to absorb the city. I would also attend a dozen gallery openings or more a month. But it was at the museums—the Met, Modern, Whitney, Jewish, Frick, Guggenheim, Natural History, and others—where I got a more comprehensive feel for what was happening, not only in abstract expressionism but among the broader panorama of artists working at the time and across history's long arc. (It would take many more years for me to discover the marvels of that art referred to as prehistoric, a term I've never subscribed to and rarely use: those powerful rock art paintings tens of thousands of years old that are found in caves and alcoves all across the world. When I did, the arc became more complete.)

Feeling rather than reason described my visceral response to art, at least back then. I remember being at the Museum of Modern Art and standing before a Mark Rothko, one of his large vertical canvases—red and black divided into two unequal color fields with blurred edges. I allowed myself to enter the painting and was suddenly shaken by an unexpected orgasm, something I had not yet experienced in my relations with men. I was wearing a light-yellow summer dress and feared the wetness between my legs must surely be obvious to the other museumgoers. The incident shamed and embarrassed me at first, but no one seemed to notice. I came to understand that art could move one physically as surely as intellectually or spiritually.

I loved Fairfield Porter's soft landscapes, Helen Frankenthaler's unique energy, and, of course, everything from Gorky's mature period; after that bathroom viewing at the Heller apartment, I'd sought out every painting by the master on exhibit anywhere in New York. I loved many painters' work—Elaine's was a prime example—because I spent time at their studios, followed their development, felt I knew what they were saying from the inside out. I absorbed the art as readily and deeply as I absorbed the place.

....

Once some friends and I strolled across the Brooklyn Bridge and back, reading Hart Crane's famous poem out loud along the way. For a few months I drove a taxi belonging to a driver friend who was ill. That too was a great way to learn the city. But the city, for me and my friends, was really Lower Manhattan. Uptown, Brooklyn, the Bronx, Queens, and Staten Island were like foreign countries. New York may have been one of the most cosmopolitan metropolises on earth, but many of its inhabitants were provincial residents of neighborhoods where only Italian or only Chinese or only Ukrainian or Polish were spoken. Through open windows in the summer one breathed in the inviting scents of old-country dishes. In those neighborhoods even the children, born and raised in America, seemed different. Orthodox Jewish boys were pale-skinned beneath their yarmulkes. On Sunday groups of pre-adolescent Polish girls could be seen clustered along the sidewalks, multicolor first-communion ribbons lacing their hair like rainbows.

I was living in a world peopled by some of the great creative artists, writers, critics, and thinkers of the day.[9] The milieu was exciting beyond belief. Looking back, I am impressed by the generosity many of those creative minds displayed with someone just starting out, such as myself. There was a general sense of solidarity. Many of the artists had yet to make a name for themselves. Knowing those people, some undoubtedly better than others, was a privilege. And because I never shied away from inserting myself into their lives and making my voracious presence felt, I visited studios, asked for reading suggestions, saw how the masters worked, and got at least some of them to share ideas that nurtured my own.

That generosity of spirit seems absent today. As economic inequality worsens and people are forced to scramble for what they need, solidarity has too often given way to self-promotion and opportunism. In the New York City of the 1950s and 1960s, secondhand bookseller Harold Briggs and Ted Willentz (who with his brother Eli owned the well-stocked Eighth Street Bookstore just east of Sixth Avenue) accepted my first books on consignment and introduced me to what was happening in the larger poetry world. Profit wasn't the bottom line with these booksellers; they often sold books at cost or gave them free to those of us who had little money to spare. This was a gesture I would later find echoed thousands of miles south of the border when I moved to Mexico City at the end of 1961. There poets knew we could always get a free meal at the Zona Rosa delicatessen belonging to an aging Jewish poet from Odessa, Jacobo Glantz. Solidarity transcended the profit motive that today keeps rich and poor so far apart. And this didn't simply mean access; it created an atmosphere in which kindness flourished and positive values bloomed.

....

Most prominent among the artists I knew and those who influenced me were the men, of course, but below the surface the women's presence was palpable and powerful. Many women artists would fight their way to success in subsequent decades. Looking back, I realize we were struggling for our own artistic recognition even as we bore the weight of millennia of unacknowledged marginalization and silence. When we could name the social forces at work it would eventually push some of us to embrace a feminist understanding of society, changing the way we thought about power.

At the time I describe, though, we doggedly thought of ourselves first and foremost as artists, irrespective of gender. Most of the female artists I knew refused to identify as "woman artists." It seemed belittling, demeaning. They wanted to be judged simply as artists, fiercely unwilling to acknowledge the effects of sexism on their ability to be taken seriously in a male-dominated world. The word "feminist" wasn't yet in our vocabulary. I was of two minds about identifying as a woman writer. On the one hand, I too hoped to be considered on the merits of my work. On the other, I was beginning to recognize not only the way that being a woman held me back but also the uniqueness of my gender, the particular consciousness it bestowed. Even in retrospect, I wouldn't describe myself as embracing biological determinism,[10] but after having Gregory, in the fall of 1960, the experience of childbirth took possession of my body and mind.

....

I had already endured one unhappy marriage and didn't anticipate marrying again, at least not anytime soon. I simply wanted a child and saw no reason not to have one. I chose Joel Oppenheimer as his father without expecting anything from him. Gregory was planned for, and wanted, by me in any case. He was a big baby, weighing more than eleven pounds at birth. It was important to me to be conscious for his delivery, and without access to the new childbirth methods, which were just beginning to emerge in 1960 but were available only to those who could pay, I refused to sign the release for administration of anesthesia in order to be awake when he arrived. Dr. Zimmer, a general practitioner who served many in the artist community and charged $100 for my entire pregnancy, didn't really understand my need to experience conscious childbirth. But he acquiesced and said he would perform an episiotomy in such a way as to help me achieve my dream: "I'll cut you at the height of a contraction," he said, "so you won't feel it as much."

It had been a thirty-six-hour labor and Gregory's arrival felt like quite a reward. But the charity hospital where I gave birth didn't pay much attention to either of our needs. Two good friends, Don and Valerie Petersen, accompanied me to the hospital but weren't allowed into the delivery room. My condition as an unmarried mother was emphasized. After giving birth, I was moved to a ward with some forty women. A young Chinese mother in the bed directly across from mine was mortified because her baby was a girl. She refused to speak the entire time she was there, even to her husband who brought her familiar foods each night. One of the rather sullen nurses on duty held up a black baby and explained to anyone interested that its skin would remain white "like everyone else's" until a few days later when pigmentation set in. They regularly fed Gregory in the nursery before bringing him to me, causing him to sleep and have no interest in nursing.

In those days it was customary to spend five days or a week in the hospital after giving birth. This meant that for my child's first few days we were mostly separated. But as soon as I was able to take Gregory home, he began demonstrating his radiant personality. He was alert and happy, rarely crying. While other babies sucked on pacifiers, he took to clutching a film spindle in his little fist, and I had to keep a jar of them on hand to replace those we lost. I took him everywhere in a white wicker basket, to art openings, even the Cedar Bar. City grime and cigarette smoke didn't seem to faze him. He was the darling of a loving community.

Since we left New York when Gregory was only ten months old, it may be hard to imagine that those early influences shaped him in any foundational way. But I believe they did. The openness and care in his first community seem to have been bedrock to his natural curiosity, lifelong equanimity, and ability to bring people together. Being raised during his first year by a single mother eliminated conflictive child-rearing methods and tensions. Much later, when he was thirteen, he orchestrated a reunion with his biological father and benefited from Joel's love as well. In fact, Gregory was always proud of having several fathers, "all of them wonderful," he would say. His great love of art could also have had its origins during his early life in New York.

But what I remember most palpably from those first days and months of my son's life was the extraordinary difference between being one human being and two. It wasn't that I thought he was exclusively mine, an extension of me who should follow my path. In fact, I believed in emotionally letting go of a child from the moment of his or her birth. Like most parents, I wanted my children to be independent, courageous, reasonably happy, and able to follow their own inclinations. But there is something indescribably wonderful about bearing and raising a child. I had that impossible-to-describe experience with each of my four.

The day before Gregory and I came home from Manhattan General, my mother arrived from Albuquerque. She stayed a week, helping with my son and warming to the idea of being a grandmother. My father had been upset during my pregnancy. He couldn't seem to get his head around single motherhood and, assuming I had become pregnant accidentally, offered me the money for an abortion. When I explained that this was a wanted child, he tried to understand, and after Gregory's birth became his most heartfelt and vocal champion.

The attitudes toward a woman having a child outside of conventional marriage and the difficulty of getting rid of an unwanted pregnancy both reflected society's hypocritical norms back then. At some point during my pregnancy with Gregory I received a surprise call from one of my old bosses at Lytle Engineering and Manufacturing Company. The man, whose name I've forgotten, spoke to me with a familiarity beyond that warranted by our previous work relationship. After a couple of questions that didn't wait for answers—How was I doing? How was life in the big city?—he guardedly, as if speaking in code, asked if he might count on my help in a delicate situation. I'm sure I was flattered. I said of course.

A young female employee had "gotten herself pregnant." There was no question about her keeping the baby. And this was well before abortion would be legalized in the United States.[11] My old boss assumed that I, the worldly young woman now living in New York, would be able to take care of the problem. I myself hadn't had reason to seek an illegal abortion, but I'd certainly heard others talk about them. They seemed accessible. And I'd been conditioned as a caretaker, the one who made things right.

I told my ex-boss to send Margie east. I'd do what I could. She arrived a day or two later, reticent, frightened, resolutely courageous, and bearing a wad of American Express traveler's checks. I probably didn't realize at the time that it was my boss who had made her pregnant. As always, Elaine was my best source of information. But, despite the many stories we'd both heard when neither of us needed them, it would prove problematic finding a solution to this common and painful dilemma.

Someone sent us to a female gynecologist in the West Village. All she did was confirm that Margie was pregnant, further along in fact than she'd said. From there we passed through at least three more doctor's offices. No one was willing to run the risk of terminating a pregnancy. I somehow obtained the Pennsylvania telephone number of Dr. Spencer, an idealist well known for helping women in trouble. His son told me he was no longer practicing.

Each day felt like a clock running down. Margie would arise from my living room couch pale and hopeful. Phone calls to and from Albuquerque kept her in touch with the man responsible. Mexico and Puerto Rico were mentioned as possibilities. Then—I've forgotten how—we were given the name and telephone number of a "Dr. Anne," somewhere on upper Broadway.

Whoever made the contact assured us Dr. Anne was practiced and safe. I called. A man's voice answered. I remember his immediate interest was money. I asked how much. He said $1,000. I offered $700, what Margie told me she had. He accepted and gave us an appointment for the next afternoon. I accompanied Margie to a run-down hotel on upper Broadway, somewhere in the nineties or low hundreds. The doorman pointed us toward a small elevator and said "805." It was clear he was used to sending young women to the apartment. No words were exchanged with the man who ushered us into a drab sitting room. Several other women waited.

After an hour or so, a large woman in a dirty T-shirt emerged from a back room. She noticed my large belly and almost took a step backward. I quickly motioned to my friend and she laughed, a quick, hollow sound. Then she told Margie to follow her. A half hour passed, and she reappeared, paler than before but upright. I looked at her face. She nodded briefly. We left. In the taxi heading back downtown she told me it hadn't been as bad as she'd anticipated. Mostly what she felt was weak and relieved.

This wasn't to be the end of it, though. Over the next few days Margie suffered severe cramping, ran a low fever, worried she might have an infection. I worried too. Would she be all right? Should she want them, would she be able to have children one day? Would it be a good idea to take her to a hospital emergency room? Had we both gotten in over our heads? We were lucky. A couple of days later Margie felt well enough to return to Albuquerque. I received one more grateful call from my ex-boss. I had performed a miracle, he said. Margie and I may have had some further communication. Then the incident folded in upon itself, a possible tragedy that remained, instead, simply a story to be told. This was as close as I would come to life before *Roe v. Wade*, what we long thought was the last whisper of an era in which women's bodies were more firmly controlled by men, our daily survival at risk.[12]

....

Casual conversations in someone's loft or late of a summer's night sitting on the cool grass in Washington Square Park provided forums for a rich exchange of ideas. And each of us was eager to show one another how those ideas expressed themselves in what we were doing. Poets read to one another and painters invited friends to their studios to see canvases they'd just finished or on which they might still be working. A frequent question was "Is it done?"

This was a question that took on a particular dimension among the abstract expressionists. Jackson Pollock had died in 1956, before my arrival in the city. His breakthrough style of throwing, dripping, and splattering paint on unstretched canvases spread out on the floor marked, in some important sense, the beginning of action painting: the ultimate freedom of gesture. Pollock was gone, but his presence was still very much felt among his contemporaries. I recognized his genius but wasn't as moved by his work as I was by that of others.

Boldness of gesture was important. Many artists—Bill de Kooning, Franz Kline, Elaine, Resnick—used large house-painter brushes to fold gesture into, around, and over gesture. Much as one sees in ancient Mayan glyphs, portions of a painting hid earlier portions without obliterating them entirely. In Elaine's bull series, for example, one could see the animal emerging from the surge of power it generated. In Bill's famous portraits of women, threat and ferocity came through an exploration that gave the impression of not really wanting to complete itself. Contrary to assumptions made by those unfamiliar with abstraction, most of these artists had come up through rigorous formal training; they were expert draftsmen (and women), confident in the skills that allowed them to depart from figurative representation while maintaining integrity of form.

When was a painting done? Occasionally that was answered by a dealer who insisted on taking an overdue canvas to the gallery for a sale or show. The artist's attitude toward the absurdities of the market might also come into play; I remember Bill's five-year-old daughter, Lisa, placing her small palm on a canvas that still had wet paint. The artist looked at the handprint, laughed, decided not to fix the accident, and announced he would add $5,000 to the picture's asking price.

Most often, though, the painters I knew were concerned with the natural evolution of their work, much as I was beginning to learn when a poem ended, resisting the temptation to go too far, say too much, not allow participation from the viewer or reader. We trusted one another enough to share unfinished efforts and listened to one another, although final decisions tended to be ours.

....

Although by the time I arrived in New York, McCarthyism had silenced most progressive political identification and people were reluctant to admit previous adherence to left-wing organizations, many of the older artists had been shaped by membership in Communist-oriented unions or professional associations. Some had belonged to the US Communist Party. Although struggles for the rights of specific social sectors were not yet on our collective agenda, most of the artists I knew naturally favored justice, opposed war, and engaged in a solidarity that crossed social lines.

Elaine was moved by the plight of accused murderer Caryl Chessman, who was on death row at San Quentin. She became involved in the struggle to save his life and the larger movement against capital punishment and was devastated when he was executed. Soon the civil rights movement in the South and a powerful nationwide opposition to the American war in Vietnam would motivate large segments of the population. Artists were involved, often donating their work to antiracist and antiwar shows, occasionally also marching or demonstrating. These larger battles eventually also included protests by women artists who demanded inclusion in the museums. But these would take place in the 1970s, at least a decade after I left New York.

Casual conversations were punctuated by more formal discussions at the Artists Club, more often referred to simply as the Club. Meetings were held in a loft located up a flight of stairs at 39 East Eighth Street, near where so many of us lived. It was jointly rented by a core group of artists; Philip Pavia might have been its founder. Fifty to one hundred visual artists, with the occasional smattering of poets, critics, and others, would crowd into folding chairs on Friday nights for formal panels or talks about anything from what art means to whatever passion occupied our attention at the moment. Men who coveted a place as kingpin of a surging movement hurled "truths" at one another, hoping to sway their followers. Some didn't speak to one another for months after. Lines were drawn and redrawn. But among those battling egos, more profound issues were pondered. Very occasionally a woman would speak. There was always plenty of food for thought. I absorbed it all.

I also remember raucous parties at the Club. Someone would take up a collection or an artist who had sold a painting might spring for what was needed. A few bottles of cheap wine, a phonograph, and some records were all that was required for a dance that might last into the early morning hours, when some of us would go off with whoever struck our momentary fancy while others retired to some sort of married life. Wives stayed home with the children while their husbands partied.

In that pre-feminist time, men were definitely the artists; their wives or female companions supported them in a variety of ways, often with full-time jobs as well as by keeping house and caring for offspring. If the women also made art, they did so in off hours and in some cramped corner of a living area. Gay male couples were part of the scene. They were accepted although I don't remember much spoken acknowledgment of their relationships. Lesbians were much more hidden. Alcohol was definitely the drug of choice, and no few artists were alcoholics—a condition we didn't recognize and a term we didn't use back then. Marijuana and hashish were easily available, but I wasn't aware that any of the painters I knew used harder drugs.

⋯⋯⋯⋯⋯⋯⋯⋯⋯⋯⋯⋯⋯⋯⋯⋯⋯⋯⋯⋯⋯⋯⋯⋯⋯⋯⋯⋯⋯⋯⋯⋯⋯

How did I fit into that community? I was almost two decades younger than Elaine and most of her friends. I was independent and had an adventurous spirit, but also poorly educated and, practically speaking, unqualified for much beside waitressing, modeling, gallery sitting, typing, or filing. The artists I knew were dedicated to their work, spending only as much time at a paid job as was necessary to earn a minimal income. In the hot summer months, artists like Elaine, who were beginning to be able to survive from selling their canvases, rented vacation homes on Long Island. Those who had already made it economically bought country homes with studio space.

One summer, so as to be near my friends, I waitressed at a restaurant called the Elm Tree Inn at the very tip of the island in Amagansett. That was the summer I spent an afternoon with Arthur Miller and his then-wife Marilyn Monroe; Elaine took me to witness their female basset hound mating with a male belonging to Philip Pavia. Elaine and I tried to engage Marilyn in conversation. She was hospitable but shy. Tennessee Williams, Eli Wallach, and Anne Jackson were doing summer stock nearby, and came to the restaurant for a meal; I waited on them, wide-eyed. Williams paid for the meal with what he thought was a $100 bill. It was new and crisp and, when I went to make change, I noticed another stuck to it. I was tempted to keep the additional hundred but returned it to the playwright. Jack Kerouac and a few friends also made an appearance one night. I had the temerity to ask Kerouac if he would read a chapter of my very bad novel. He was politely encouraging, as I remember.

Like most such jobs, the work at the Elm Tree was exploitative and poorly paid. The cook was edgy, even cruel at times. A fellow waitress and I were expected to run out back between shifts and change the bedding in a row of cabins rented by gay couples for brief encounters. One night that woman, with whom I shared a room, was raped by a man she'd met on the beach. She was devastated and left the following day. I was discouraged by the lack of support the restaurant's owners showed her and decided to leave as well.

I packed my small suitcase and walked to the nearby highway to hitch a ride into the city. It was after my shift and late at night, but I felt safe on the highway shoulder, my thumb held out to the straggle of passing cars. Soon one stopped and picked me up. The driver turned out to be an off-duty New York City policeman who had been camping on the island with his sons. He drove me straight home, then carried my bag up the three flights of stairs. A very different and much safer time.

I felt fully integrated into that community of mostly older and much more successful artists, albeit at its younger, less experienced, and poorer edge. Although I was just beginning to write and many of my friends were starting to earn from their art, that difference never seemed awkward. I had to struggle to make a meager living but being close to Elaine and her friends gave me full membership in a world that opened doors and expanded my consciousness.

....

The concentration on creativity as opposed to being expected to prepare for one's future by getting a university degree or—if you were female—landing a husband who could support you, struck a chord that had long vibrated in my rebellious spirit. Growing up, my parents appreciated art and encouraged me to write. Still, they wanted "success" for their children, and hoped we would first establish ourselves in more conventional ways.

Mother was an artist but hadn't been educated to believe that could be her primary identity. As a result, she didn't take her art seriously. She hated being a housekeeper and, in many ways, also resented being a wife. I desperately needed another sort of female role model. Dad, always supportive, made me feel I could be whomever I wanted to be. But he was shocked to discover how I was living in New York. He believed he had raised me to "do better." I remember a visit by him and my younger brother during which they were visibly repulsed by my fourth-floor Lower East Side walkup with its bathtub in the kitchen and army of tiny cockroaches. I had lovingly prepared a sumptuous meal with ingredients from the nearby First Avenue market. I think it was my signature paella. They hardly touched the food. I was disappointed and probably ashamed.

I also made paella when Fidel Castro came to New York in September of 1960. He and his retinue ended up at the Hotel Theresa in Harlem. I decided to bring the feast as a gift to my hero. When I told the market vendors whom I was cooking it for, they threw in some of their choicest red bell peppers and fresh lobster tails. I carefully prepared the dish, then hauled it on the subway all the way up to 125th Street where I emerged above ground, my heavy platter covered in aluminum foil. But I was unable to deliver the gift. A line of "New York's finest" stopped me at the subway exit and wouldn't let me through. I had to return home, souring food in hand. I later learned that Malcolm X and Langston Hughes had been invited to visit Fidel. As a young woman with neither literary nor political credentials, I hadn't been so lucky.

What one did to pay cheap rent and put food on the table could be anything at all. As some artists became more successful, they often hired those just starting out to do odd jobs. Women worked as models, men as studio assistants, stretching canvases or doing carpentry. My friend Mark di Suvero, who would survive to become a world-renowned sculptor, was working as a carpenter's assistant at an uptown commercial site. He was guiding a pile of lumber atop a freight elevator when someone yelled "up" instead of "down," sending him into the elevator works. It took firemen hours to cut him loose. He was taken to Roosevelt Hospital, where they said he wouldn't walk again. Fortunately, they were wrong. I was one of a small group of friends who took turns looking after Mark at the hospital. I was already pregnant with Gregory at the time. It was frightening.

I had many good friends among the artists: Elaine, Pat, Milton, Al Leslie, Al Held, George Sugarman, and others. Gradually, I also came to know some of the writers: Robert Kelly, Jerome Rothenberg, Hettie Jones, Ginsberg, and

Joel Oppenheimer. Joel was a fine poet, part of the Black Mountain school in which Robert Creeley figured prominently; he would later become the biological father of my son, Gregory, born in October 1960. David McReynolds of *Liberation* magazine and Bill Ward of the *Provincetown Review* published my incipient poems. After a few years I began to read my work at some of the open mics at Greenwich Village cafés and bars. And I produced two slim books of bad poetry.[13]

An important moment in my poetic development was a visit to see William Carlos Williams, still living across the river in Rutherford, just outside Paterson, New Jersey. I admired his work and, with my usual forthrightness, sent him a few of my poems. He responded generously, inviting me to pay him a call. I remember taking the interstate bus, buying a sprig of pussy willows at the station, and knocking at the poet's door. His wife, Flossie, opened and welcomed me inside. Williams had suffered a debilitating stroke several years earlier and had trouble writing, even speaking without effort. He was also going blind. He asked me to read him some of his recent poems, which I found thrilling. Then he listened to several of mine. Those aspects in my work he chose to encourage—writing about what I knew, listening to the sounds of my words, and breaking my lines to accommodate my breath—helped me understand where I might try to go from there. He introduced me to his concept of the variable foot.[14]

After a year or so I also graduated from the stopgap jobs I'd held when I'd first arrived in the city: modeling for artists, typing or filing, working for a while at the feather factory, and sitting at some of the independent galleries. Among the latter, my experience at the City Gallery, in a small building at the corner of 24th Street and Sixth Avenue, was noteworthy. Artists Lester Johnson, Red Grooms, and Jay Milder had rented the space. Johnson was older than the other two and already somewhat known. Grooms would later become one of the stars of the Pop Art movement, but at the time he was just a gangly young redhead from somewhere in the Midwest. A jazz musician lived on the same floor: a good neighbor, whose long practice sessions I remember as hauntingly beautiful.

The artists let me sleep on a cot in a small back room in exchange for keeping their gallery open every afternoon. Almost no one showed up at the rather isolated location, so I had plenty of time to practice Milton Resnick's disciplinary instructions. There was no toilet in the loft, requiring me to make periodic runs to a bar across the street. I kept that job for several months. I vividly remember the day I lost it; the three artists had painted an exuberant mural in the stairwell leading to the second-floor gallery, and the building's owner was furious. He had no idea how much that mural would have been worth had he possessed the foresight to preserve it until those young men achieved fame. In a fury he painted over it and kicked us all out. The building was eventually torn down.

As I say, though, I graduated from those makeshift jobs to more steady employment. This happened when I went to work for Nancy Macdonald at Spanish Refugee Aid. I've often thought of that as the first paid job at which I felt truly useful, doing work of which I could be proud. SRA had been established at the end of the Spanish Civil War to help care for the thousands of refugees still living in displaced persons camps in southern France and northern Africa. These were the defeated Republicans whose loss signaled the end of a dream shared by so many around the world.

About a year after Nancy hired me, we took on another young woman, Rhoda Clark (now Rhoda Nashama Waller). Rhoda had become pregnant very young and had been forced into an unhappy marriage, but she soon divorced and was raising her daughter on her own. We had single motherhood among other things in common and became lifelong friends. Eventually we also brought another young woman, Joan Herbst, on board. The SRA advisory committee included such luminaries as Hannah Arendt, Mary McCarthy, and Dwight Macdonald. I sometimes got to attend board meetings but was too young and unschooled to appreciate the approximation to minds as stellar as Arendt's.

Dwight's ex-wife, Nancy, ran the tiny office and I became her assistant. We were the organization's working members. We collected warm winter clothing and "sponsors" who were willing to commit to sending a small amount of money to be forwarded to an individual refugee each month. I translated their accompanying letters into Spanish; Nancy did the same into French. Just a few years ago I was giving a reading in New York, after which a man came up and introduced himself as Nick, one of Nancy's two sons. His mother had been dead for years, but he remembered our friendship.

Nancy and Dwight owned a summer cottage on a lake in the woods near Wellfleet, Massachusetts. Following their divorce, they alternated using it. Nancy once invited me to spend a few days with her there. She even went out the weekend before to try to rid the surroundings of mushrooms. After dinner at the home of neighbor Arthur Schlesinger Jr., Nancy, Francis Biddle, Stephen Spender, Norman Mailer, and other venerable men and women of various ages got naked and went skinny-dipping in the moonlit water. Close to full-term in my pregnancy with Gregory by then, I remained clothed and on the sidelines. Observing, always observing.

Spanish Refugee Aid occupied an office in a small building at the corner of Broadway and Eleventh Street. That building also housed the original chapter of the Fair Play for Cuba Committee, which became active after that Caribbean nation's 1959 revolution. It sponsored an early trip to Cuba. I was tempted to go, but motherhood made me hold back; maybe I was afraid. Elaine de Kooning, LeRoi Jones, Lawrence Ferlinghetti, Norman Mailer, Marc Schleifer (later Abdallah Schleifer), and I wrote a strong letter protesting the 1961 Bay of Pigs invasion; hundreds of artists and writers signed on and it was published in *Monthly Review*.

A group of Hassidic men, with their wide-brimmed black hats, long Payot (ritual sideburns), and black coats, had the office right below ours. I never knew exactly what they did, but it had something to do with the rite that accompanies the kosher butchery of poultry. When we coincided in the building's elevator, they rarely returned a greeting. The Hassidic seemed remote, but I think they were shy. One day they delivered a bundle of carefully mended black coats and warm gloves to us to be donated to our refugees.

....

Nancy Macdonald, as I say, became a mentor and good friend. She was as supportive as my artist friends when I gave birth to Gregory, encouraging me to bring him to work before I found childcare solutions (there weren't many of those in 1960s New York). We even had the same lover at one point, which was oddly interesting. Sex and the possibility of finding love were separate experiences in the New York in which I lived. In that pre-HIV era we made casual physical alliances that might last anywhere from a night to a few weeks or months, rarely longer. Individual freedom was the ideal, but, of course, that ideal played out differently in the lives of the women than in those of the men.

An intimate loneliness underscored all but a few of my many experiences of that sort. How could it have been otherwise? A skewed idea of sexual freedom too often hid within an assumption that physical and emotional intimacy could be as casual as conversation. Sex was simply another experience, wasn't it? Men and women were attracted to one another or, perhaps more accurately, it was the men who went from conquest to conquest, satisfying the macho need and sense of entitlement they'd been conditioned to cultivate since birth. The most painful part of this equation was the sense, also socially conditioned, that women chose "no" at our peril. In our culture, women and men hadn't yet learned how to relate to one another other than sexually, which encouraged competition and jealousies. Looking back, most of the men with whom I was intimate in those years remain disappointing or frustrating memories. It was the women—Elaine, Pat, Nancy, Rhoda—whose mentorship and/or friendship endures. It would be decades before I assumed my lesbian identity.

I remember throwing one man from my bed after casual conversation revealed his fascist leanings. A few men, although our sexual relationship was short-lived, did become friends. Jason Harvey was one of these. Our connection and his deep kindness induced me to give my son Jason as a middle name. Light was Harvey's palette; he was a designer of lamps. Decades after I left New York, I received a letter from his son telling me he had died. It seems I had also retained a place in his heart, and his son took the trouble to track me down.

The cultural critic Seymour Krim was another friend. We had a brief sexual relationship, almost as if we had to get it out of the way. It was Seymour who suggested that if neither of us had found the right partner by then we might come together and care for one another when we were old. I seem to recall that we thought of thirty as old. We eventually lost touch. Seymour died long ago, taking his own life when confronted with a fatal disease.

Although rarely very satisfying, some of those brief sexual liaisons are interesting in retrospect. Jaakov Kohn was a silversmith in the Village. He was also a widower with several small children, the youngest of whom suffered from a rare condition from which he continually became immobilized as a result of breaking his overly brittle bones. Jaakov was their sole support, rarely able to leave the apartment above his small shop. Sometimes late at night when his children were asleep, he would call to ask if he could come over. I always said yes. We had in common our need for human warmth.

Another strange bedfellow was a novelist named Alan Kapelner. When we met—I can't remember how—I'd already read his *Lonely Boy Blues*. Alan was quite a bit older than I was. He was a gentle and sensitive lover. For whatever reason, he was also a liar. He told me he was the illegitimate son of Mabel Dodge Luhan, a well-known patron of the arts who had been influential in New Mexico during the early years of the twentieth century. Alan offered all sorts of details. The story was intriguing, and it never occurred to me that it wasn't true. Many years later, back in New Mexico myself, I was able to research his claim and discovered it had been a total fabrication. I've always wondered what induced him to pass himself off as someone he was not.

My most memorable experience at SRA concerned a benefit art show I organized in 1960. We were always trying to raise money for the refugees; why not take advantage of the fact that I knew so many artists whose work had become saleable? I made good use of my contacts and was able to get an uptown gallery to donate space for several weeks. A wealthy friend provided funds that paid for engraved invitations and a gala champagne opening. I was enormously pregnant with Gregory at the time and remember I made myself a veritable tent out of drapery material to hide my unwieldy belly. I worried that my grandparents might show up at the opening; they didn't.

I'd somehow connected with a woman named Tana de Gamez, a Zionist who sold bonds for Israel at the time and who had a great deal of organizing experience and was willing to share it with me in this endeavor. Tana thought big. It was she who one night suggested that we ask Pablo Picasso for a drawing or print. His *Guernica* was iconic, and his allegiance to the Spanish Republican cause well known. I remember us sitting together, I think it was at her apartment, in that era of dial telephones and international operators who were actual human beings. I called Information in Spain and explained I needed Picasso's number. Next thing I knew I was speaking with Jacqueline, the woman living with the artist at the time. I explained my request, heard her speaking off-phone to the artist, and in minutes had the promise of an original drawing that would be sent to the New York address I provided.

I can still feel my excitement the next morning when I went to work fairly bursting with my news. An original Picasso! I had no doubt Nancy would be as elated as I was. I didn't understand her concerned expression and long silence until she explained that we couldn't accept the Picasso. He was a member of the Spanish Communist Party, she said, and in post-McCarthy America any association with him would likely lose us our tax-deductible status. I was stunned. And angry. But there was no budging Nancy, who knew our "democracy" far better than I. Calling Jacqueline to explain why we couldn't accept a drawing I myself had asked for was surely one of the more humiliating things I've had to do.

Despite that wrinkle, the benefit exhibition was a huge success, earning more than $10,000 for the refugees. I remember a small mobile by Alexander Calder and another sculpture by David Smith. Almost all the artists I knew contributed. And since we set prices low, most of it sold. I continued to work at the Spanish Refugee Aid until I left the city in the fall of 1961, gradually parting political ways with Nancy although we remained friends for many years.

....

Nancy, who had been soured on Communism by Stalin, distrusted the ideology. Cuba was bringing me closer to it. Our politics diverged, yet she wanted us to learn to think for ourselves and often let Rhoda and me off work to attend a march or rally. The main issue of the day was nuclear war, and we protested the absurd little antinuclear shelters the government was encouraging people to buy or build.

I was working for Nancy when I attended my first political demonstration. It took place in front of the Portuguese consular office at Rockefeller Center and was organized in protest of that country's government after the crew of a cargo ship mutinied and tried to seek refuge in Goulart's Brazil. Salazar wanted the ship and crew returned to Portugal. The demonstration consisted of only about a dozen determined men and women. It was a bitter cold night in early 1961. Gregory was just a few months old and I marched with him in my arms. A city policeman took off his gloves and urged me to wear them. The experience inspired one of my first decent poems, "The Gloves," one I still sometimes read in public these many years later.

....

THE GLOVES
FOR RHODA

Yes, we did march around somewhere and yes it was cold,
we shared our gloves because we had a pair between us
and a New York city cop also shared his big gloves
with me—strange,
he was there to keep our order
and he could do that
and I could take that
back then.
We were marching for the *Santa María*, Rhoda,
a Portuguese ship whose crew had mutinied.
They demanded asylum in Goulart's Brazil
and we marched in support of that demand,

in winter, in New York City,
back and forth before the Portuguese Consulate,
Rockefeller Center, 1961.
I gauge the date by my first child
—Gregory was born late in 1960—as I gauge
so many dates by the first, the second, the third, the fourth,
and I feel his body now, again, close to my breast,
held against cold to our strong steps of dignity.
That was my first public protest, Rhoda,
strange you should retrieve it now
in a letter out of this love of ours
alive these many years.
How many protests since that one, how many
marches and rallies
for greater causes, larger wars, deeper wounds
cleansed or untouched by our rage.
Today a cop would never unbuckle his gloves
and press them around my blue-red hands.
Today a baby held to breast
would be a child of my child, a generation removed.
The world is older and I in it
am older,
burning, slower, with the same passions.
The passions are older and so I am also younger
for knowing them more deeply and moving in them
pregnant with fear and fighting.
The gloves are still there, in the cold,
passing from hand to hand.

I am writing this just as my *Time's Language: Selected Poems (1959–2018)*
makes its appearance. Sixty years of poetry collected in a single book. Having
the 450-page volume in hand has naturally sent me back to my early days in
poetry, most prominently those New York years in which I struggled to turn
my incipient work into something personally authentic. The collection begins
with work from my first two slim books. It is embarrassing to me now, but
I remind myself it's important to reveal one's journey, especially to younger
writers.

My first two books were illustrated by some of the important artists of those times: Elaine, Al Held, Ronald Bladen, Robert Mallary, and Joop Sanders. I've long wondered why they were willing to lend their talent to a beginner's awkward lines. I can only imagine they must have seen something in me, some indication of the poet I might become. That generosity of spirit is something I learned in that world. I have tried hard to carry it forward.

For many years, one way I did that was by following a practice I observed in Elaine almost from the moment we met. Each time she sold a painting, she took 25 percent of what she earned and purchased one by a younger artist. Often it was that person's first sale and the encouragement was probably as important as the money. I followed her example until I ran out of wall space for the art I was acquiring. And I continue to mentor upcoming artists and writers in other ways: by sharing publishing information, devoting as much time as possible to critiquing manuscripts, writing prologues and introductions, lending support in the form of blurbs, and—in recent years—by translating Cuban and other literature from the Spanish.

More important questions that come to me now, as I hold my *Selected Poems* in hand, concern the ways in which living among that group of New York artists nurtured my writing, how their attitudes and values helped shape my own. I owe them a great deal, yet it's been easier for me to describe other influences—the 1960s itself as a particular time period, my later involvement in several Latin American political struggles, giving birth to and raising my children, coming home and having to fight for reinstatement of my US citizenship, coming out as a lesbian—than it has been to define exactly what I received from those visual artists. Perhaps more than anything else it was their total commitment. And their conviction that art in and of itself—when it is good and goes all the way—can be life-changing.

....

There were few social services for single mothers with infants in New York City back then, and that meant few childcare possibilities. After Gregory was born—he and I were charity cases at Manhattan General Hospital on Second Avenue—I was able to leave my son with another new mother who took in a few babies as a way of earning some cash. She kept them clean, fed them, and took them to the park each day, which was all one could expect under the circumstances. But Elaine, who had an almost magical talent for solving problems, soon had a better idea. The Dalton School was an expensive private institution popular among the sons and daughters of those artists who were now making enough money to give their children elite educations.

To teach its high school girls to care for the offspring they would presumably have one day, the school ran a penthouse nursery for three infants between the ages of six weeks and six months. The service was free. It may also have been a way for the school to believe it was doing something for the needy. It was light and airy, provided clothing and meals, and included the on-site presence of a nurse as well as regular visits by a pediatrician. A privileged find.

Elaine, who was enthralled by Gregory from the moment of his birth, fought for him to be admitted to Dalton's nursery. She argued that the school would be doing a good deed by caring for the child of a single mother. Elaine rarely failed when she put her mind to something, and I was thrilled to be able to bring my son to the school each day, even if it meant taking him all the way uptown on a combination of subway and buses, going back downtown to work, and then retracing my steps to pick him up each afternoon. When Gregory was six months old, though, the Dalton would no longer take him. I was back to having to figure out his care once more.

Someone told me about Jewish Philanthropies and its subsidiary daycare program for Jewish children. They required proof of the child's Jewishness, which in Gregory's case meant being able to show that he'd had a bris. In line with the custom of the times, I'd had my child circumcised while still in the hospital, but by a doctor rather than a rabbi. So, no bris. At the time I believed my throwing a fit right there in the Jewish Philanthropies office was what made the woman interviewing me relent and accept my son into the program. Later I realized it was more likely because the charity sought Jewish babies for adoption by childless Jewish parents.

From the time he was six months old, each morning I brought Gregory to the apartment of an Italian family who lived in the projects on Avenue D. The father was a garbage collector and the mother augmented the family income by offering childcare. I paid a minimal sliding scale in line with my salary at SRA. When my Jewish Philanthropies case worker began talking to me about the benefits of Gregory being adopted by a nice Jewish couple, though, I became uneasy. Shortly after that, Gregory and I left New York, boarding a bus bound for Mexico City.

Before we did, I had one last Lower East Side experience that I remember with gratitude. Poet and friend Paul Blackburn ran one of the reading series at a local café—I think it was Les Deux Magots—and invited me to do a set.

This would be my first opportunity to be a featured poet, but the date offered was scheduled after I would leave the city. I hoped another poet would be willing to change dates with me. Paul told me that Joel Oppenheimer had an earlier slot and suggested I call him.

Joel and I had only seen one another once since Gregory's birth; he'd come to our apartment somewhat drunk one night when our son was three weeks old, stood for a while staring down into the crib where Gregory slept, then left without saying much. He'd brought the novelist Hubert Selby Jr. along for reinforcement or comfort. Selby was as silent as Joel. It took some courage for me to make the call. Joel, not at all drunk when we spoke, generously agreed to switch dates and I was able to enjoy a featured reader's spot before saying goodbye to an exceptional period in my life.

I should say that years later, brought together by Gregory himself, Joel and I became friends. In many ways he had always considered Gregory a son. In 1988, when he was dying of lung cancer in New Hampshire, his soon-to-be-widow, Theresa, called me in New Mexico to tell me Joel wanted to say goodbye to Gregory. His other sons were at his bedside. My son lived in Paris at the time. I called him there, he phoned Joel, and they had a brief but deeply felt farewell. The poem I wrote about that Albuquerque/New Hampshire/Paris connection is another I still like to read.

....

JOEL OPPENHEIMER 1930–1988

The strong wife of my firstborn's father
calls to tell us it's time.
Tomorrow or the next day
a week at most.
He talks and is not in pain,
has prepared well to die.

And you? I ask.
There's no preparing . . .
I search for words.
Come on, you're the poet,
she challenges my craft, laughs.
Tears gripping this wire
between women who have never met.

The children's visit meant so much,
tell them they're stuck with me . . .
Her voice is warm
from New Hampshire's first signs of winter.
Here, on this autumn desert
feathery Apache plume and flowering sage
it is almost dusk.
Two a.m. in Paris
where my son picks up the phone.
I have moved through my tears,
relay the message.

Time zones and languages contract, expand,
replay the shared granddaughter
just now completing
the cycle of her first year.

We are poets who walked briefly
in each other's lives,
grow old in New Hampshire, New Mexico,
our children and their children
testing the words we leave behind.

May the words grow with them
and keep singing, Joel,
crossing time zones
powerful against corrupt statistics,
beaten babies, lies
that fake this rallying beat of truth.

No one is fooled.
Death only lives
when the language of life is gone.

At the Les Deux Magots reading, as it turned out, I met US Beat poet Philip Lamantia, who lived in Mexico but was spending a few days in New York. Philip and his then-wife, Lucille, hosted an almost nightly salon of poets and artists at their Mexico City apartment. He scribbled his telephone number on a scrap of paper and told me to call when I got to town. The creative spirits I met at that salon—writers and artists from several Latin American countries as well as Mexico itself—opened me to a whole new poetic experience. It was at those nightly gatherings that the idea for a bilingual journal was born, and Mexican poet Sergio Mondragón and I launched *El Corno Emplumado / The Plumed Horn*, a magazine that would enjoy an eight-year run and publish some of the most exciting work of the 1960s. My personal and creative lives were always deeply entwined; Sergio and I were married for seven years and he is the father of my daughters Sarah and Ximena.

The world of New York artists and writers with whom I lived in the late 1950s and early 1960s gave me much of value, much that I still treasure. It made me confident I would someday be the writer I needed to be, and that I could learn to be her anywhere.

Chapter Five

WHERE
STONES WEEP

Mexico, 1961–1969

Do we really live on this earth?
Not forever on earth,
only briefly here!
Although made of jade, one shatters,
although of gold, one breaks
and even the Quetzal feather can tear:
Not forever on earth:
only briefly here!
—NEZAHUALCÓYOTL (1402–1472)

Mexico is an ancient thing that will still go on forever telling its own story in slabs of color leaves and fruits and proud naked Indians in a history without shame. Their great city of Tenochtitlán is still here beneath our shoes and history was always just like today full of markets and waiting.
—BARBARA KINGSOLVER, *THE LACUNA*

I often think about the ease and determination, indeed the relative lack of nostalgia and heightened anticipation of what may lie ahead, that I carried with me throughout my first half-century of life. In the mid-1950s, when I wasn't yet twenty years old, my first husband and I headed for India on a Lambretta motor scooter with $400 in our pockets. We didn't get there but spent the next year and a half in Spain, first in Madrid and later Seville. We worked at whatever we could find, and I acquired my first familiarity with the Spanish language.

Soon after our return to Albuquerque, that marriage fell apart. I remember a brief sense of loss or disappointment followed by immense relief. In retrospect I knew I had married Sam as a way of escaping my familial home—parents who were loving and supportive but whose own uncomfortable marriage clothed in outer sparkle confused and suffocated me. Back then marriage was the only way a young woman of my class and culture could leave her parental home. At the end of that decade I made my next big move: following my friend and mentor Elaine de Kooning to New York City. More explicitly, to the artist community in Lower Manhattan where she was queen.

In 1961, with my first child in tow and with the sense that I'd probably gotten all I was going to get from New York, I moved on to Mexico City. Almost a decade later it was Cuba and after Cuba, Nicaragua; until at the beginning of 1984 I finally made my last big move: home to the New Mexican landscape where my parents had brought my brother, sister, and me in 1947 when I was ten. The circle had closed.

My years in Mexico are the ones I want to evoke now.

But first I will say something about otherness, the ways in which perceiving myself as other has isolated me from time to time but also made me more acutely aware of who I am in relationship to place. From my earliest memories, I felt strangely different in my family of origin: unwilling or unable to fulfill the expectations of class and culture, the facade my parents constructed, even resentful of such pretense. In Spain I was certainly other, although, because of my age and lack of experience, I was mostly relegated to a realm of superficial foreignness. I thought I understood the country better than I did. Among the New York artists and writers of the late 1950s and early 1960s, my youth and provincialism also set me apart, yet I experienced a feeling of belonging I hadn't known before.

Mexico upped the ante. There, my small son and I were other in ways as confusing as they were challenging. I was the gringa woman, desirable as well as disreputable, even dangerous. A single mother in a place where the condition was certainly less acceptable than it had been in New York, I possessed that aura of white exoticism even as I was a constant reminder of supposed superiority and conquest. My son was the beautiful little blonde boy exclaimed over by everyone who saw him.

I remember chatting with a market woman sometime during my first year in the country. She remarked on my accent and asked if I was from another part of Mexico. "No," I lied, "I'm Italian." At the time I had no idea why I'd said that. My shame, I suppose, at belonging to a nation that had so ravaged the one I was now coming to know.

Many years later, feminist biologist Ruth Hubbard and I collaborated on a book we called *The Shape of Red: Insider/Outsider Reflections*.[1] Writing in the form of alternating letters to one another, we hoped to explore the ways in which we'd experienced the insider/outsider moments of our lives. Ruth was an Austrian Jew, forced to escape her war-torn nation for the United States at the age of fourteen. I had left home more willingly, lived elsewhere for close to three decades, and had recently returned to a place I recognized and needed but that attempted to deport me because of my ideas. In important but often unac-knowledged ways, many of us move between feelings of belonging and wishing to remain outside a cultural milieu that may feel safe but also stultifying.

I had been familiar with the US-Mexican border area since childhood. Even in that era of the fifty-five-mile-per-hour speed limit, Ciudad Juárez was only a half day's drive from Albuquerque, and my parents took us down oc-casionally. We never ventured much beyond the tourist strip, with its bright curio shops and restaurants, but Mother and Dad—ever eager for a bargain—saw a dentist there for a while, had their eyes examined, and bought glasses at the city's vastly reduced prices. If my family hadn't been influenced by the fact that my maternal grandfather was a Christian Science practitioner who believed in spiritual rather than medical solutions to health issues, we prob-ably would have purchased medications there as well.

Later, as I've written, I continued to visit Juárez on my own and also with Elaine during the time she was a visiting art professor at the University of New Mexico. We would spend a carefree weekend, which always included a Sunday morning visit to the bullfight at the city's large Plaza Monumental. I had acquired a taste for the bulls in Spain, something I would reject later in life when its barbarism came to repel more than its pageantry thrilled me. But I will always remember Elaine sitting beside me in those sun-drenched bleach-ers, rendering the force—the very nature—of those magnificent animals in sure strokes of charcoal or pen on paper.

....

Gregory and I made a brief exploratory trip to Mexico City sometime in the summer of 1961. My friend Rhoda joined us, and we stayed at the apartment of Catalan refugee poet Agustí Bartra and his wife, Ana. I'd met Agustí and Ana in New York, perhaps through my work at Spanish Refugee Aid. We'd become friends and, although they wouldn't be in Mexico at the time, generously offered us their home. I think their son Roger and daughter Ana welcomed us.

That must have been when Beat poet and prison escapee Ray Bremser arrived in Mexico City and, along with his wife Bonnie, also camped for a while at the Bartras' place. Allen Ginsberg had asked if I could help them in Mexico. Ray and Bonnie had a little girl, not much older than Gregory. Bonnie was turning tricks to support their small family, the child was wantonly neglected, and when Ray and Bonnie themselves decided they wanted to sell—yes, sell— her to people better able to parent, it was Elaine as always who came to their aid. She placed the vacant-eyed little girl with a childless couple, collectors of her art, somewhere in Texas.

It was a wild scene at the Bartras' that summer. Years later, Bonnie wrote a memoir, *For Love of Ray*,[2] in which she described me as a naive and bourgeois woman, too uptight to approve of prostitution or of raising a small child amid clouds of marijuana smoke. I was certainly naive in many ways, and clearly bourgeois compared with Ray and Bonnie. But I'd supported Ray's evasion of prison time, played a part in putting them in contact with people south of the border, and don't remember making a judgment about Bonnie's decision to prostitute herself if it was the only way they could survive. I did wonder if it might not be coercion on Ray's part, rather than Bonnie's choice. What I found most deeply troubling was their treatment of their daughter, and also that they were bringing some pretty unsavory characters into a home I respected and had made available.

For Gregory and me, that summer visit was a prelude to our later Mexican experience. I was testing the waters, imagining what our lives might be like if I decided on a permanent move. Mexico's colonial churches were filled with treasures and pungent with the scent of copal. A nation of corn, the air smelled of *nixtamal*, and roasted chile-sprinkled *mazorcas* could be eaten at stalls along city streets. Ancient stones seemed to speak, telling stories one could only absorb as one became familiar with the landscape and its people. Two imposing snow-capped volcanoes—Popocatepetl and Ixtaccihuatl— dominated the horizon to the south of the city.

Another world, but one with which I immediately identified. I was attracted by what I saw of the strong indigenous presence, multiple cultures, and generosity of spirit. The other thing I took in was Mexico's natural beauty: its great diversity of countryside and multicolor houses lining cobble streets. Purple, red, and white bougainvillea vines, tall as trees, cascaded over volcanic garden walls and the violet lace of the jacaranda canopy spread its ample branches.

....

CORNER OF LATIN AMERICA

La esquina de Latinoamérica
it's called
where a weathered fence of rusted metal
cuts white sand, then disappears
into water that has no knowledge
of borders.

Metal recycled
from Vietnam-era tanks and planes,
gap-toothed and bearing improbable image
of cactus and skeleton.
Broken pilings, a division
that once was: what? Shabby, imposing,
makeshift, or absurd bravado?

This corner of Latin America,
where lines on a map
translate to searchlights, guns,
pickup beds heavy with hunched men and women
caught, taken back to their point of origin
only to try again tomorrow
or next week.

Corner, as in the uppermost and outermost
point on a map
once inhabited by Kiet Seel to the north
Casas Grandes to the south.
Not a place that gathers,
enfolds, comforts or protects.
Not refuge but exposure.
Danger writ large in global script.

One side of the worn fence
a young man lifts his body in push-ups,

strains against twisted pieces
of a cement platform, crumbling.
Woman and child
sleep in the fence's long shadow.
Far side: San Diego's powerful skyline
disappearing in mist.

La esquina de Latinoamérica,
containment vs. we don't want you—
except to watch our children, clean
our floors, keep our profit high.
Like a hologram, this place
emptied of itself,
waits restive for change.

In dreams and in grief
I am riding that corner fence,
its rusted metal cuts the flesh
of my thighs.
Blood runs to the sand
then disappears
as high tide takes the beach.

And it wasn't only the country's physical beauty. Like others with significant indigenous populations—Guatemala, Bolivia, Peru, South Africa, Mali, China, Vietnam, Cambodia, Laos—Mexico is a nation of artists. In every village I saw experts creating beautifully crafted textiles, pottery, hand-blown glass, carved native woods, and objects made of silver, jade, and onyx. In the 1960s, a corrosive tourist taste hadn't yet invaded the markets where this array of art was made and sold, and generations of creative spirits still followed ancient methods of production, sometimes introducing their own more contemporary designs.

The prospective move felt enticing. Several months later Gregory and I departed New York on that Greyhound headed south.

....

Albuquerque was on the way, and we stopped for a week with my parents who, by that time, had taken completely to their first grandchild. They had long since become accustomed to my adventurous decisions, and I remember a great deal more excitement than concern about our move. I arrived in the Mexican capital knowing we had a few welcoming friends and armed with two important connections: the scribbled phone number Philip Lamantia had placed in my hand when I'd read at Les Deux Magots and a list of names and phone numbers Nancy Macdonald had given me, introductions to people she thought I might want to look up.

Nancy's list deserves further explanation. She and her brother Selden Rodman had spent a good deal of their family money helping Jewish intellectuals escape Nazi-occupied Europe during the Second World War. In that important work they were part of an international network composed of individuals in many countries. Mexico had long been a nation welcoming to endangered immigrants; Benito Juárez's famous dictate "El respeto al derecho ajeno es la paz" (Respect for the rights of others is peace) wasn't mere rhetoric. It played itself out in the acceptance of thousands of refugees from Spain's Civil War, European fascism, and, years later, those forced to flee the Latin American genocides. It was in the context of this refugee network that Nancy knew Mexico's ex-president Lázaro Cardenas, German psychoanalyst Erich Fromm, Argentine editor Arnaldo Orfila, and others. These were among the dozen or so names on the list she handed me before we said goodbye.

I was adventurous but also shy. When it was time to contact the people on Nancy's list, I couldn't work up the courage to call an ex-president or world-renowned psychoanalyst. I didn't recognize Arnaldo Orfila Reynal's name or that of his French wife, anthropologist Laurette Séjourné. If I had, I might have hesitated to approach them as well. Arnaldo, from Argentina, had been active in the important 1918 Reforma Universitaria in the city of Córdoba, a movement that continues to have a lasting impact on the way the university is conceived of throughout Latin America. When I got to Mexico, he was the director of El Fondo de Cultura Económica, the country's most important publishing house, partially funded by the government. He was a cultural reference and a man of great humanity. Laurette was one of the few anthropologists at the time who was exploring the country's pre-Colombian past without forcing it through a reductive contemporary lens. Her books were revelations. Needless to say, she had powerful enemies as well as devoted admirers.

Since I didn't know any of this, once Gregory and I were settled in a small apartment in Colonia Narvarte, and I realized Arnaldo and Laurette lived mere blocks away on Avenida Universidad, I decided to take the plunge. I

Magician's Pyramid, Uxmal (photo by Margaret Randall).

had no telephone number for them, only an address, so Gregory and I took a walk one afternoon and knocked on their door. Because of Arnaldo's directorship of El Fondo de Cultura Económica, the couple lived in a large apartment above its offices.

Neither was at home when we showed up. A friendly, older indigenous woman who worked for them answered the door. I left a brief note, explaining I was a friend of Nancy's. I knew that Nancy and her brother had posted bond for Laurette when she and an earlier husband, Victor Serge, had to flee occupied France. Only a few hours after that tentative visit, my own doorbell rang and Laurette and Arnaldo stood there smiling. I seem to remember them bearing a welcoming box of chocolates. They would be among my closest friends throughout my eight years in Mexico.

Mexico in the 1960s was quiet serenity laced with desperation. The pace was slower than in New York. People worked hard, but within a more casual sense of time. Manhattan had always seemed to me a grid, a crisscrossing of straight lines, explosive boxes of energy. In contrast, Mexico City was concentric circles spiraling out from discrete points of consciousness. One walked in and out of temporal dimensions; you never knew when you might find yourself inhabiting another plane. Here the pulse had a different beat: more ancient, less readymade, magical.

I was fortunate in that I immediately found people who weren't only helpful but immensely interesting, among the best and most creative minds in Mexico at the time. The famous muralists, Frida Kahlo, Tina Modotti, and others had been stars of previous decades. Their presence could still be felt, and in fact a couple of the muralists were still active during my first years in the country. Some of their successors were just as exciting. I've already mentioned my friendship with Agustí and Ana Bartra. Early on I also got to know Anita Brenner and Leonora Carrington.

I can't remember who introduced me to Ruth Stavenhagen and Nicolás Bodek. Ruth was born in Germany. Her father, Kurt Stavenhagen, possessed one of the largest and most valuable private collections of pre-Colombian artifacts in the country. He once asked me to take a jade mask to New York. I must have been traveling back for some reason I no longer remember, and he wondered if I would deliver it to a friend. He asked the favor in a very offhand way, never mentioning the fact that removing archaeological treasures from Mexico was a crime.

I didn't know that either, and I willingly carried the mask in my suitcase. In those much more relaxed times no one even noticed. I called Stavenhagen's friend and delivered the goods. Only later did I come to understand that the old man had used me for a task he not only knew was wrong but also must have known would involve me in something in which I might not want to participate. I never confronted him but stopped pursuing the friendship.

On the other hand, I liked Ruth and Nicolás immensely. After a few days at the Bartras' home, Gregory and I moved in with them and they extended their warm hospitality for a month or so until we found our own place. One vivid memory I have from that time was Ruth asking me if I would accompany her to the building's rooftop one evening to take a look at a maid who had died in her small cubicle. She had been working for another one of the families in the complex, had apparently gotten pregnant and hidden it successfully; however, when she gave birth alone in that small room, something went terribly wrong. The mother died; her baby lived.

Ruth was a psychologist. I never understood why she took me to see that poor young woman, ghostly gray-yellow in premature death. There was nothing either of us could do. But the experience initiated my growing awareness of the horrors embedded in a system in which domestic help is servitude rather than service. Throughout Latin America, and in many other parts of the world, live-in maids work long hours for minimal pay and no benefits, sometimes from early adolescence on. Even the poor exploit those poorer than themselves. Employers with some degree of social consciousness or liberal shame assuage their guilt by claiming to pay these women better than the going rate, sometimes even insisting they join them at the dinner table or otherwise pretending they are "part of the family."

I was guilty of such behavior. A big reason I'd left New York was that I wanted to spend more time with my son. In Mexico, rather than patch together childcare possibilities, I could count on a live-in maid who would care for him whenever I needed to work or go out. It was a welcome solution, and I took full advantage. And, yes, I too justified the arrangement, believing I treated Antonia and then Ermelinda and then Juanita and then Concha, her sister Helena and their mother, Serafina, with absolute respect. I tried hard to limit asking anything after hours of the women who worked for me, although there really was no such thing as after hours in that system. I encouraged several to go to night school, without wondering if they really wanted to or what benefits a night course might offer. Many domestic servants must leave their own children in the care of others while they attend to the children of their employers. What I eventually learned is that no such relationship, however generous it may seem, remedies a profoundly unjust system.

On the other hand, my associations with some of the women who worked in our home gave me insights into their worlds. Ermelinda was a bright young woman from the mountains of Puebla. She invited us to visit her family who lived in a remote area, reachable only by horseback. My daughter Sarah was six months old at the time, and I was still nursing. It was during those hours astride the horse that I suddenly realized my milk had dried up. I had bought the old adage about not being able to get pregnant while nursing. Wrong. I had become pregnant with Ximena and that had cut my milk supply. There was nothing for it but to wash an old whiskey bottle we found, fill it with diluted cow's milk, dribble it into Sarah's mouth and hope for the best.

The couple of days we spent with Ermelinda's family were a revelation. In that dramatically remote countryside, they lived in very primitive conditions, but their hospitality was enormous. Ermelinda's father had been suffering for months from an open sore that wouldn't heal on his foot. Walking had become intolerable. We persuaded him to accompany us back to the capital, where we hoped we could get him medical attention.

Don Rodolfo had never traveled farther than the provincial city of Puebla, and then only by horse. He had never been in an automobile and had not seen electric lighting or other modern conveniences up close. It was hard convincing him to leave his home for a few months, but he was suffering and ultimately consented. We did find a doctor willing to see him at no cost. The diagnosis was advanced tuberculosis of the bone. All they could do was make him comfortable and send him home to die.

While Don Rodolfo was with us, though, we got a glimpse of the world as he saw it. I remember him "reading" to Gregory although he had never learned how. He sat with my son on his lap, holding a book—sometimes right-side up, sometimes not—slowly turning the pages as he invented marvelous tales of mountain life complete with mysterious animals and magical beings. I once entered the kitchen to find him repeatedly dropping a slice of bread into the toaster, fascinated by how dark it got. One night we took him to a drive-in theater, where we watched *Aladdin's Lamp* and he tried to figure out how the actors had gotten inside the screen.

....

Mexico was politically and culturally illuminating. Living south of the border I learned fast about the relationship between US domination and the dependent nations in its orbit. In those early 1960s, the country was alive in ways I hadn't experienced. The ancient Mayan and Aztec sites were still being avidly explored, their secrets only very partially unearthed. Mexico City itself was built over the great pre-Columbian city of Tenochtitlán, and the membrane of time between the two was astonishingly thin. The capital city's air was crisp and clear, its population only half of the twenty-four million who live there today. Stark contrast defined the country: between rich and poor, ancient and modern, resentment and pride, violence and sensibility, one of the world's great metropolises and bucolic villages that seemed to exist in a bygone century.

Poets as well as philosophers and writers from other countries were also active in the Mexico to which I'd arrived. They'd found refuge from the Spanish Civil War, the Nazi occupation of Europe, and other death traps.[3] Looking back, I believe that Mexico's long tradition of sheltering people in trouble, which later extended to its embrace of Latin Americans fleeing the brutal dictatorships of the 1970s and 1980s, helped to create a milieu in which creativity flourished.

....

My life in Mexico began to take shape and consolidate itself soon after our arrival, at the almost nightly salons hosted by Philip Lamantia and his wife, Lucille. Their apartment, centrally located in the Zona Rosa, an upscale neighborhood in Colonia Cuauhtémoc, was spacious and inviting—an ideal venue for a dozen or so young poets to gather, meet, and share new work with one another. I remember those sessions as exhilarating, necessary. Soon I was a regular.

The word spread and, before I knew it, we were poets from several different latitudes getting to know one another and eager to have a feel for what each was writing. I should add that the core group was almost entirely male. Chilean-born poet Raquel Jodorowsky, then living in Peru, was a presence for a while. Mexican poet Homero Aridjis's wife, Betty, often accompanied him, but she wasn't a poet. Lucille, also not a poet, was a good hostess, serving drinks and making us comfortable. As always, I occupied my place without questioning the fact that I was one of only a couple of women writers.

The more brilliant attendees included Ernesto Cardenal, a Nicaraguan who would eventually rank among the greatest Latin American writers of his generation. This was before he became a Catholic priest, took part in his country's Sandinista revolution, and, when it triumphed in 1979, became its first minister of culture. Nicaragua is a nation of poets, and a couple of others from that country also showed up occasionally: Ernesto Mejía Sánchez, who had been exiled in Mexico for a number of years by then, a young Francisco Valle, and a troubled genius named Beltrán Morales.

A few US Americans found their way, as I did, to those salons. I remember Howard Frankl and Harvey Wolin in particular. The majority were Mexicans, of course. These included Homero, Juan Bañuelos, and Juan Martínez. Homero had already begun to find his rather classical voice. Juan's poems were more socially oriented, often referencing the political as well as physical landscape of his native Tuxtla Gutiérrez in the southern state of Chiapas. Juan wrote long mystical lines. Mexico supported a range of poetic styles.

Felipe Ehrenberg and I may also have met for the first time at Lamantia's. Ehrenberg was a powerful presence, someone who quickly filled whatever space he entered. His wife, Martha Hellion, radiated an indigenous beauty, quiet wisdom, and unacknowledged creativity. Felipe was beginning to make his mark as a visual artist; we would collaborate on many projects during my years in Mexico. After they separated, Martha became a world-renowned designer of theater and opera sets. Their son Mathias and daughter Yael were roughly my own children's ages, and family relationships continued from generation to generation.

Another visual artist by the name of Carlos Coffeen Serpas dropped by at times. He was as retiring as Felipe was outgoing, and fascinating in his own right. Already in his thirties, Carlos still lived with his mother in a single squalid room. They slept in the same bed. He appeared not to have any visible means of support, something common to many artists who find it impossible to function by society's rules. Carlos seemed wedded to suffering, and beneath his shirt and pants a tight rope cut the flesh of his waist in permanent self-mortification. His drawings were tortured but marvelous.

Undoubtedly, the poet I met at Philip's who most impacted my life was the Mexican Sergio Mondragón. Rather than begin with my initial impression of him, I'll reproduce what he had to say about his introduction to Lamantia's salon on a commemorative panel we shared in 2015:

> Toward the end of 1961 I was finishing up my journalism studies and doing some reporting for the Mexican magazine *Revista de América*. It was October, and I'd just interviewed the painter David Alfaro Siqueiros in prison; he was a political detainee at the time. Among much else, I'd asked him about his relationship with the US painter Jackson Pollock, and the supposed influence the Mexican muralists had on that school of which Pollock was a pioneer, the school that in the United States would later be known as "action painting." I was immersed in writing and researching that interview, when my classmate at the school of journalism, the poet Homero Aridjis—who had just published his first book—invited me to meet the "beat" poet from San Francisco, California, Philip Lamantia. Philip had arrived in Mexico City shortly before.
>
> That meeting was a revelation. The group of poets who were gathered there immediately began to read in their respective languages. Soon after, Lamantia called to say he wanted us to meet Margaret Randall, recently arrived from New York. That very night we were once again reading our poems. The walls of Margaret's apartment were covered with paintings she'd brought with her, abstract expressionist works. This was a painting style I was seeing for the first time (outside of books). . . . All this helped me put the finishing touches on my feature about Siqueiros.[4]

A powerful cartography linked the world I had come from to the one in which I'd arrived. Sergio and I hit it off immediately. He was a year older than I. I was attracted to his passion for poetry, interest in creating a community of creative people, dark indigenous looks, and what seemed a solid commitment to family life. Although I'd tried hard to endure New York's endless series of brief sexual encounters, I longed for a stable relationship. What I failed to recognize was that I was about to trade freedom for control.

At Philip's we not only shared our own work but from time to time also something by a poet we admired. Most of us had a rudimentary knowledge of the others' language but not their culture: not enough to grasp nuance, trace influences, or fully understand what we were hearing. We quickly realized the need for some sort of venue or forum—a bilingual magazine, perhaps— where good translation could provide the necessary bridge. Most of the Latin Americans were unfamiliar with Whitman, H. D., Pound, or Williams. The US Americans were woefully ignorant of Vallejo, Neruda, Huidobro, or Mistral. In the United States, at least, some translations of the "greats" had been published, but they were inadequate or frankly bad, distorting the work of those poets rather than presenting them as anything approaching their intensity, beauty, or meaning. The same was true about English-language poetry in Spanish.

Everyone agreed on the need for a remedy to this situation. Sergio and I decided to do something about it. *El Corno Emplumado / The Plumed Horn* was born. It may have been Harvey Wolin, briefly involved at the beginning, who suggested the journal's name. The *corno* was the jazz horn so important to the best of our cultural offerings then exploding north of the border. The *plumas* were the feathers of Quetzalcoatl, the plumed serpent who was the iconic god of Mesoamerica's pre-Hispanic cultures. Such unexpected word pairings were popular in Mexico at the time, for literary magazines, theater groups, even restaurants and bars. The Cross-Eyed Cat and Crazy Coyote were cafés where artists gathered. *El pájaro cascabel* (Rattlesnake bird) was Mexican poet Thelma Nava's independent poetry broadside.

El Corno, as our journal was most often called, was different. Its bilingual nature set it apart. Our ambitions were also immense. We dreamed of a quarterly averaging two hundred pages per issue, publishing the best new work from South and North America and later also from farther afield: Europe, Africa, Asia, and Australia. We never managed to make more than a few of our thirty-one issues completely bilingual; more often they included work in both languages but not necessarily the same texts in translation.

From left to right: Felipe Ehrenberg, the author, and Sergio Mondragón at the commemoration of *El Corno Emplumado*, Mexico City, 2015 (photo by María Vázquez Valdez).

Once production of our first issue showed we were serious, we began receiving submissions in the post office box we visited each day, eager to see what writing and money might have arrived. We sustained the endeavor for almost eight years, invigorated by a worldwide web of creativity and consumed by a constant struggle for funding. Our youth, characterized by unstoppable energy and drive, allowed us to create the impossible. Our vision linked us to those with similar interests around the world.

After we launched the project, no obstacle was too daunting. We walked the streets of that great metropolis, explaining our goals and begging for poetry and money. I remember visiting José Gorostiza, then Mexico's undersecretary of foreign relations and author of a major poem called "Muerte sin fin" (Death without end). After hearing us out, he reached into his desk drawer, pulled out a thousand-peso note, and placed it in our hands. That was back when a thousand pesos was real money. It would be hard to imagine getting in to see such a high-level government official in the United States, much less expecting him or her to be interested in supporting an alternative literary journal.

We hosted a benefit reading at a private home in Coyoacán. In retrospect, it was historic. Ernesto Cardenal was among the handful of readers. I believe we raised the equivalent of US$6. Subscriptions weren't readily forthcoming to a magazine that didn't yet have a history, but a few early believers took out small ads. Amazingly, we were able to raise the thousand dollars or so that enabled us to produce our first one-hundred-page issue in January 1962.

That issue included original work by Ernesto Cardenal, Laurette Séjourné, Spanish poet León Felipe, English surrealist painter Leonora Carrington, and US abstract expressionists Elaine de Kooning and Milton Resnick—all later considered luminaries in their fields. By issue #2, we had added work by my US contemporaries Robert Creeley, Paul Blackburn, and Robert Kelly; the Mexican poet and novelist Rosario Castellanos; the German Werner Bruenner; and the great Peruvian poet César Vallejo (the latter in English translation).

The magazine didn't only attract young poets. Those who were more established also sent us their work. Ernesto Cardenal and Julio Cortázar were avid supporters. Samuel Beckett and Norman Mailer mailed checks. We published such greats as Rafael Alberti, Thomas Merton, Ezra Pound, William Carlos Williams, Nicolás Guillén, Rainer Gerhardt, Kenneth Patchen, Pablo Neruda, José Lezama Lima, Nicanor Parra, Eugenio Montale, Louis Zukofsky, Octavio Paz, Walter Lowenfels, and André Breton. Nobel laureate Hermann Hesse sent us an unpublished poem. We printed it bilingually in July 1962; he died a month later, so it's possible it was the last poem he ever sent out. Many important writers and artists appeared in our pages.[5]

What's most interesting, though, is that although many of these men and women were already well known, others weren't. We discovered new talent as delightedly as we published the famous writers who honored us with their texts. I've always been proud of this, especially when it allowed our readers to experience work written in one language accurately and elegantly translated into another.

We also had some significant misses. Early on, Cassius Clay (later known as Muhammad Ali) sent us a collection of haiku-like poems against the American war in Vietnam; they didn't correspond to my sense of good poetry, and I made the mistake of rejecting them! Norman Mailer also sent poems I didn't like; when I sent them back, he responded, bemused, with a $15 check. Sergio and I always prided ourselves on not letting friendship or fame get in the way of our criteria for accepting submissions. This was a good policy that occasionally backfired.

....

Several questions emerge as I write these lines: What cultural history—in Mexico, throughout the Americas, and farther afield—created the perfect storm in which a journal such as *El Corno*, unaffiliated with a university or writing program, was born and could prosper for almost eight years? What needs did it fulfill? How could two young people (Sergio was twenty-six when we launched the journal; I was twenty-five) successfully keep it going without institutional support? Was our freedom from a single sponsorship, in fact, one of the things that allowed the magazine to engage such a diversity of styles? What percentage of our project was imagination, what part passion, what hard work? What was the connection between our personal relationship and our curatorial decisions? What impact on the project did our diverging views eventually have? How did Sergio and I balance and complement one another, how did we grow apart, and what did those patterns mean for the journal? And, finally, what is *El Corno*'s legacy?

Of course, none of this was on our minds as the 1960s dawned. Sergio and I remained serious and disciplined; the magazine became a central part of our life together. Like clockwork, and against all odds, we produced an issue every three months. The first had one hundred pages, and they soon averaged between two and three hundred. Poetry was central, but essays, short stories, journals, artwork, cartoons, comic strips, manifestoes, reviews, contributors' notes, and a letter section were also part of the package. Each issue opened with an editor's note, which was either written by both editors and published in the original and translation, or written separately as a note by each of the editors. These were meant to set the tone for what was to follow. Some critics have suggested that by reading those notes one can trace the journal's development and internal struggles.

One of the magazine's most eagerly anticipated features was its letter section, a dozen or so pages at the back of each issue in which poets from different latitudes wrote about what was going on in their lives and communities. They described cultural contexts, discussed ideas and dilemmas. Travel has always been important to writers, even poor ones, and on occasion these poets were also writing far from home. In our issue #5 (January 1963) we published a letter from Gary Snyder, then living in Kyoto, Japan:

> America five hundred years ago was clouds of birds, miles of bison, endless forests and grass and clear water. Today it is the tired ground of the world's dominant culture.... Industrial-urban society is not "evil" but there is no progress either. As a poet I hold the most archaic values on earth. They go back to the Neolithic: the fertility of the soil, the magic of animals, the power-vision in solitude, the terrifying initiation and rebirth, the love and ecstasy of the dance, the common work of the tribe. A gas turbine or an electric motor is a finely crafted flint knife in the hand. It is useful and full of wonder, but it is not our whole life.

After only the first two issues, in #3 (July 1962), Kathleen Fraser wrote from Paris:

> Today, walking along the Seine to soak up last remnants of bookstalls faces fish towers I happened into the Mistral Bookshop where one always goes to get warm even if all the recent periodicals have been devoured twice around. Today, luck. In the reading room, your new first issue. I read it from cover to cover and was delighted with the offering. Not just one kind of sound. Room to stretch.

Jackson [Mac Low] also appreciated *El Corno*'s diversity: "I like the breadth of work you include; you don't restrict yourselves to any one group. [Werner] Bruenner and [John William] Corrington were real discoveries for me."

And Ernesto Cardenal, in the first of what would be many letters, promised:

> I'll publicize the magazine everywhere. I imagine you'll continue energizing Mexico. You will energize all of Latin America as well. We must create

a movement that renovates, that puts an end to complacency, the idea of a consecrated literature, the rhetoric they have imposed on us, the dogma, the conspiracies of silence.

From much farther away, in Bihar, India, Malay Roy Choudhury wrote,

We have started a literary rebellion here, calling ourselves HUNGRYALISTS. Allen Ginsberg who came to India and stayed with us for about a year introduced us to his fellow Beats. I shall be glad, naturally, if you please send your works translated into English so that we can translate them in our languages and introduce you to a large and interested audience down here. You know perhaps, people in India speak many languages: Bengali, Hindi, Tamil, Telugu, Kanari, Malayalam, Gujarati, Marathi, Gurmukhi, Urdu, etc. (#9, January 1964)

In issue #11 (July 1964), Lawrence Ferlinghetti wrote, "No. 10 of CORNO is great. Much better than any former issue, I think. Especially the drawings by Topor, the Indian primitive poetry, and the Brazilian concretions." And he went on to request an address for Topor so he could ask him for a drawing he wanted to use on the cover of a book he was about to publish.

Poets shared the essence of their wanderings. Matti Rossi, the Finn who translated the rich selection of Finnish poetry that appeared in issue #14 (April 1965), wrote us often. In a letter in the issue that included that anthology, he explained he had learned Spanish in Mexico some years before:

I learned to speak. It took me a month. Puebla, Yucatan, Chiapas. The places I most loved. I traced the old pathways of the Mayab, saw a lot, suffered some, made great friends, didn't want to miss out on a single day, even slept with my eyes open.

The writer and social analyst Thomas Merton was a Cistercian monk living at Gethsemani, a Trappist abbey in Kentucky. We often published his poems, drawings, and correspondence. These fragments from a letter that appeared in our issue #24 (October 1967) reveal much of what he was about, and they are also eerily prophetic:

Every once in a while, someone wonders why I am a monk, and I don't want to be always justifying . . . because then I get the false idea that I am a monk. Perhaps when I entered here, I believed I was, and kept it up for five, ten, fifteen years, even allowed myself to become novice master and tell others what it was all about. No more. I live alone in the woods and have as far as feasible for me copped out of the monastic institution. Of course, that too is delusion. That is why I understand what you feel about Cuba. But, unfortunately, all the big societies now seem to me to be so built on lies and fake rituals. They are really unlivable. . . . I wonder if we are getting around to one of those times when we ought to be saying goodbye and getting ready for God knows what, the bombs, the camps, another round of the same. For the US, if it is not nuclear war that lies ahead then it is some form of fascist violence, I think. Whatever it is, I'll stay in it, and try to keep in contact with the poetic underground! I look forward to the next *Corno*, Love, Tom.

This sense of impending doom and desperation, counterbalanced by the hope our passionate poetic vision embraced, permeated every one of the journal's issues. As did the ever-expanding concentric circles of appreciation for what we were doing. In issue #28 (October 1968), Walter Lowenfels wrote,

> We are surrounded by barrages of what to do to stay young. But the problem nobody seems to write about, or teach us about, is how to grow old, how to wage daily battles against nostalgia. For poets & editors it's a very practical affair: how to keep up with tomorrow. Among the 90,000 "best poets of our generation" that throng the publishing highways of the USA, there are innumerable circles, few of which are aware of the others. In the Lowell-Auden-Kunitz circle, the Sonia Sanchez-Olga Cabral-Clarence Major circle doesn't exist.

Many letters gave news of deeply rooted struggles for justice. In issue #26 (April 1968), the incomparable people's artist Rini Templeton wrote from northern New Mexico:

> It was very good to see your issue #23 with the work of Cuban poets. How much light pours through when someone does make a hole in the blockade-blackout. Things have been happening here: the armed attack at Tierra Amarilla in the spring, the growing militancy and unity in the Mexican-American people since then.

Our letter section was also a place where poets could express opposing views and defend divergent ideas about art and society. We encouraged these discussions. In issue #17 (January 1966), Roger Taus urged the magazine to stand solidly against "the main enemy of the peoples of the world: US imperialism." He saw no room for any other stance. Two issues later (#19, July 1966), this brought a response by Ted Enslin from his refuge in Maine's woods:

I am disturbed by the increasing instance of political insistence. I know these pressures exist, and certainly I feel as strongly as any about Viet Nam or the incredible USA Machine, but [politics] has absolutely no place in poetry or art of any kind, no didactic cant does.

Enslin interpreted as political cant, or jargon, all concern with social issues. British-American Denise Levertov was eloquent in her response. In issue #21 (January 1967) she rebutted Enslin's argument point by point, and then went on to differentiate between art and the writing of propaganda:

> What is wrong (and ultimately useless) is the deliberate use of something that seems to be poetry (but isn't) for propaganda purposes. The difference is that on the one hand one has a poet *impelled towards words*, the words of a poem, by feelings and convictions that may or may not insist, within him, on the didactic; and on the other, a person *deciding* that a poem on some political theme might be "effective." The latter person may be sincere in his beliefs, but he is misusing poetry.

The consistent use of the male pronoun, even by such a strong female poet as Levertov, was standard at the time.

From 1962 to 1965, the last issue each year was a bilingual book devoted to the work of a single poet; alternating years showcased those writing in Spanish and English: Catalan Agustí Bartra's *Marsias & Adila*, US American Robert Kelly's *Her Body against Time*, Chilean Raquel Jodorowsky's *Ajy Tojen*, and *The Man in Yellow Boots* by Canadian George Bowering. Those volumes also contained letters between the author and editors, revealing discussions from the manuscript's preparation all the way through to the moment of publication. Process was always important to us: how things came about, how the work was made, what changes might be introduced along the way, and why.

Those end-of-year books were no longer necessary after *El Corno* developed its own publishing imprint. We eventually published more than twenty titles, many of them bilingual. Particularly significant among these were Jerome Rothenberg's *The Gorky Poems*, translated by Sergio and me; *Land of Roseberries / Tierra de Moras* by Walter Lowenfels with original drawings by David Alfaro Siqueiros; and *Majakuagymoukeia*, a Spanish rendering of the creation story according to the Cora Indians of Nayarit. Ana Mairena wrote the latter. Married to the governor of that state at the time, she felt the pseudonym necessary. My mother did the English translations of the Lowenfels and Mairena books.[6]

In 1965 I published *October* under *El Corno*'s imprint. I now consider it to be my first successful poetry collection. It had an interesting history. Among our many visitors over the years were Japanese-American sculptor Shinkichi Tajiri; his Dutch wife, Ferdi, who made whimsical jewelry and other art constructions; and their two young daughters, Giotta and Ryu. Shinkichi also traveled with two studio assistants, one Japanese, the other German. It was as if their extended family was determined to heal the wounds of World War II. They stayed longer than most, and we collaborated on several projects. I included a series of Shinkichi's sexually explicit images in *October*. The printer we were using at the time was shocked and threw the great unbound signatures into the street, refusing to complete the press run. On several occasions our avant-garde sensibility came up against the more conventional side of Mexican society.

....

When I speak about *El Corno*, I speak primarily about Sergio and myself. This is because we were the driving and sustaining forces behind the project. Harvey Wolin was with us for our first issue but withdrew right after the second. Robert Cohen had a longer and more influential tenure at the end, helping me edit the last three issues. From time to time we had editorial assistants, poets and artists who volunteered to help out for a few months. But the initiative, glory, and weaknesses rightfully belong to Sergio and to me.

Our cultural histories, personal as well as those of our respective countries, could not have been more different. I came, as I've said, from a nation submerged in Cold War bias. Art was not supposed to reflect so-called political concerns. The myth of impartiality, which had long kept journalists in line, now weighed on writers and artists as well. Senator McCarthy himself had been discredited, but his influence lingered. Newly established MFA programs at several universities were producing apolitical writers cut from a male mold. All the major literary grants were awarded to safely sanitized poetry or prose that promised not to make waves. Experiments in form were in vogue but diversity of content discouraged. Publishing, whether of books, anthologies, or magazines, rewarded that which didn't threaten the status quo. Except in places such as *El Corno*, creative people were hesitant to discuss the fabricated clash between poetry and politics.

Some important books were condemned in the courts or by the United States Customs Service, and banned as pornographic.[7] Meanwhile, US society wallowed in postwar affluence, technocracy, and hypocrisy. Texts by or featuring strong women were unpublishable. It wasn't acceptable to write or talk publicly about such topics as sex, unless it reflected male lust. Shame, domestic violence, woman abuse, and male infidelity crossed every class and cultural line. But writing about them was taboo. Silence was rewarded, truth unacceptable. Writers of color, gay artists, and those with disabilities were also largely ignored.

Young US poets—those of the San Francisco Renaissance, the Beat movement, Black Mountain, Deep Image, and others—rebelled against these strictures. We exposed the hypocrisy and refused to speak the language of those who would confine us to a Levittown of the mind. A few women creatives were asserting our power. We were interested in memory and history. Many of us experimented with hallucinatory substances. Personally, I had grown up on the New Mexican desert but moved to New York City where I quickly fell in with poets and painters who were seeking the new. I was a free-spirited, outspoken young woman, on the cusp of a world I absolutely expected to be able to change.

In Sergio's Mexico, on the other hand, young poets had access to an unbroken legacy of artistic expression. They lived in a country with a very long history of appreciating and respecting the arts. In the early 1960s they were beginning to look to their own cultural past rather than Europe, which had long been the source of inspiration for twentieth-century writers in our countries. Indigenous poets and ancient cultures began to have a vital presence in contemporary creativity. This was also happening in the United States, although to a lesser extent.

In Mexico, this mix of the indigenous, a fragile line between the real and surreal, and an inborn ability to suspend disbelief gave birth to a writing style that some years later, when Latin American literature experienced the Boom, came to be known as magic realism.[8] At the same time, as liberation movements gained momentum across Latin America, some guerrilla fighters were also producing powerful poetry. I'm thinking especially of El Salvador's Roque Dalton, Peru's Javier Heraud, Nicaragua's Leonel Rugama and Daisy Zamora, Guatemala's Otto-René Castillo, Argentina's Paco Urondo, and Uruguay's Carlos María Gutiérrez.

As I've mentioned, Mexico's tradition of welcoming poets fleeing repressive regimes added to a rich tapestry of talent. Sergio was a young poet living and writing in the midst of this vortex. When we met, he was already beginning to project a unique voice. I was powerfully attracted to its timbre.

By moving to Mexico, I saved myself from the poetic tedium I might have inherited had I remained in the United States, majored in literature at a university, or tried to insert myself into an institutional cultural setting typical of that time and place. I was influenced by the Beats, Black Mountain, and Deep Image, but wasn't really part of those movements. I could have continued to live and learn in New York City, and my work would have developed, albeit differently. But Mexico broadened my perspective. My imagination soared in ways that were qualitatively different from those ignited by my earlier, more insular experience. And *El Corno* put me in touch with poets from across the globe.

I brought my New York verve, energy, and organizational sense to Sergio's much greater knowledge of Latin America. Those evenings at Lamantia's had given us both a strong sense of what we and other young poets needed: a vehicle through which we could come to know each other's work. Who can say why we came together, grabbed the moment, and responded so explicitly to our conviction that birthing a bilingual poetry magazine was urgent and possible? Perhaps it had to do with chemistry. Each of us was at a transitional point in our lives, unburdened by a 9 to 5 job. The energy of new love certainly helped, and later the family we created. The historic moment and interlocking communities were key. Excitement at discovering cutting-edge work pushed us to make that work broadly available. Looking back, I think our success also had a lot to do with the fact that we were young. We simply never considered that what we were attempting to do might be impossible. Once our first issue appeared, news spread, poets and artists began contacting us, and soon our post office box was receiving letters and submissions by the hundreds.

When I think about what communication was like back then, it's hard to re-create its tortoise-like pace. A letter or envelope of poems typically took three months to travel from Buenos Aires or New York to Mexico City. Cost considerations meant that heavier packages traveled by sea. As *El Corno*'s fame spread, poets and others dropped by to see us, often unannounced. An elegantly dressed couple from Tucson, founders of the Arizona-Sonora Desert Museum, introduced us to the joys of keeping a tarantula as a pet. Chilean painter Roberto Matta visited, as did South African poet Dennis Brutus and the Peruvian economist Hilda Gadea, who was Che Guevara's first wife.

On one occasion a ramshackle old station wagon pulled into our driveway. I watched intrigued from an upstairs window as the driver got out and carefully placed two wooden cages beside the car before ringing our bell. They contained a pair of coatimundis, raccoonlike animals that he explained must be kept separate, because after mating the female would devour the male. The man was Roy Brigham, his wife was Besmilr, and a visit to us had been recommended to them by their daughter Heloise, whom I knew from New Mexico. A union linotype operator, Roy could travel anywhere and earn enough to keep going. Besmilr was an extraordinary poet; after hearing her read, we immediately offered to publish her long "Yaqui Deer" in our issue #19 (July 1966). Our house was always full of US or Canadian poets on their way south, Latin Americans traveling north, or those from Europe or some other part of the world who were drawn to Mexico as if by a magnet. Long-distance telephone calls were out of the question. Email was beyond our wildest imaginings.

The interlocking webs of creative contact we established were as significant as the internet would be decades into the future. Perhaps more so because, unable to make use of instantaneous digital communication, we looked into each other's eyes, read our poems aloud to one another, and shared meals, hallucinations, the joy of our growing families, and the languages we were reinvigorating and making our own.

Every day one of us stopped at the post office where we rented a box that invariably held surprises. Even the postal workers knew and loved the magazine. In its last year, when Mexico's political forces were particularly antagonistic, our mail was often withheld for days at a time. Eventually we'd receive a large bundle all at once. We always assumed government agents were behind this erratic delivery. But a few years back I received an email from a man who said his father had worked at that office and had recently died in an accident, leaving several copies of *El Corno* among his things. The son told me it was his father who, all those years before, had hidden our mail when government agents came around, returning it to us after they left the premises.

One morning I parked illegally in front of that post office, as I always did, opened the driver's side door, and inadvertently caught the leg of a young cyclist riding by. He fell to the ground, his bike in shambles. I could see that his leg was badly broken; a shard of bone had pierced the skin. A small crowd gathered. People urged me to flee before the cops came. But how could I leave that boy lying there? I ran into the post office to call an ambulance, and when I emerged, the police were already on the scene.

I was taken to the nearest precinct and locked in a holding cell. I'd managed to call some friends who tried to come to my defense. Someone I knew in San Francisco wired me $200 to try to bribe the authorities to let me go. Felipe Ehrenberg hunted down the boy's grandparents, who didn't want to press charges. All they cared about was making the boy's injuries right. But the wheels of injustice were already turning, and they kept me in that cell overnight. With me was a bleary-eyed offender, who observed me with curiosity. One of the precinct cops pulled a chair up to the cell bars, eager to see how my cellmate might react to my presence. I too looked at the man with whom I occupied that small space. Despite our class and cultural differences, I was sure he knew we shared a bond against authority. I curled up in the corner of the cell and confidently fell asleep.

The next morning the ominous black vehicle they called by a woman's name, Julia, picked me up and delivered me to City Hall's basement jail, where they put me in a larger cell with half a dozen other women. I was getting desperate. I knew it would only be a day or so before I would be taken to Lecumberri, the notorious prison where formal proceedings would commence, and I would be in the system. Did the authorities want more money than we had offered, or was this a serious assault on my foreignness, femaleness, or politics?

All of a sudden, I heard my name called. A guard unlocked the cell door and motioned me out. At the end of a long hallway I saw the great Mexican poet Efraín Huerta standing with his arms open. I ran into them. Whom you knew and what influences you could muster had worked at last. I was free. During the years I lived in Mexico I never really understood exactly how such influences worked, but somehow I learned to live by their rules.

Was *El Corno Emplumado* an underground magazine, in the honorable tradition of so many leftist publications? No, because it was sent through the mail, sold in bookstores worldwide, and overt political ideas were only one part of what we put out. Poetry and art were our currency, and our aim was to reach as many readers as possible. Still, as Merton had remarked, the journal did have something of the underground spirit; if by that we mean unorthodox, unreserved, unapologetic. We chose to print works of literary communities carving out places for themselves on every continent.

Although we had no special training in design, we were also graphically adventurous for the times. We believed that typography should support content, not the other way around, and we printed poems with long lines sideways rather than breaking them to conform to the standard page size. Occasionally we included pages that unfolded, accordion-style. We also sometimes positioned drawings this way, as in issue #5 (January 1963), which was illustrated with reproductions from Mexico's ancient codices. Issue #30 (April 1969) had an insert, a single folded sheet with anonymous sketches smuggled out of one of the country's overflowing political prisons. Our early covers featured continuous lines of repeated lowercase type; later we incorporated some stunning paintings and photographs, ignoring copyright and simply taking what we liked wherever we found it.

....

El Corno became an institution, and Sergio and I a couple. The first issue appeared in January 1962 and we were married the following month by a hung-over small-town judge in the charming village of Tepoztlán. Laurette and a fine cultural critic named Ida Rodríguez Prampolini were our witnesses. I sold the small tract home in which Sam and I had lived in Albuquerque, and we bought a house in Prado Churubusco, on the city's south side. I would have preferred an old adobe in Tlalpan or Coyoacán, but Sergio wanted a place where no one had lived before; he was sensitive to energy fields and feared the presence of ghosts.

Although he took to Gregory immediately—for years, and against my pleading, refusing to tell my son that he wasn't his biological father—Sergio also wanted children of his own. I was delighted to have more. Our daughter Sarah was born in 1963 and Ximena the following year. Our family of five was flourishing. I had no reason to believe it wouldn't continue to do so. In search of better job opportunities, I took out Mexican citizenship in 1967—an easy formality by the wife of a Mexican. I didn't want to lose my American citizenship, but found I already had. This decision would cause me tremendous problems down the road.

Our passion for the project and each other was enough for a while. Sergio and I had created something much bigger than ourselves. We did a lot of translation together. Gradually, though, his ideological quest and literary preferences moved toward Eastern mysticism while I began identifying more with leftist revolutionary struggle. In the Spanish half of the journal, he published somewhat esoteric work, in line with his interests. In the English section, I accepted more socially conscious work motivated by my own. Sometimes we presented these texts bilingually. But toward the end of our joint tenure, the magazine gradually became two distinct showcases between a single set of covers.

This dichotomy affected our personal relationship as well. Sergio's mother had died giving birth to his younger brother, and his father sent him away when he was very young. Unresolved childhood trauma cried out in Sergio, often making him tense and moody. His unwarranted jealous rages shocked me from time to time, and I didn't yet have a language to counter his particular brand of misogyny. When he joined a group that believed nirvana could be achieved by men only, I was horrified. He had trouble with my northern directness and incipient feminism. We grew apart, then separated.

Sergio left our home and the journal, and I eventually started a relationship with a US American poet who was passing through—one of hundreds who stopped in to visit *El Corno*, which, after a few short years, had become a place of reunion for many of the talents who read or contributed to it. Robert Cohen helped edit the magazine's last issues. My intimate and family life and the one I inhabited through poetry continued to remain of a piece.

Robert was nine years younger than I. Like many travelers from north of the border, he had set out in the mythical footsteps of Che Guevara in search of his own Sierra Maestra. He arrived in Mexico accompanied by a friend named Gordon Bishop. They dropped in one night, and Robert never left. He is the father of my daughter Ana, born in the spring of 1969. Robert and I would spend some intense years together. He was with me during the repression and escape from Mexico. He accompanied me and our family to Cuba and lived with us there for a number of years. As with Sergio, Robert and I eventually separated. But also as with Sergio, we have a better friendship now than we did when trying to combine our lives.

The magazine eventually died beneath the boot of an authoritarian state. It was destroyed by the repression that followed the Mexican Student Movement of 1968. Toward the end of the 1960s throughout the world, young people rose up in opposition to rampant injustice, demanding greater social participation. In Mexico the movement of 1968 began in July with a march in support of the Cuban revolution. The authorities came down hard, killing a high school student. The struggle escalated. University autonomy was an issue, and then others. Workers and farmers joined in. Sharper division, more deaths, rapid mobilization. Upheaval spread throughout the country.

Mexico had been preparing to host the 1968 Summer Olympics, due to begin on October 12th. As our movement strengthened and grew, hotel cancellations began coming in. The authorities feared they would lose money on the expensive sports installations and new lodgings that had been built in anticipation of the international event. Something had to be done. On October 2, ten days before the games were to start, military and paramilitary forces attacked a peaceful demonstration at a place called Tlatelolco, or Plaza of Three Cultures: high-rise working-class housing surrounding a colonial church and built over pre-Colombian ruins. After five hours, with blood still seeping into the stones, the government spoke of twenty-six dead. The number was estimated at closer to one thousand.

In *El Corno*'s editorial notes as well as in the work by others, Sergio and I and then Robert and I supported the students. Along with a vast majority of Mexican artists and intellectuals, Sergio and I had also taken part in the movement. I worked with students at the National Autonomous University of Mexico's school of medicine, translating, participating in information brigades, and boarding city buses to explain our demands. At one point some friends and I tried to get into Olympic Village, where the world's athletes were being housed. We naively believed that if we told them what was going on in Mexico, some might refuse to compete. During the awards ceremony, Olympic gold medalist Tommie Smith and bronze medalist John Carlos famously raised gloved fists in a Black Power salute. We wanted to believe the gesture was for us. In reality the two US athletes were protesting South African apartheid and racism within the Olympic movement. Smith and Carlos were forced to relinquish their medals but eventually were able to reclaim them.

Mexico has a long tradition of supporting the arts. After we began producing an exciting product every three months, various governmental agencies started lending their aid: Mexico's presidency, Bellas Artes, the ministry of education, and the public university, among others. They had no problem with our progressive positions with regard to civil rights in the United States or in protest against the American war in Vietnam, nor with our rejection of social hypocrisy generally. But when we sided with the students those subsidies ended abruptly. This happened to every independent cultural project in the country that took a similar position. Because translation was an important part of *El Corno*, funding from outside the country allowed us to continue into the summer of 1969, a bit longer than most. But our involvement with the movement finally forced us to stop publishing.

....

There are a few more things I want to say about those years, dominated by the ongoing excitement of the magazine but not limited to its pages. In February 1964, energized by the tremendous reception *El Corno* enjoyed throughout the creative world and in conjunction with Argentina's Miguel Grinberg and Mexico's Thelma Nava, we hosted El Encuentro Internacional de Poesía, an international gathering of poets. The two-week-long event brought creative people from a dozen countries. Many of them "flew now and paid later" or sold a piano or automobile to be able to afford the trip. They slept on our couches and floors. Puerto Rican artist Jaime Carrero kept busy sketching the participants. Salvadoran Roque Dalton showed up with a knapsack of poems and a story about barely having escaped with his life from a CIA prison when an earthquake cracked open its walls. Venezuelan poets from the group Techo de la Ballena (The Whale's Roof) appeared on our doorstep and slept on our floor. Ecuadorians, Panamanians, Colombians, and Chileans arrived. One piece of that 1964 gathering was an open-mic reading in Chapultepec Park that lasted more than thirty hours.

Allen Ginsberg stayed a week with us in mid-1965. He was on his way to Cuba. I remember a late breakfast around our kitchen table. Venezuelan poet Edmundo Aray and his wife, Sonia, were also visiting then, and Allen started singing the praises of his electric toothbrush, at the time quite a new-fangled device. He wanted to show us how it worked so he brought it to that breakfast table laden with huevos rancheros and freshly made tortillas. He plugged it in and immediately began demonstrating its virtues, offering it around for the rest of us to try. "Ayeee!" cried Sonia, jumping back as the quivering tool clattered to the floor. "It's like having a short circuit in your mouth!"

Allen sat cross-legged for hours on our living room sofa, intoning the chants he had learned on a recent trip to India. He spoke about the pyres of bodies burning in Benares. He went on to Havana, where he had been invited to judge poetry in that year's Casa de las Américas literary contest. There his iconoclastic homosexual wit played out as disrespect. After publicly challenging Raul Castro to sex, and pinching Haydée Santamaría on the bottom, his welcome was revoked. He was put on a plane for Prague, where he continued to act in a similar vein and was thrown out of that country as well. "King of the May," he shrieked across continents. "I am King of the May!"

Very important to our diverse readership was the space we gave to what was going on in the arts in Cuba. The Caribbean island had overthrown a US-client dictatorship in 1959 and artistic innovation was being supported there as never before. Fearing Communism, however, almost nothing about Cuba appeared in the US media. The work of its poets and visual artists was even less accessible.

Sergio and I had been invited to the island in 1967, to a small gathering honoring the hundredth anniversary of the great Nicaraguan modernist Rubén Darío. We were impressed with what we saw. When the event ended, Sergio returned to Mexico and I stayed on to travel a bit. The following year, I attended a much larger meeting, the 1968 Cultural Congress of Havana. Some six hundred philosophers, writers, artists, and civic and religious leaders came together to discuss the pressing issues facing creative people at the time. More than one thousand journalists attended. These visits and the

Chichén Itzá (photo by Margaret Randall).

ongoing relationships we established made it possible for us to feature a section of Cuban work in an early issue of the magazine and then devote our entire issue #23 (July 1967) to new Cuban poetry and visual arts.

Making this work available didn't sit well with everyone. We had been in contact with Rafael Squirru, an Argentine poet who headed the Pan American Union, the cultural arm of the Organization of American States. Because he liked what we were doing, and also perhaps because his job was to infiltrate and try to influence left-wing cultural projects and bring them under US control, he ordered five hundred subscriptions to *El Corno*. The support would have kept us afloat for several issues. When Squirru found out we planned on featuring work from Cuba, though, he threatened to cancel those subscriptions. We refused to oblige and lost the support.

I've mentioned Laurette Séjourné and Arnaldo Orfila. We spent a lot of time together; in many ways they were mentors as well as friends. We often picnicked in the lovely countryside. They would pick us up in their gray Peugeot, with an elegantly prepared wicker basket containing patés and French cheeses in the trunk. When we first arrived, Gregory and I had been fortunate to accompany Laurette once a week to her dig out at Teotihuacán, where my toddler played among four-thousand-year-old relics and I learned about a culture that impressed me with its complexity.

Laurette was exploring what she called the Palace of the Butterflies, an area where the ancient inhabitants of Teotihuacán had lived. After lunch she would confer with a group of trained workmen who showed her what they had unearthed during the previous week. We would observe as she decided which pieces to leave on site and which to take home for further study. We learned a lot from those afternoons. I am sure that was when both Gregory and I acquired our ongoing interest in pre-Contact culture.

....

CHICHÉN ITZÁ

Where crossed eyes among stone skulls
meant wisdom,
vision or a higher destiny,
where glyphs still hide within glyphs
danger and certainty walked in this jungle
twelve centuries ago.

Today vendors screech like the howlers
once leaping through these courtyards,
fake a raucous jaguar growl
on whistles made in Taiwan,
shout *cómprame cómprame*
as they push a gaudy mask at the tourist
who pleads *no money* and walks on.

Both sides of every path circling every vestige
of every pyramid or temple
are lined with stalls: men hawking
the real thing, women unfolding
colors woven of tears, their voices
rising with those of a hundred guides,

each in the center of his huddle, ears
that come from every latitude,
tourists waving their *selfie* sticks,
listening to crude tales of human sacrifice
and contorting their bodies

so the shot captures them
leaping from atop the great staircase.

Large pink umbrellas bob across the grass
shielding from midday heat
and historical exhaustion.
The guide who works eight tours a day
peppers his tale with promises:
I don't show this to everyone,
will take you where others don't go.

He dares you to believe him, wagers the ruse
may be worth an extra hundred pesos.
Chichén's dynasties of glory
now a Disneyland that draws 1.2 million
to stones that will not reveal their secrets
through the insulting din.

I think of Sir Edward dredging the sacred *cenote*
for treasure, using his diplomatic pouch
to send stolen bounty north
and Alma's campaign for return
of what belongs here:
right of occupancy, pride of place.

I curl against Chaak Mool's reclining body,
meet the eyes of one hundred
braided limestone snakes,
imagine elbows and hips
blasting a small hard ball
through the ornate stone hoop,
spin my silence down sluices of time.

Could Chichén's seers have imagined
this cleaning of overgrowth
and clearing of roads,
new rules suspicious of old,
Sound & Light gaudy enough to eclipse
the sun descending like a dagger
on their calendar's perfect dawn?

UXMAL

we came at once upon a large open field
strewed with mounds of ruins, and vast
buildings on terraces, and pyramidal
structures, grand and in good preservation,
richly ornamented without a bush to obstruct
the view, and in picturesque effect almost
equal to the ruins of Thebes.

—JOHN LLOYD STEPHENS, *INCIDENTS OF TRAVEL IN
THE YUCATÁN* (1843)

Even the visitor who loved it most
evoked Old World splendor,
impossible to believe
those graceful facades
were conceived by the ancestors
of those who led him to this place.

Listen and you will hear the sounds
of wooden trumpets, conch shells,
drums and rattle,
breathe clouds of copal incense,
gaze upon the blue-green and gold
sheen of Quetzal plumes.

Ask a Dwarf, a boy not born of woman,
to build a pyramid in a single night
and don't be surprised
when that being
hatched from an iguana egg
achieves the impossible.

For here, right here, is the impossible:
Uxmal where snakes make love
on polished limestone
and feathered gargoyles
converse across patios
filled with ancient light.

Lord Chaak was first
but then Tutul Xiu
installed his family line
for generations,
and when the Spaniards arrived
allied himself with them,

which may or may not be why
this city presents itself
in such perfection,
stories we cannot bear to hear
where eyes and ears open wide
to snag storm rays from sky.

Despite the 1863 guardians
covering male genitalia
in deference to Empress Carlota,
a dance of grace and power
never stopped moving
across these walls.

Blood never stops running
from tongues pierced
by stinger rays,
rituals we don't understand
and condemn
through our prism of now.

Believe in the Dwarf, magician
whose rounded shoulders
anchor your line of sight.
Believe in Uxmal leading the *Ruta Puuc*
as it retraces its steps
through a jungle of brilliant green.

In 1965, Arnaldo became the target of US political designs in Mexico and of Mexico's own nationalism. Quite suddenly one day he was ordered to abandon his post as director of El Fondo de Cultura Económica. He was given seventeen hours to clear out his office and he and Laurette not much longer to vacate their apartment. El Fondo had published two books that, for different reasons, infuriated the Mexican authorities. One was C. Wright Mills's *Listen Yankee*, an important anti-imperialist text. Mexico sustained diplomatic relations with Cuba, indeed it was the only Latin American country back then that did. But those relations were as much a conduit for the flow of covert information as they were a sign of political independence. The other book to which the Mexican government objected was *The Children of Sánchez* by anthropologist Oscar Lewis. It exposed a Mexican culture of poverty the authorities preferred to keep hidden.

As is true in most places, Mexico's intellectuals and artists disagreed about many things. But almost all shared a deep respect for Orfila and what he had done for the country. People who in other circumstances barely spoke to one another came together in a tremendous effort to remedy what we considered a terrible injustice. We sold bonds, raised money, and enabled our friend to start his own publishing house, free from government control. He called it Siglo XXI, and it soon became a reference throughout the Spanish-speaking world.

We held a celebratory dinner with some fifty writers and artists in attendance. At that dinner the great Mexican novelist Elena Poniatowska offered her home to house the venture. Arnaldo accepted, moved. Arnaldo headed Siglo XXI almost up to his death at the age of one hundred. He became my publisher then, as well as my friend. I produced a number of books under his brilliant editorship.[9]

....

Culturally important in our small family nucleus was the unique and wonderful school my three oldest children attended. Mexico, like most countries with deep class divisions, failed to support a decent public education system. Poorly paid teachers were forced to hold two or three jobs and sometimes failed to show up to class. The wealthy enrolled their children in expensive private schools; they still do. Religious institutions claimed many students as well. Neither was an option for us. Through friends we found out about the Manuel Bartolomé Cossío, an elementary school that later also added a high school and was based on the teaching philosophy of a Frenchman named Célestin Freinet. In Mexico, Manuel Bartolomé Cossío's founders were José de Tapia and his wife, Graciela González de Tapia. We were fortunate to be there during their tenure.

Freinet was born in 1896 in Gars, a small French village near the Italian border. His extremely progressive and interactive teaching method was based on the idea that children know their own needs and rhythms. They learn responsibility by caring for their school, its environment, and each other. They are not all expected to read and write at the same age, but progress individually through the hands-on use of movable type and the writing of daily journals. They engage in serious research. Both individual aptitude and community spirit are stressed. By the time they are ready to move on to a more conventional school, most graduates have acquired skills beyond that of their contemporaries and, more importantly, are accustomed to critical thinking.

Gregory completed fourth grade at Manuel Bartolomé Cossío; Sarah, second; and Ximena, kindergarten. We left Mexico before Ana could be enrolled. The Cossío was a close community of students and their mostly left-wing parents, many of whom became good friends. Gregory's English teacher, Maru Uhthoff, and I remained close until her death in 2017. Another of his teachers, Cristina Payán, hid us for a while during the repression that forced us out of the country. Film star Guillermo Murray and his wife, Lidia, also parents at the school, tried to help us during that difficult time. When my daughter Ximena returned to Mexico and had a family of her own, she sent her son and daughter to the Cossío, where they studied with the sons and daughters of others who had been students there so many decades before.

For a while Sergio and I earned a modest living translating comic books that arrived from the United States with their word bubbles blank. We'd drive out to Navarro Publishers on the far north industrial side of the city, deliver the translation we'd just completed, and pick up the next. We had to count the letters in what was the much longer Spanish and fit them into the bubbles that had originally contained the English. Some of the themes shocked me, though they shouldn't have. Khrushchev was the villain in a Superman story. US agents were always heroes.

We had to patch our finances together. Sergio won a few writing grants and wrote articles and books commissioned by the Secretariat of Education; I taught English and also managed to pen a few cultural reviews. When Robert and I began living together, although his Spanish was still rudimentary at the time, he surprised me by getting a full-time job at a news agency. He was my first partner who shared economic responsibility for our family.

Although Mexico resented US imperialist domination, everyday life was complex. Mexicans never forgot that the United States had stolen a third of its territory in the Mexican-American War (1846–1848). This was a land grab, pure and simple. Yet they also had a love/hate, passive/aggressive, push/pull attitude toward US Americans. The racism provoked by ongoing inequality created a desire for whiteness that played itself out in advertising slogans such as the one for a popular brand of beer, "La rubia de categoria" (the high-class blonde). We experienced this bias in our own family. Sarah and Ximena were only fourteen months apart. Sarah was blonde and blue-eyed, while Ximena had dark hair and eyes. When I took them both out, strangers often complimented Sarah and then, looking at Ximena, inquired, "Is she yours too?"

During the decade I lived in Mexico these experiences and others like them provided hands-on lessons in understanding neocolonialism. Not from books, but life.

....

El Corno's last issue (#31) appeared in the summer of 1969, just before feminism's second wave exploded across the face of Western consciousness. As we'd solicited and selected work for the journal, we didn't think about the gender of those who wrote it. Like almost everyone else at the time, we were mired in the patriarchal idea that most good writers and artists were male, with the occasional woman who "wrote or painted like a man." When I look at the magazine today, this lack of gender consciousness stares back at me. I believe it was our greatest failing. In our defense, I can say that very few possessed a gender consciousness back then. But we prided ourselves on being ahead of the curve, and I've always felt critical that I was incapable of challenging that particular bias. We also lacked a consciousness of race, but the very nature of the journal meant we published writers and artists of different ethnicities.

Another failing was our careless proofing. Too many typographical errors appeared on our pages. This attained such dramatic proportions with a particular book that the author demanded all copies be destroyed. Two people did almost everything, but there really is no justification for sloppy editing.

We did better in other areas. We were conscious of wanting to present a range of political and spiritual ideologies, and so we published Beats alongside Language Poets, Communists and guerrilla fighters beside Catholic priests and mystics, indigenous poetry and writing by academics with something interesting to say. One of our poets described himself as a carpenter, another as a farmer. We were proud of this diversity even after Sergio and I began moving in different ideological directions. Each of us continued to publish the work he or she favored, and each favored work of quality.

Neither Sergio nor I ever took a salary. *El Corno* was a labor of love. On several occasions we ourselves paid a printer's last installment or otherwise made up a deficit. Poets organized readings in support of the journal and visual artists donated their drawings and paintings to be sold on its behalf.

Needless to say, we couldn't afford to pay our contributors. I strongly believe in poets and artists being paid for their work, but our utopianism back then made such remuneration impossible.

Financing the magazine was always a problem. We had no business sense, nor did we necessarily want any, since we saw sound business practice as indicative of capitalist greed. In this respect, our youthful idealism got in our way. We sold copies in each country for what we were told a young poet there could afford. Mostly this meant $1 a copy, sometimes less. Bookstores ordered the journal, but in many cases failed to pay. We had a few ads from generous businesses that believed in what we were doing. A small amount of what we needed came from subscriptions, which were $3 a year, mostly from libraries, and I don't think our subscription list ever exceeded three hundred. A diverse group of individuals often helped out economically. When you consider that each issue cost on average $1,500 to print, the problem is obvious. And I'm not even including the cost of postage to recipients around the world, or our own considerable labor.

El Corno Emplumado filled a tremendous need for poets, writers, and readers of literature in many countries. Along with a number of other independent magazines flourishing then, it was a voice of nonconformity, resistance to a stultifying status quo, and a loud answer to those who told us poems could only be written about subjects approved of by whatever academy was in vogue. We believed poetry could be written about anything: that a poem was good if it grabbed you, bad if it didn't. It must be well-crafted, original. Ideas about craft aren't static. They change with the times and it's unlikely that I would have appreciated back then some of what excites me today.

I want to stress that we were not alone but part of a global surge in rebellious artistic energy. The 1960s and 1970s saw a great renaissance of independent cultural projects. Among the literary magazines in Mexico were *Pájaro cascabel* and *El Cuento. Eco contemporáneo* and *Airón* in Buenos Aires; *El techo de la Ballena* in Caracas; *Pucuna* in Quito; *Casa de las Américas, Signos*, and *Santiago* in Cuba; and *Trojan, The Floating Bear, Caterpillar, Ikon, The Outsider, Monk's Pond, The Sixties* (earlier called *The Fifties*), and many others in the United States were just a few of the several hundred with which we regularly traded issues. This exchange was an important part of the network we were creating, and it allowed us to keep up with what poets were doing beyond our borders.

One big difference between these journals and *El Corno Emplumado*, though, was that we bridged cultures. And it wasn't just that we published in Spanish and English; we produced translations from a number of other languages, including several indigenous tongues, both north and south of the Rio Grande and from Mesoamerica. We took seriously the notion that we could connect people of diverse experiences, ideologies, generations, languages, language usage, and ways of constructing the poem.

We also believed that poetry could change the world. We subscribed to a loosely defined sense of freedom through the word. We talked about "the new man" (it didn't yet occur to us that we explicitly needed to include woman in the term). Early on, that meant a more spiritual and egalitarian human being, in touch with his or her imagination, uninterested in consumerism, resistant to solving problems through war or other forms of violence, and opposed to the hypocrisy around us.

Later, this New Man, at least for me, was more aligned with the person Che Guevara wrote about in *Man and Socialism in Cuba*. Revolutionary sacrifice—the ultimate sacrifice if necessary—rather than more personal concerns. My more practical Yankee nature wanted palpable results, and I believed revolution to be the surest road to them. Sergio admired Guevara's concept, but was also interested in the Buddhist principles of mindfulness and nirvana. He saw spiritual change as more important. Interestingly, long after *El Corno Emplumado* stopped publishing, our poet selves brought us closer again. I believe that today each of our visions of a new human being includes something of what was important to the other back then. I know my own concept of what constitutes a good poem is more inclusive.

Poetry is either good or bad, works or doesn't. *El Corno* included a great deal of excellent work in a range of voices. We regularly published US, Canadian, Uruguayan, Guatemalan, and Peruvian poets, the *Nadaistas* of Colombia, and the Concrete Poets of Brazil. We featured the great Haitian poet René Depestre. We produced anthologies of new work from Mexico, Argentina, Finland, Cuba, Canada, Brazil, Colombia, Greece, Venezuela, Nicaragua, Guatemala, Chile, Uruguay, Algeria, France, the Netherlands, Norway, Spain, and Russia; and individual poets from China, Rumania, Poland, India, Australia, Israel, Japan, and Panama.

In Mexico, Juan Rulfo, Rosario Castellanos, Felipe Ehrenberg, Laurette Séjourné, Leonora Carrington, José Luis Cuevas, Octavio Paz, Carlos Pellicer, Juan Soriano, José Emilio Pacheco, José Carlos Becerra, Homero Aridjis, Thelma Nava, Juan Bañuelos, Juan Martínez, Efraín Huerta, and others were important repeat contributors. We broke through the US-imposed cultural blockade and made Cuban poetry available to a Western readership. *El Corno*

Emplumado published major work by Allen Ginsberg for the first time in Spanish and by Ernesto Cardenal for the first time in English. This is nowhere near a complete list. Over our eight-year run, we published more than seven hundred poets, fiction writers, and visual artists from thirty-seven countries, many of them several times.

....

It was in Mexico that I first met some of the Latin American revolutionaries who were intent on changing their societies. Many had been forced into exile there; others came and went. Ecuadorian Miguel Donoso Pareja and his wife, Judith Gutiérrez, come to mind: he was a poet; she, a painter. Gradually they were able to bring their five children to safety, but they always struggled. One of their beautiful teenage daughters killed herself at the age of fourteen.

I desperately wanted to be part of the effort aimed at creating a more just world. Toward the end of my stay, this desire led to my agreeing to drive a comrade to Tapachula on the southern border with Guatemala, retrieve a commander who needed to cross over, and bring him back to Mexico City. I had a car that worked, and I suppose those asking the favor thought a US woman wouldn't attract unwanted attention. Naive and gullible, and lacking membership in an experienced political organization that might have provided some guidance, I asked far too few questions. Through sheer ingenuity and luck, we made it, but were almost caught. In Mexico I wasn't able to insert myself into the continental struggle in any viable way.

Still, the drama and sacrifice of the times became a part of who I was beginning to be. When Che Guevara was murdered in Bolivia in October of 1967, it affected me deeply. In Mexico City many of us went out into the streets that night, writing our anguish on the walls. The Mexican authorities covered our slogans with thickly stenciled white doves of peace. The following night we went out again, slinging red paint at those doves' breasts. I still sometimes see those "bloodied" breasts in my dreams, vivid symbols of a shattered hope.

A few weeks later a Canadian film crew came to the country. It was making a documentary about one of the important muralists, Rufino Tamayo. I was hired on as an interpreter. The filming took place on the tiny island of Janitzio on Lake Patzcuaro, Michoacán, during the weekend of the Days of the Dead. As we wound our slow way through throngs of poor fishermen and their families carrying ornate bread dough *ofrendas* to the cemetery at the highest point of the island, I thought of Bolivia's poor, as needy, inhabiting a world of their own rituals, and disconnected from the movements hoping to set them free as these people were.

Mexico's celebration of the Days of the Dead, which takes place each year on the last day of October and first two of November, provides a window into the way Mexicans regard death. Many households erect small altars, upon which photos of those recently departed are accompanied by their favorite foods, special sugar skulls, pieces of cane, and seasonal breads. A pathway of orange *cempasúchil*, or marigolds, runs across the floor from the home's front door to the altar, leading the souls to their welcome. Large altars in public places often allude to shared tragedies, such as the numbers of women murdered that year in incidents of domestic violence or the country's increasing siege of murders at the hands of the drug cartels. Art and social commentary are deeply intertwined. Death, whether from poverty or violence, is commonplace in Mexico and so it is also part of life. People do not avoid talking about it or shy away from its embrace. This attitude gradually became a part of my belief system.

I can't say that death touched me personally during my years in Mexico more than it did later in my life, when war suddenly took friends or age naturally removed people close to me. There was a dramatic exception, though. At the Bartolomé Cossío Sarah had a classmate named Marcela. She was Lidia and Guillermo Murray's youngest child and only daughter. I think she and Sarah were in first grade together when the events I am about to relate took place. That year a neighborhood friend of Marcela's fell from an upper-floor apartment window, dying tragically.

Lidia and Guillermo were stricken and naturally concerned about the effect the child's death could have on their daughter. They were afraid she might mimic her playmate. Although they took Marcela to see a psychologist, other parents pitched in to make sure she was somewhere safe each day after school. She frequently spent time at our house, playing with Sarah. Meanwhile, Lidia and Guillermo—who lived in a high-rise apartment themselves—were looking hard for one on the ground floor.

About a month after her friend's death and before they had been able to move, the Murray family was hanging out at home after dinner one night. They had wired all their windows shut except for one in Guillermo's office. Marcela's two older brothers, Guillermo Jr. and Rodrigo, were with their parents in the living room. Suddenly they realized Marcela had wandered off. When they looked in the office, they saw a small chair pushed up against an open window. Wordless, they knew what had happened. Marcela's broken body lay motionless on the pavement below.

Can a five-year-old commit suicide? And, if so, what does that mean? Did Marcela want to join her friend? Had she perhaps pushed her and felt guilty about perpetrating an event she could not have known would be irreversible? We will never know. Felipe and Martha Ehrenberg and I went to the child's burial, high on a hill with a distant view of the volcanoes. I didn't take Sarah, a decision I would later regret. I guess I was not yet attuned to Mexico's intimate relationship with death, especially in the case of a child. Because I didn't give her the opportunity of being present at her friend's funeral, Sarah lacked the comfort of a ritual that might have provided some sort of closure. For months she asked, "Where did Marcela go?"

In the Mexico I knew honor killings were also common. Age-old customs applied, and the rule of law didn't seem to have as much to say about those acts as popular culture did. Two indigenous artists from the mountains of Guerrero came to our home one day. They painted the wonderful flowers and birds that can be found on bark paper, and we had asked them to make original drawings for an issue of *El Corno* that included a section of indigenous poetry (#10, April 1964). I remember one of the men asking what a poem was; I explained it was like a song without the music.

Felipe Ehrenberg, who had invited the artists to collaborate with *El Corno*, told me that a few months earlier one of them had come home to discover his wife in bed with another man. He shot the interloper. Everyone in the village, including the man's wife and the family of her dead lover, saw this as an honor killing and, as such, acceptable. But it was also considered prudent for the one who had killed to absent himself from his community for a number of months until passions calmed. During my years in Mexico, and in many different areas of life, I always felt popular tradition more palpably than modern-day convention.

....

Nineteen-sixty-eight was a watershed year in Mexico. Students, ultimately joined by workers and farmers, staged giant protests against governmental overreach and wrongdoing. The vast majority of the country's intellectuals and artists sided with the students. Similar upheavals took place that year in the United States, France, South Africa, and other parts of the world. But because it was about to host the Olympics, the Díaz Ordaz administration unleashed a deadly crackdown ten days before the games began. This provided me with a lifelong lesson in how far a regime is willing to go to protect its economic interests.

I won't forget one of our movement rallies at which two Tarahumara men from the northern state of Chihuahua showed up unexpectedly. Famous for their extraordinary ability to run, they had traveled hundreds of miles on foot. They approached a microphone, where the older began to speak in his native language, the younger translating his words into Spanish. Their solidarity was brief but stunning: "We have always known they hated us. But now we know they are truly evil because they are murdering their own children." Message delivered, they turned around and ran home.

The Mexican Student Movement didn't take place only in the capital. It exploded across the country. Lawrence Ferlinghetti visited in the late summer of 1968 and wanted to travel to Oaxaca. I told him if he paid our expenses, I would provide the car and children. We spent a few days in that city, observing the ways in which the movement was expressing itself in the provinces. Ferlinghetti later wrote about that excursion.[10]

Sergio, again from his panel participation in 2015, summed up the defeat of 1968:

[It was] a wound in Mexico's heart that has bled for decades and may never close, putting an end to the golden dream of the Sixties and to . . . *El Corno Emplumado*. Because that was the beginning of the end of the magazine. The economic support from government institutions ended abruptly, and the "forces of order" hunted down the movement's protagonists and many of its sympathizers, those who had escaped with our lives. They dispersed people, forced them to flee, submerged them in silence and into a long and humiliating assimilation of the tragedy. One voice, as we know, raised itself the day after the massacre and in the midst of the confusion that followed. It's important to remember it. From his diplomatic post in India, Octavio Paz renounced his position as Mexico's ambassador to that country in protest against that which had been perpetrated.[11]

The depth of the historic insult inflicted upon our youth was of such a magnitude that today, almost 50 years later, [we] continue to question, interview, and write about the Student Movement of 1968, as opposed to the oblivion and indifferent demands in which some still wish to embalm that horrendous history. . . . We can listen to people, weathered by age, with broken voices and holding back their tears, speak of the details of their participation and of the quota of suffering they have had to endure.

El Corno had remained true to its principles and as a result been forced out of existence. But its legacy multiplied. The most reliable evidence of this legacy can be found in the hundreds of young poets who have written to me over the years. They say *El Corno* was the inspiration for their own projects: literary journals, translation, art collectives, and film and theater groups, all of them independent, searing, and cutting-edge, and all exploring new ways of linking creativity and change. Many of these endeavors credit our efforts with paving the way.

In 2005, two young filmmakers, Anne Mette Nielsen of Denmark and Mexican Nicolenka Beltrán, produced a wonderful documentary called *El Corno Emplumado: Una historia de los sesenta.* Anne Mette and Nicolenka were the same ages Sergio and I had been when we started the journal. With few resources and having to deal with the obstacles all first-time filmmakers confront, they traveled two continents in order to tell our story. The result is a beautiful fifty-four-minute film.

I was moved to tears by the original footage from the aftermath of the massacre at Tlatelolco, footage that hadn't been shown in Mexico in the thirty years following that brutal attack. Another scene I remember is the one in which Sergio takes the filmmakers to a small print shop, one of only a few still like it operating in Mexico City at the time, where the owner demonstrates the old linotype hot-lead method of reproduction now practiced almost nowhere. The slow methodical rhythm of that process reminds me of how artisanal our work was back then, how technically primitive but hands-on. The type falling into place gave physicality to the words. I saw this film for the first time at the 2006 Guadalajara Book Fair, one of its inaugural showings. In a standing-room-only crowd, dozens of young poets paid tribute to *El Corno* and its importance in their lives.

It was museum curator and cultural analyst Robert Schweitzer who had suggested the idea of the film to Nielsen and Beltrán, and he vigorously supported their project. Speaking of the journal, he describes one way in which it also informed his own work:

> I came to *El Corno* somewhat late, not when it was the link and lifeline connecting North to South in ways that would help shatter the intellectual and creative divide that characterized the long history of imbalance and arrogance perpetuated by the North. Although I knew of it before then, it wasn't until

the mid-8os, when I was a museum curator, that the meaning, significance, and profound value of this little magazine became most clear and relevant to me. I was involved in the expanding dialogue on cultural and social issues regarding "the other" and post-colonialism. *El Corno* had been a touchstone for what was possible, especially during the period before the computer and the networking that would eventually come through that technology. Some years later the journal became a major conceptual component for an exhibition I curated in 2002.

El Corno Emplumado stood apart from, and in many ways against, the academy. But the academy took note of *El Corno*. Many university libraries hold complete sets of the magazine. Its partial papers (those we thought to save) are housed at New York University's Fales Special Collections Library and the Harry Ransom Center at the University of Texas, Austin. And in 1994, University of Utah Ph.D. candidate Alan R. Davison wrote his dissertation on the journal. He too viewed it as speaking for the decade. He titled his study *El Corno Emplumado, The Plumed Horn: A Voice of the Sixties*. I asked Davison if it had been difficult to convince his doctoral committee to approve his rather unorthodox dissertation topic. In a November 2014 letter, he reminisced,

> There was no resistance from my committee members to the project as a whole, but one member withdrew a month before my oral defense, citing my "lack of attention to feminist issues." Fortunately, several weeks after she withdrew, I received the letter in which you [explained the lack of feminist consciousness at the time]. With that letter in hand, I successfully defended the project.
>
> As for *El Corno*'s importance in the literary history of the Americas, I believe that story is still being written. Although your and Sergio's efforts were little short of Herculean at the time, it is entirely possible that the journal (in its digital form) will reach a greater audience in the future. *El Corno* is an inexhaustible compendium of attempts (both failed and successful) to broaden the poetic canvas; many of its first-time translations of seminal poems are unsurpassed; it is a living document of the importance of hopefulness in the process of social and personal development. In short, *El Corno*'s message is as important today (maybe even more important?) as it was in the 1960s.

One way in which the journal's legacy remains alive is in the memories of those who contributed to it, some many times over. Davison's theme of hopefulness echoes in the following testimony by a poet who appeared often in our pages. Jerome Rothenberg sent me the text he'd delivered at New York University's King Juan Carlos I of Spain Center a few years back. The event was built around a showing of Nielsen and Beltrán's documentary. Nielsen moderated a discussion that included Sergio Mondragón, Rothenberg, and Cecilia Vicuña. Fragments from Rothenberg's contribution give a vivid sense of the magazine and his involvement with it:

> The Sixties as such is also an idea, and the idea gets repeated and modified over the intervening years, until it becomes, in anyone's mind, more real and clearly more enduring than the time itself was. The difference between then and now, for me, is that *then* I lived with hope and *now* with only a kind of desperation. Yet it was at the beginning of the 1960s—which weren't yet the 1960s as we speak of them—that Robert Kelly proclaimed for me (for us) a "poetics of desperation" in which we came to share. In relation to that and what followed, the *real* 1960s (which included also the early 1970s) were a kind of time *between*—a liminal moment, as we liked to say, in which what was possible and hopeful dared to assert itself *against the odds*. And those odds, that oddness, meant a real war then in progress and a real clash of ideas in which we called for change and transformation—not just a change of political parties as now, but "a total assault on the culture."
>
> It was in that milieu of desperation and hope that *El Corno* began— part of a cultural underground that thought it was finally coming to the surface (to the light). Many of us had magazines and presses then (it was part of our privilege where we lived and worked) but with *El Corno* there was also something different. In the US the greatest exultation among poets was over the flowering—and the domination—of North American poetry. (The "American grain" clearly as William Carlos Williams had it—not an imperial venture but pretty close.) But what *Corno* did, what it brought together, were the two Americas—not only an international perspective but a truly collaborative venture across two or more languages and cultures.
>
> For six or seven years . . . I was a recipient of the amazing mix of images and voices that was *El Corno Emplumado*. I had a place in nine or ten of their issues, and they were the publishers as well of my fourth book of poems, *The Gorky Poems (Poemas Gorky)* in 1966, a bilingual work with translations into Spanish by Sergio and Meg.

Until his death at the age of eighty-nine, Roberto Fernández Retamar presided over Cuba's Casa de las Américas, the extraordinary cultural institution that continues to break through the cultural blockade imposed by the United States for more than half a century. In response to my inquiry, he wrote,

> I remember *El Corno Emplumado* very well. . . . The magazine contributed admirably to the production of poetic texts by authors from Latin America and the United States. And you frequently published Cuban poets, most notably when you devoted an entire issue to the Cuban poetry of the moment.
>
> Of course, I also remember my letter you published knowing that the consequences of doing so would be the loss of 500 subscriptions promised by the man who at that time was cultural director of the Pan American Union. We always thought of your magazine as a sister publication to our own *Casa de las Américas*, and considered it a great accomplishment, that we read gratefully each time we received an issue.

Ernesto Cardenal published in *El Corno*'s first issue and many subsequent ones. Today he is more than ninety-five, and one of the greatest living voices of the language. In response to my asking him to send his memories of the journal, he wrote,

> In the Sixties and Seventies of the past century Latin America saw the proliferation of literary movements and magazines, some with names that were strange if not downright bizarre, such as *El techo de la Ballena* (The Whale's Roof), *El topo con gafas* (The Mole with Spectacles), *Cormorán y Delfín* (The Cormorant and the Dolphin) edited by an Argentine poet who had been a ship's captain, and *Sol cuello cortado* (Beheaded Sun, a Venezuelan journal that was involved in the strange case of the kidnapping of a US military official). Among them was the bilingual magazine *El Corno Emplumado* (which also had a strange name), edited by poets Sergio Mondragón and Margaret Randall. He was Mexican and she from the United States. This was the journal that lasted the longest and also the one that exerted the greatest influence throughout Latin America. Many of us first published in *El Corno*, and we also communicated with one another through its pages. *El Corno Emplumado* contributed a great deal to Latin American literature, and I deeply regret its demise.

More than a few of the contacts I made through *El Corno* turned into deep personal friendships. Such was the case with Susan Sherman. When I asked her to describe her relationship to the journal, she touched on several aspects:

> El Corno opened a new cultural and political space to me and served as inspiration for the founding of *Ikon* magazine in 1967. But most important, it was through sending poems to *El Corno* in the early Sixties that I began a correspondence with Margaret Randall. I finally met her in person when I traveled to the Cuban Cultural Congress in 1968, where we cemented a lifelong friendship. Without *El Corno*, and without Margaret, I would never have been exposed to the conjunction between the artistic and the political that literally changed my life.

El Corno was a bridge, but it was also the beginning of my thinking of myself as a builder of bridges. More than a half-century later, that's still true. And the thing about bridges is that they multiply: when you walk across one, another appears. Perhaps no one evokes this sense of circles rippling outward toward other circles better than Silvia Gil, the longtime Casa de las Américas librarian now retired. When I asked her to reminisce about her first memories of the journal, she wrote,

> I think of my first years at *Casa*'s library, the institution I've worked at for fifty years. When I started there, dozens of publications arrived from all over the world. Those were the Revolution's early years, and editors everywhere wanted Cuba to know what they were publishing. This was especially true for Latin America and the Caribbean. One after another, the magazines came. The one that particularly sparked our curiosity was *El Corno*.
>
> Right away I wondered about its name: what in the world was a plumed horn? And what did all those crazy journal names from all over Latin America mean: *Pájaro cascabel* (Rattlesnake Bird), *La rosa blindada* (The Armored Rose), *El Escarabajo de oro* (The Golden Scarab), *El pez y la serpiente* (The Fish and the Serpent), *La bufanda del sol* (The Sun's Muffler), *Los huevos del Plata* (La Plata's Eggs), *Alcor* (Little Hill), *Rayado sobre el techo* (The Stripe on the Roof), *El grillo de papel* (The Paper Cricket), and dozens of others? They were the "*eco contemporáneo*" (contemporary echo)[12] of groups of restless and talented young people who, from one end of the Continent to the other, were intent on changing the world and believed that literature and art were their weapons.
>
> In 1969, when *El Corno Emplumado* ceased publishing, Margaret had to leave Mexico and came to live in Cuba. Here she was my neighbor. Her apart-

ment immediately became a gathering place for young people who aspired to be writers. Many of them have gained fame in Cuba and beyond. Not one of them has forgotten those gatherings.

I still receive news of the ways in which the journal continues to impact readers. US writer and translator Matt Gleeson teaches literature in Oaxaca, Mexico. In mid-2018 he told me he was planning a class on *El Corno Emplumado*, and toward the end of the year I asked how it had gone. This is part of his response:

It's astonishing what a wide-ranging microcosm of the poetry world we're able to dip into through the pages of the magazine. (The class draws from the Spanish-language side of things, so it's a different *El Corno* than a lot of U.S. people know, yet it's still a marvelous way to clue them in to some great English-language poets, from Creeley to Kelly to Rothenberg, etc.) It's also astonishing how much history it illuminates....

I get the sense they're enjoying the variety. (Reading Ezra Pound's third canto and José Agustín Goytisolo in the same hour is like hitting two opposite poles of poetry.) And I think that the political stances of *El Corno* are important to us all, the moral (ethical) compass it has, and the fire. Some reactions I've seen.... Yesterday we finally read the editors' note from October 1968 that was the beginning of the end of things, and there was lots of commentary. Most called the essay brave. Many feel like nothing's changed in Mexico. An older member of the class came to Mexico as a Spanish exile when young and lived through 1968, and he said that piece excited and moved him like few others from the time. Cecilia Vicuña's early poems unleashed a surprising amount of discussion yesterday.... They were fascinated and very affected by the anonymous Colombian poet (another poem that's terribly current). A few are extremely interested in liberation theology already and they really got going as soon as we started reading Cardenal. (Something that comes up every time I teach poetry from that era is how easy it is today to lazily think of "the 60s counterculture" as some kind of libertine thing incompatible with Catholicism, yet there are so many radical, countercultural Catholics.)

Speaking as someone who's hell-bent on becoming fully and broadly Nuestramericano, I'm not aware of another literary journal—then or today—that so totally embodies the crossing of national borders through the Americas (and beyond).... Maybe what's most inspiring to me is that palpable hunger for community and the way it's obviously achieved. It strikes me as richer than today's interconnection. I can tell that all of you read each other's words carefully and hungrily and sought out real connection. Today we can all be a million-legged spider at the middle of a social-media web of connections, but I get the sense that people don't read each other's words quite as carefully amid the glut of text, and that everyone's still just as hungry for community.

Remembering a project that consumed me for eight extraordinary years almost half a century ago, I've tried to reimagine its daily presence and significance as I experienced it then, and simultaneously through the filter of today's perspective. Perhaps the most important thing I can say about *El Corno Emplumado* now is that it fearlessly honored integrity and imagination, was an example of youthful vision and belief in the power of poetry, and a splendid map across which many creative spirits moved. Although the journal was forced to stop publishing a half-century ago, that bridge has multiplied many times over and points in directions we could not have imagined back then.

....

When we think about female imagery throughout Mexico's history, we must reconsider and reimagine the lives of real women as well as the culture's symbolic figures. Coatlique is an enormous stone block of a statue more than eight feet tall on display in the great room at Mexico City's Museum of Anthropology and History. I cannot think of a more powerful or raw embodiment of womanhood. She wears a skirt of writhing snakes and a necklace of human hearts, hands, and skulls. Her feet and fingers are adorned with claws and her breasts are depicted as hanging flaccid from pregnancy or age. Diverse legends define her, but she is most often understood as portraying the mother who devoured her children rather than see them enslaved.

La Malinche is another myth that deserves radical reinterpretation. Born sometime between 1496 and 1501, the girl who would enter history with that name was Doña Marina, a Nahua from Mexico's Gulf Coast. In 1519 she was one of twenty slaves given to the Spanish conqueror Hernán Cortés, becoming his interpreter, advisor, and intermediary. Later she gave birth to Cortés's oldest son, Martín, considered the country's first *mestizo*, or person of mixed race. This story of her "sleeping with the enemy" made her a symbol of betrayal when in fact she was a victim of injustice. In Mexican popular discourse the term *malinchista* came to mean a disloyal compatriot or traitor. Over time, the historical figure mixed with Aztec legends such as that of *La Llorona*, the

Convent of Sor Juana, Mexico City, 2015 (photo by Margaret Randall).

ghost woman who weeps for her lost children. In recent years, feminists have protested *La Malinche*'s definition of treachery and reimagined her as the symbolic mother of the new Mexican people.

It is interesting that among Mexico's many illustrious poets, the outstanding figure is Sor Juana Inés de la Cruz. Born out of wedlock at San Miguel Nepantla, near Mexico City, in 1648, she was registered as a "daughter of the Church." She herself turned down several marriage proposals and at the age of twenty entered a cloistered convent in order to be able to study literature, philosophy, and the sciences, becoming fluent in Latin, Nahuatl, and a number of other languages. Sor Juana left volumes of poetry and prose on such topics as love, feminism, and religion. Her searing critique of misogyny and male hypocrisy led to her condemnation by the Bishop of Puebla.

Sor Juana has often been called Mexico's first feminist. Eventually her radical consciousness brought official rebuke. She was forced to stop writing and devote herself to charity work. She died in 1695. This self-taught seventeenth-century intellect had a powerful benefactor in the Countess of Pareda, and there is evidence that the women were lovers. Sor Juana's great talent was recognized during her lifetime, and she has been called "the tenth muse." Her image appears on several Mexican bank notes as well as a postage stamp.

Throughout time, this deeply misogynist nation has given the world many other extraordinary women: the twentieth-century painter Frida Kahlo, the visionary photographer Tina Modotti (born in Italy but lived and died in Mexico), and more contemporary artists and writers such as those we knew and published in the pages of *El Corno*. Together, they provided an inspiring backdrop to my discovery of feminism.

Living in a tremendously sexist society, toward the end of my time in Mexico I experienced a shift in gender consciousness that changed me profoundly. It was 1968–1969, and the early texts of Second Wave feminism were beginning to trickle down from the north. I read those texts, and something clicked. *Las mujeres* was the 1970 compendium of essays I published with Siglo XXI. Arnaldo wisely suggested the book's nonthreatening name. He knew back then that if we used the word feminism in its title, the book wouldn't make it past the censors in many Latin American countries. *Las mujeres* has enjoyed eleven editions and remains in print. I still occasionally receive letters from women who tell me it was their introduction to thinking differently about their lives.

· ·

Mexico remains an indelible part of our family's story. My middle daughters, Sarah and Ximena, returned as adults to the country of their birth. They married Mexican men, settled, and had their families there. The rest of us visit often, drawn by their presence, a world of ancient stone ruins, dramatic diversity of landscape, lilt of language, and collective as well as personal memory. Southern Mexico's Mayan culture remains a fascinating source of inspiration to me. I have explored most of the large and some of the smaller sites and return often to the story of breaking the Mayan code, a complex riddle that began giving itself up not that many years back.[13]

Ximena, especially, has adopted the Mexican aesthetic. A professional chef, she is an expert in the country's rich cuisine. Outsiders tend to think of Mexican food in terms of tacos and tamales while ignoring the complexity of its more sophisticated dishes such as its exquisite *moles*, those sauces containing chocolate, peanuts, sesame seeds, and a variety of chiles. Some *moles* combine more than twenty-eight ingredients. Ximena has lately been attempting to revive a variation of a chile in danger of extinction that is native to Cuicatlán Canyon in the state of Oaxaca. Called *Chilhuacle*, it is one of the main ingredients in all seven Oaxacan *moles*.

In recent years, a succession of Mexican administrations has become increasingly corrupt and implicated in perpetrating or protecting their crimes. Disappearances and murders are everyday occurrences. In the past couple decades alone, more than 1,500 young women—many of them textile workers—have vanished from the streets of Ciudad Juárez, the border town where my parents took us as children and where I later introduced Elaine to the bullfights. Between 2012 and 2018 the number of attacks against politicians increased by more than 2,400 percent. Some dozen journalists are assassinated in Mexico each year, making it one of the deadliest countries in which to work in the media. Today mafias of organized crime control whole cities and towns. But the Mexican people have demonstrated an extraordinary defiance and resilience. In the summer of 2018 they voted in a president who may well be capable of turning things around.[14]

Chapter Six

INTERLUDE

Escape

There where you don't understand,
in the white spaces, in the emptiness,
write: I love you.
—ELENA PONIATOWSKA

Interlude as in limbo, a place no longer mine. I had been evicted but not allowed to leave. And I was not yet anywhere else. It wasn't like having one foot in one place and one in another. More like not being able to feel the ground beneath my feet. No longer in possession of place.

In the summer of 1969, *El Corno Emplumado* was forced to cease publication and I was forced underground. When my youngest daughter, Ana, was just three months old, armed paramilitary operatives came to our home. I was upstairs in bed, ill with what would turn out to be severe kidney disease, and never saw their faces. Robert handled the intrusion alone. But in the intervening years I came to imagine that I had seen those two men, one of them wielding a pistol. I could describe them physically, what they looked like and wore, how they sounded and moved, the threat they brought into our lives.

They came to our home accusing me of being a foreigner who was running a sweatshop and wasn't paying social security benefits to my employees. Robert naively invited them in, explaining that we had no sweatshop or any exploited employees, and assuring the intruders that in any case I wasn't a foreigner but a Mexican citizen. He would get my passport as proof. As soon as he handed it over, one of the men said he had to go out to his car for some paperwork. He would make this right, he insisted.

The next thing I knew, Robert was running up the stairs toward our bedroom, shouting: "They have your passport! They have your passport! They got away!" I roused myself. Gregory was traveling with friends, but our first impulse was to collect our two older girls from school. If the repression was upon us, we wanted as much of the family as possible together. Waiting for Gregory to come home was agony. A week later he did. Meanwhile, I reported the passport theft at our local precinct and was told to apply for another. When I did so, it was declined.

Laurette Séjourné sat beside me through the long slow emptying out of a vast waiting room at Relaciones Exteriores. Until we were the only ones in that immense space. A man wearing knee-high leather boots came to where we sat, clicked his heels in fascistic gesture, and told us I would not be issued a new passport: "You have lost three," he accused, "and we must investigate." It wasn't true. At first, I didn't know who was behind this attack on my person. Years later, in Nicaragua, I met ex-CIA agent Philip Agee. When I told him my story, he said it sounded very much like one of the operations based in the US embassy in Mexico during the 1960s.

We react to events as they unfold. In this case there was no time to allow for full emotional response, nor did I even grasp the implications of what was happening. Mexico had been my home for the better part of a decade. It was probable that my son had no conscious memory of a time before living there. My three daughters had been born in the country. For Robert the shock of being evicted from a place he was just beginning to know must have been disconcerting, even painful, but his ties were only a year or so deep. I was being forced into a kind of exile, something I would not be able to allow myself to feel for many years. Perhaps not until writing these lines.

Waiting characterized this time. Waiting followed by more waiting. Robert had to leave his job; he was the one who went out, tried to make contacts, acted as liaison with our friends at the Cuban embassy and others. I mostly stayed behind closed doors and curtained windows. Who could we talk to about what was happening to us? Only a few close friends. We felt we had to be careful, as well, with visitors from outside the country. It was hard to know whom to trust. I remember a visit from Saul Landau and Nina Serrano; at first, we hesitated to give them a full account of what was going on, then heard ourselves pouring the story out in all its messiness.

We waited. Then waited some more. I must have wondered if this was it, if I would die in this unexpected trap set for me by who knew which antagonistic forces; because at one point I found myself writing with a sort of desperation, attempting to set down a record of what my life had been to that point. Were the unspeakable to happen, I think I wanted to leave my story, my version of events, for those coming later. I no longer have the sixty-plus pages I wrote in little more than one feverish session: my first premature attempt at memoir.

I've mentioned that my son, Gregory, eight years old at the time, was not at home when the repression hit. Among the hundreds of people who visited us during those years were Bob and Alice, a young couple traveling through Latin America. He was Canadian, she from the United States, and they stayed with us just prior to the repression. They fashioned simple leather sandals and sold them along the way. Gregory, who was always interested in learning something new, started helping them make those sandals. It was summer vacation and when they were ready to head further south, he asked if he could accompany them. I said yes, but only as far as the Guatemalan border. I couldn't have imagined the drama about to grip us.

As it turned out, the travelers had their own problems after leaving Mexico City. When they arrived at the area where María Sabina had popularized the hallucinogenic mushroom, they stopped to experience it. Dozens of visitors were there at the time. They continued on, and several days later Bob, Alice, and Gregory were rounded up along with other hippie adventurers and returned to the capital in a bus, its windows papered over with newsprint. Our guests were deported. Gregory spent one night in jail and the next morning was unceremoniously delivered to our home. In retrospect it is clear that the government was cracking down on foreigners, youth, and anyone else suspected of having been sympathetic to the Movement of 1968.

The week between my son's return and having to leave our home for good was tense and filled with "solutions" that fell apart one after another. I had a call from someone saying he had my passport and wanted to return it but I was too frightened to explore that option. We thought the magazine might be the problem and got a friend who worked for one of Mexico's large dailies to insert an article about its demise. That had no impact.

By this time, it was clear we would not be able to remake our lives in Mexico. We had been planning to spend a year or two in Cuba and decided to move those plans ahead. Everyone else in the family had their passports in order. I was the only one who needed a way out of the country. If I had become persona non grata, we thought, the Mexican government should be happy to let me go.

Several friends with connections in high places tried to use their influence on our behalf. Arnaldo Orfila went to see Gorostiza, by then the secretary of foreign relations. He said my problem originated in the United States and was out of his hands. Lidia Murray, our friend from the Bartolomé Cossío, got an appointment with Luis Echevarria, the person many believed had been responsible for the massacre at Tlatelolco the year before. He would succeed Díaz Ordaz as president of Mexico but in 1969 was still its secretary of the interior. Echeverria, too, said he could do nothing.

We had a large art collection—probably close to one hundred canvases—from my years in New York as well as more recent work given to us by Mexican and Latin American painters. We also had El Corno's files; in those years that meant several hundred 3 × 5 index cards with poets' names, addresses, and telephone numbers, all alphabetized in two oblong wooden boxes. After the paramilitary attack at the house, we were afraid the men might return. We were particularly concerned about those index cards falling into the wrong hands. It wasn't that all our poets were politically vulnerable, but many were, and we didn't want to cause trouble for anyone.

....

Concha and Elena, sisters who worked for us at the time, remained at the house. I gave them what money I had on hand and told them to leave as well. They did, but not before the same paramilitary agents who had attacked us returned and threatened them. They tried to get information about our activities and whereabouts. Neither sister knew anything; there was nothing they could tell. Those young women's lives were brutally disrupted. They were battered psychologically, perhaps also physically. And from one day to the next, through no fault of their own, they were without work. They are among the millions of ordinary Mexican women, hardworking poor who sell in the great markets or work in the homes of others, cleaning, cooking, and raising children from the time they are practically children themselves. Over the years, Sergio managed to keep in touch with Concha, Elena, and their family, living in a shantytown at the edge of the great metropolis.

I never stopped thinking about those women, wondering what had become of their lives. And then, as I was writing this book, Gregory visited

From left to right: Elena, Sarah, Concha, and Ximena, Mexico City, 1966 (attribution unknown).

Mexico. Sergio took him out to see the sisters, fifty years older now than when he was eight and they had suddenly been ripped from his childhood. Five family members inhabit a single bedroom and small living area, modest but clean and welcoming. Through the years they have managed to replace zinc and cardboard with better building materials; their home has electricity and running water. Neighbors have organized to build stone steps leading up to where they live, beyond the road that is accessible by automobile.

Both had married. Elena's husband died two years ago, and she moved back in with her sister. Concha had been on her own for years, and is now the matriarch of a large, woman-centered family. She helps support them all by getting up at four each morning and making tacos, which she sells at a small roadside stand. But this day she took off work and cooked for Gregory and his wife, Laura; Sergio and his wife, Marina; and her own numerous clan. She made chicken tacos, fresh cheese and cream, cabbage salad, black beans, homemade tortillas, and two types of pie. That kind of feast requires a week's income or more and marks a special occasion.

Memories flowed throughout that visit. Gregory says the sisters remembered me delivering babies in our old neighborhood, baking bread, trusting my children and the two of them in ways they hadn't experienced before, lending them my clothing on occasion. They said I didn't differentiate between people of their class and my own, and because of this I was known in the old neighborhood as someone unusual. As I read my son's description of that visit, some of my old guilt melted away. There is no pretending that system of household labor is fair but knowing that a half-century later Concha and Elena retain such positive memories helped me access the humanity in our relationship. They have children and grandchildren, many of whom have

From left to right: Elena, Gregory, and Concha, Mexico City, 2019 (photo by Laura Carlevaro).

followed education out of that cycle of household labor; several are studying trades and two are the first family members who hope to attend university.

....

After we all abandoned the house, our friend Maru spent almost a day there, retrieving the file boxes and packing up the art. Maru was one of the most courageous people I've known. Our friends at the Cuban embassy agreed to ship the paintings to Havana, where I wanted to donate them to the National Art Museum. Sadly, I never saw them again. Were they sold? Distributed to high-level officials for their personal collections? I learned the hard way that revolutions, too, can be guilty of corruption.

Without doubt our greatest problem was hiding with four young children. It was hard to explain to the oldest three why they had been taken out of school so abruptly, why they could no longer play with beloved friends, why it was even imprudent for them to peer out the windows from our various hiding places. Ana was an infant but certainly intuited something. Within a couple of weeks Robert and I made the painful decision to send them all to Cuba.

The Revolution was taking in thousands of youngsters at the time, sons and daughters of leftist activists who were engaged on the front lines of a variety of Third World struggles. The parents of some of those children were imprisoned or dead. Others were still fighting. Gregory was eight; Sarah, five; Ximena, four; and Ana, a newborn. We believed that putting them in the Revolution's care was the only way of keeping them safe. Too many bodies of movement children had shown up on the *pedregal*, the city's volcanic outskirts: macabre warnings to their activist parents.

This was a hard decision, but we felt we had no choice. I had tried to get my parents in Albuquerque to receive my children temporarily; they said no.[1] We might have entrusted them to Sergio, who was hurt and angry that we didn't. Still, our goal was to stay together as a family and—despite the emotional upheaval and other options we might have pursued—we did what we thought best. Gregory was the only one of the four who understood something of what was happening. He had to leave his best friend, Juan Christián; I know that was painful. Years later, when they reconnected as young adults, they were surprised to find their tastes and beliefs had followed almost identical paths. The bedrock of political culture we had acquired in Mexico had been formative for them both.

For Sarah and Ximena, the sudden rupture was more confusing and left deeper scars. They too had to abandon school, teachers, and close childhood friends. They had to choose only a couple of favorite toys to bring with them, and were thrust into uncertainty without their parents in a land they didn't know for what must have seemed like an eternity—until Robert and then I caught up with them. An infant, Ana couldn't possibly have understood why her mother and father disappeared. I am sure the separation marked her in ways it has taken her a lifetime to disentangle. My own life has taught me that what we experience before we have the use of language affects us profoundly.

We made our arrangements. I had to wean Ana from one day to the next. I vividly remember watching Robert depart with her and the older children as they left for the Mexico City airport, where the Cubans had arranged for them to board a flight to Havana. In that more humane time, Robert was able to accompany our kids to the plane itself, even board it, get them settled, and kiss them goodbye. In the depths of her cellular memory, I know that Ana has never forgotten that moment. In my last image of her she was wearing a pale pink onesie with a white collar. As the car disappeared, I tasted a mix of anguish and relief.

Those two and a half months during which I attempted to buy my way out of Mexico remain surreal in memory. At Laurette and Arnaldo's home, adjacent to Siglo XXI, we could hear the busy murmur of a publishing house and, of course, imagined its employees might also hear us if we spoke above a whisper. At the end of each workday, Laurette and Arnaldo invited us out of hiding and into the warmth of their living room where we shared supper and speculation. One evening Rolando Rodríguez visited. He was the director of Cuba's Book Institute at the time and assured me I would have a job there once we arrived on the island. That moment still seemed impossibly remote.

It was also while we were at Laurette and Arnaldo's that we received the tragic news that René Vallejo had suffered a severe stroke and was not expected to live. Vallejo was Fidel's personal physician and had become a friend during my 1968 trip to Cuba. It was at his urging that I'd decided my family might benefit from a year or two on the island. Knowing he and I would never see one another again, especially in circumstances in which I felt assaulted by loss, was hard for me to accept.

At the Payán home, on the outskirts of the city, we hid in a third-floor cupola. One morning I looked out the window on a funeral procession slowly bordering a field below. The coffin was small and white. It held the body of a child. That image remains with me all these years later. At Maru's, on July 20th we gathered before a little black-and-white television and watched the first human land on the moon. "That's one small step for a man, one giant leap for mankind."[2] The words echoed, the scratchy image both distant and immediate. It was a toss-up as to whether that extraordinary event or our own situation seemed more bizarre. We also took refuge for a few days with Rita Siegel, now Rita Pomade, a friend from my New York days with whom I have remained close.

A cigarette habit had consumed me at the rate of three packs a day for fifteen years. After Ana's birth I'd finally managed to stop smoking. By then I was coughing more readily than speaking. Nursing my baby, I happened to catch a glimpse of myself in a large mirror across the room. A tenuous piece of ash seemed about to fall on Ana's newborn head. That image was what motivated me to give up the habit.

Quitting cold turkey had been difficult and I continued to suffer extreme symptoms of withdrawal. My hand shook for a year, and I often burst into tears for no apparent reason. It was a challenge not to start smoking again during my time in hiding. Robert and I took on a couple of translation projects to help pass the interminable hours, days, weeks between meeting with someone who might be able to help me acquire false papers or—more often—coming up against some dead-end. I remember putting the finishing touches on a translation of Jorge Ricardo Masetti's *Los que luchan y los que lloran*, but the manuscript was later lost.

I needed to obtain a replacement passport, fake or real. It turned out to be much more complicated than I could have imagined. With our movement in shambles, old channels that might have handled such problems no longer existed. A month passed, and then two. A third began. I was starting to feel numb, as if the impasse might go on forever. My longing for the children, uncertainty around when we would be reunited, periodic kidney attacks, and nicotine withdrawal were the outward signs of inner anguish.

Finally, an acquaintance introduced us to someone with contacts in the Mexican Mafia. He assured us he knew a man who could help. It seemed we were about to find a solution to months of frustration. I left my hideout and went to a beauty parlor in a part of vast Mexico City where I wasn't likely to run into anyone I knew. "I think my husband is seeing another woman," I told the attendant as she placed the plastic cape about my shoulders. "I want a complete makeover." When I emerged from the salon several hours later, my long brown braid had been cut and my hair dyed a shiny blue-black and teased into a fashionable bob. My unruly eyebrows were tweezed pencil thin. Lip color and nail polish completed the disguise.

I believed my own mother would have been hard put to recognize me on the street had we run into one another that day. Wearing a conventional navy-and-gold-striped knit dress, unlike the indigenous *huipiles* that were my trademark, I opened my eyes as wide as possible and had half a dozen passport-size pictures taken in one of those little shopping mall photo booths. Then, purchasing our tickets under false names, Robert and I flew north.

My departure from Mexico City is summed up for me in the taxi ride Robert and I took from our last hiding place to the airport, from where we would fly to the city of Chihuahua where the comrade who helped with my escape would be waiting. I remember looking out the window of that taxi, wondering if I would ever see those familiar streets again. A terrible nostalgia filled me.

Our Cuban comrades had assured me that, once outside Mexico, they could help me get to the island via Czechoslovakia. This was one of the only viable routes at the time, and the safest given my situation. In Chihuahua

City we were met by Señor García. We'd been told we would recognize him because he was missing half the little finger on his left hand, but when the plane rolled to a stop at the small provincial airport, we didn't have to guess. He was waiting on the tarmac.

Although he asked no questions about our situation, García was expansive and hospitable. He took us to dinner, put us in a good hotel, and picked us up the following morning to take us to the man we'd been told could fix my document problem—for a price. It was then that the operation began to unravel. García's friend, who worked in local government, couldn't provide me with a real Mexican passport, only a ridiculous pale blue cardboard booklet issued to border residents who routinely crossed from one side to the other. To be legal, it had to be registered at the consul on the US side, something I could not risk attempting.

Our hopes shattered, Robert and I looked at each other trying to decide what to do. On a whim, or perhaps because I saw no alternative, I said, "Fine, I'll take it." We paid the $200 we'd been quoted in Mexico City and the apologetic official promised to wait until the following month to note my name on the list he sent to his home office in the capital. That would give me more time, he said.

What followed was a blur of days, nights, different modes of transportation, and further anxious waits. Because I had not been able to obtain the official Mexican passport, García had to smuggle me past the twenty-eight-mile checkpoint in the back of a refrigerated meat truck. I rode with him in the cab until just a few miles before we had to stop, and he released me, shivering, a few miles past the danger point. I clutched my thin sweater about my shoulders and climbed back into the truck's cab.

Meanwhile, Robert had taken a bus to Juárez where we met him for dinner at a prearranged Chinese restaurant. In Juárez as in Chihuahua, García seemed to know everyone. Once again, he insisted on paying for our meal— we referred to it as "the last supper"—and directed us to a nearby thoroughfare leading to the international bridge. A few blocks and half an hour later we walked across, answering the routine "Nationality?" with an equally routine "USA."

Once in the United States, Robert flew to New York for a brief visit with his parents, then on to Madrid and finally Havana. Without a legal passport my travel plans were more complicated. I flew to Chicago, transferred to a Greyhound bus and crossed the Canadian border at Windsor, using my old US birth certificate as identification. I remember flashes of that journey:

fragments of my conversation with a thin Bible-reading young man sitting next to me on the long ride north, occasional naps and jolts back to consciousness. I was still suffering from the kidney problem that had plagued me since before Ana's birth, and I spiked a fever on and off.

Those were the days before credit cards. I was carrying several thousand dollars in cash. At the Toronto airport I purchased a ticket to Paris. Now I close my eyes and once again see that rapidly changing sky over the Atlantic, darkening almost as soon as we took off. Brilliant oranges and pinks soon announced sunrise on the other shore. In Paris I stayed outside the immigration barrier and bought a ticket to Prague. No one had asked to see my useless travel document. Just as my Cuban contacts had promised, passports weren't examined on departure, only on arrival.

Which meant that my arrival in Prague would be my moment of truth. I very much hoped the Cubans there had been notified of my coming. When I got to the head of the immigration line and handed over the pale blue book, the official receiving it shook his head, stared at me, then called a fellow officer over. Apparently neither of them had seen a document like it, and I had no visa for Czechoslovakia. I kept asking for someone from the Cuban embassy.

After a few minutes I was ushered into a small room. Although the official doing the ushering spoke no English, I understood she wanted me to wait. I remember having to urinate and being afraid to ask where the restroom was. Eventually a young woman appeared with a small medical kit in hand. It seemed the Czechs were more concerned that I didn't have an international health card than about anything else. The woman asked if I was pregnant. I said no. For months I would have a recurrent nightmare in which I dreamt I was in fact pregnant and, by allowing them to revaccinate me against smallpox, had murdered my unborn child.

The Cubans had been notified of my arrival, and someone from the embassy eventually arrived. A man of few words, that comrade barely inquired about my trip. The drive from the airport took about half an hour, mostly over narrow cobblestone streets through neat neighborhoods of small rowhouses. Innocently believing that once I arrived in Havana all my and my family's needs would be met, I gratefully gave the considerable amount of money I had left to the Cuban embassy official. "For the Revolution," I said. He took it without offering a receipt. Today I wonder where that money ended up; it was more than a thousand dollars.

My savior deposited me at a hotel on the outskirts of the city where I stayed for several days, accompanied only by recurrent kidney attacks. There

I did little more than shiver, eat, and sleep, although I did venture out on a streetcar one day wearing a long black overcoat one of the hotel employees lent me against an autumn cold for which my light cotton dress was no match.

Even in Prague my ordeal dragged on. A single flight a week connected that city with Havana. It departed every Saturday morning. Week after week, at the very last minute I would be bumped from one plane and then another in deference to travelers with higher political status. In all, I would end up spending nineteen days in Prague, the last thirteen of them at the Hotel International. There I would meet Cubans and other Latin Americans passing through for one reason or another. I would learn patience from them.

Some of those Cuban guests were returning from courses of study in the Soviet Union. A well-known composer had just completed a concert tour in Eastern Europe. Some of the Latin Americans were making their circuitous ways from Cuba back to distant home-country battlefronts. A Cuban pilot was waiting for a replacement part from a Russian aircraft factory he needed for his aging Ilyushin Il-18. With him I would experience one of the great magical realist episodes of my life.

The story about the pilot is as good a prelude as any to my years in Cuba. We had introduced ourselves a few days before. Francisco was as frustrated as I; his replacement part had been promised for several weeks and waiting was getting tiresome. One night at dinner he asked me what my story was. I mentioned my children and the fact that they had preceded me to Havana. Francisco stared at me: "Do you have photographs?" I pulled out the fraying images I'd kept with me over the preceding months and pushed them across the table.

Francisco looked at the pictures and began to laugh. "I can't believe this," he exclaimed. "Your youngest peed on my trousers when the stewardess brought them into the cockpit. The boy wanted a look at the controls."

It took me a moment to realize that the man sitting across from me had seen my children more recently than I. He had flown them from Mexico City to Havana. Immediately our interaction became excited, overflowing with a complicit exchange of details and images. Others at the table stopped talking, stunned by our conversation. "I knew they were traveling alone," Francisco said. "The four of them were being taken care of by the plane's stewardess, and a government official met the flight." He looked at my pictures again. "I'll bet you miss them," he said.

When we'd parted almost three months before, I had promised Gregory I would catch up with them all by his ninth birthday, October 14th. I arrived in Havana one day early.

WITH GRATITUDE TO VALLEJO

One day, it will be my turn. Luck of the draw even for me.
One day, almost certainly not in Paris,
a chance in seven on a Thursday,
the door that burst open on December 6, 1936, will close.

It will slam shut or settle like velvet
until its light dims completely,
the rhythms of its tongue gone still.

My turn, not because I have tied my wrist bones on wrong,
braided anxious fingers,
stumbled into the abyss
or laughed when I might have cried.

I breathed available air,
loved in every way I knew
followed my map to a place beyond canyon walls.

After the door
swung open between my mother's thighs
and before my turn's arrival
my children and their children will reach
for places I cannot know
while I am warmed
by a love that dares speak its name,
black words on white pages,
this nest woven of numbers and sky.

Chapter Seven

FIRST FREE
TERRITORY

Cuba, 1969–1980

Nothing is lost to us.
Ours the land.
Ours the sea and the sky.
Ours the magic and the rage.
My equals, here I watch you dance
around the tree we planted for communism.
Its prodigious wood already sounds.
—NANCY MOREJÓN, "BLACK WOMAN,"
FROM *ONLY THE ROAD/SOLO EL CAMINO*

This is a time-travel chapter. I lived the experience of the Cuban Revolution in the 1970s, wrote a memoir about it in the early 2000s, and now want to revisit the meaning of those years from my 2018 perspective even as I try to re-create the sense of wonder and possibility that existed on that Caribbean island during my decade there. I continue to believe that living with my family in Cuba during the Revolution's second decade was the privilege of a lifetime— for us all. Quite simply it allowed us to experience a place and a time when the quest for justice was at the forefront of daily life. I travel to the island frequently, have seen it struggle to retain its major achievements while making the complicated transition to a global economy in which capitalism was victorious. Since then the world has changed, the Cuban Revolution has changed, I have changed—and I've also gained new insight into a few old issues.

The Cubana crew had been kind. They clearly knew something about my situation. I'd been warned not to deplane, especially in Greenland, then a hub of US military activity, and one of the flight attendants brought me a meal on board. After thirty-some-odd hours, I arrived at Havana's José Martí International Airport exhausted but relieved. In contrast with previous arrivals, when I had been received as an invited guest with all the attendant pomp and circumstance, this time I found myself in a cavernous, almost silent terminal. Although I assumed the Cuban comrades in Prague had wired ahead, no one was there to meet me.

When I announced myself to the lone immigration official, he told me to take a seat and wait. Twenty minutes later an affable elderly representative of the Foreign Ministry showed up in one of the many wine-colored Alfa Romeos so common among Cuban government officials at the time. I no longer remember the man's name, but he was able to answer my eager questions: Robert had arrived a week before and he and the three older children were waiting for me at the Hotel Caprí. We would be there soon.

Cuba is a tropical island populated by a mix of Spanish immigrants, African slaves, and, to a lesser extent, Chinese laborers and Haitian sugarcane workers. Beaches are inviting and Royal palm trees dot the landscape. The Cuban people have an islander's vision of the world and of themselves. During the years my family and I lived in the country, one also saw many Eastern European technicians and Vietnamese and other residents who had come to study.

Images and feelings surge to the surface now: the interminable ride along Avenida Rancho Boyeros, observing the shabby buildings, desperate cleanliness, people congregated at bus stops or headed to market, empty *jabas* hanging from their arms. Pride in the midst of shabbiness is always moving. Through imposing Revolution Square with its large silhouette of Che overlooking everything in sight. My first sight of the Caprí. A warm greeting in the lobby from a large black woman who introduced herself as the hotel's *ama de llaves*. The elevator door opening on the fifth floor almost simultaneous with the opening of the door to room 506.

The warm rush of Gregory, Sarah, and Ximena against my body. Ximena wrapping her small arms around my leg and not letting go. Sarah standing to one side for a moment and then throwing herself headfirst into our collective hug. Smiling tears glistening in Gregory's eyes. Robert's expression was a mixture of exhaustion and relief. Each of us has his or her own memory of that moment, so significant in all our lives. We were together once more, and that very afternoon took a bus out to Miramar, to the old Bacardi rum mansion where Ana spent her days. She was plump and smelled of lavender and seemed to recognize me in some deep part of herself. I held her close. She cried for a long time.

....

My 2009 memoir is filled with impressions and anecdotes, all I wanted or was able to say at the time.[1] Now that I am trying to reawaken memory, recall the places I've lived and when, how those places and people changed me—how they made me feel then and since—those Cuban years are next in line. Already having covered my time on the Caribbean island poses a problem: What can I add today? Is there anything left to say? Should I simply skip the decade of the 1970s and move on to Nicaragua? No, because doing so would leave a gaping hole in this narrative.

The Cuban Revolution of 1959 changed Latin America, the United States, and certainly my own life. There isn't a liberation movement in this hemisphere that wasn't inspired by Cuba's victory nor an individual involved in working for social change who didn't look to the Cuban war of liberation as a model—most trying to follow in its footsteps, a scant few careful to acknowledge historical and cultural differences. All over the world, people sat up and took notice. But Cuba isn't static, and any description may be relevant only to a particular moment.

The Cuba that had moved and excited me in 1967 and 1968, and to which I arrived with my family in the fall of 1969, was little short of astonishing. A nation had learned how to read, and culture was a priority. Education was free, and at every workplace people were released for hours in order to study without forfeiting salary. Healthcare was free and accessible. Food was rationed but equitably distributed so that no one had appreciably more than anyone else. Neighbors eagerly joined voluntary work brigades, proud to be improving life for everyone. Leadership and Party members set examples of participation and sacrifice; there was little that we recognized as corrupt.

It's impossible to describe what living in that aura of fairness felt like, how simple the solutions to social inequities seemed if the will to change was there. All the fabricated reasons why such solutions weren't possible in the other countries where I'd lived suddenly seemed coverups for obscene corruption and greed. By then the Revolution had been remaking society for ten years.

Looking back, I think of the decade we lived on the island as the Revolution's glory years.

I won't list all the changes the new government made. You can read them in hundreds of books from every political point of view. I'll just briefly say it nationalized the sugar mills and other major industries, and new labor laws favored workers. Soon the vast majority of adults had jobs, and unemployment was all but eliminated. Efforts were being made to address racism and gender inequity. The great literacy campaign of 1961 reduced those who could neither read nor write from between 60 percent and 76 percent to only 4 percent of the population,[2] and many Cubans who once lacked a future beyond the drudgery of daily toil could now look to opportunities about which they could not have dreamed prior to 1959. Public education was broadened and strengthened, with the result that close to 100 percent of the country's children were now in school. Many adults were also studying. And the emphasis on culture and the arts gave people a dignified sense of self as well as inspired in them their own creativity. Housing was still in short supply, but the micro brigades were working at full intensity and it looked like they might eventually build modest but decent and affordable homes for all.[3]

Back then there was a sense of transparency as well. I was impressed by the nationalizations, the emphasis on education and health, all the big changes. But it was the transparency that touched me most. The Revolution's central figures, from Fidel Castro on down, seemed honest and disinterested in personal gain. As they constantly traveled the country, engaging in meaningful exchange with ordinary citizens, they listened to problems and considered suggested solutions. People called them by their first names. They didn't live in mansions, nor were they surrounded by heavy security. I felt a oneness between the leadership and general population. Support for the Revolution was overwhelming.

I breathed a humanity I hadn't experienced in my native United States. Not even during my years in Mexico. The sordid world of US crime syndication, that had once controlled Cuba's gambling interests and trapped its poorest and most vulnerable women into prostitution, had been replaced by rebels who'd shown they were willing to give their lives to create a more just society. I was impressed with the disinterest in personal gain, but didn't really think about the issue of power, how it could be abused in socialism as well as capitalism, what structural inequalities might be setting the stage for future problems.

Girl with shoes, Alamar, Havana, 1978 (photo by Margaret Randall).

I would like to evoke how I personally felt during those first weeks and months. There I was, a middle-class white woman from the United States, who suddenly found herself living among people whose Revolution my country was trying to destroy. Yet I don't remember experiencing the overwhelming guilt I'd felt in Mexico. For one thing, Cuba's revolutionary leadership made a point of differentiating between US government policy and US people. For another, a nation that has waged a successful war of liberation has a self-confidence that promotes a generosity of spirit.

The tiny Caribbean island had become the center of a solar system. In the 1960s, 1970s, and 1980s the world was divided into two camps: one driven by what we believed was a dying capitalism, the other fueled by Communism's promise of equality. We were an army of Davids fighting a Goliath of capitalist exploitation and imperialist plunder. Our struggle would require courage and sacrifice, but it empowered us. We were filled with a sense of entitlement. Not the entitlement that comes from class privilege or an androcentric domination, but from working to create a better society. One in which justice would prevail.

I was eager to do my part and the Cubans with whom I came in contact accepted my intentions as genuine. Some friends laughingly accused Robert and me of having *sarampión* (measles), the term they used when talking about outsiders who displayed an exaggerated eagerness and acritical attitude. I may have felt that I understood more than I did.

....

The block committee, or CDR (Committee for the Defense of the Revolution), organized citizens to beautify and patrol their neighborhood, defend its security, discuss new laws and other governmental initiatives, make sure families with special problems had what they needed, recycle, and organize preventative health campaigns and voluntary work brigades. Outside Cuba, these committees were depicted as "Big Brother," the collective spirit diminishing individuality. Inside the country, it depended on who was in charge. If it was a small-minded person who enjoyed his or her quota of power, there could be some truth to the portrayal.

Masa, our committee president, was a large, jovial, fair-minded, and immensely wise black man who'd grown up on a sugar plantation in Camagüey. He was of a social class and generation for whom the Revolution was everything. He often told stories from his childhood, stories of hunger and racial suffering. I never knew him to invade anyone's privacy. His first gesture on our behalf was to make sure we were absolved from securing a blood donation when I had my damaged kidney removed; the donation was the only requirement when someone needed an operation. Masa lived with his wife, Helena, and daughter, Krupskaya,[4] in a building at the far end of our block.

To Masa we were just another family in his care. "How's it going?" he would ask when we'd run into one another. "How's that book coming along?" Or, if he knew I'd had a long day at work, "Do you want Helena to pick up your rations when she goes to market in the morning?" He never failed to place his strong hand on my shoulder, listen to my needs or concerns. Although our backgrounds and cultures could not have been more dissimilar, I always felt that he saw me, respected me, believed I was there to do my best.

I remember a few block committee meetings to discuss new laws, at which I articulated opinions almost unintelligible to most of those present. I'm not sure Masa got what I was saying either. But he would hear me out and then call on Mercy, a neighbor with an ideology similar to mine but a Cuban's ability to make herself understood in that time and place. I often wondered where he stood on those issues. His even-handedness and equanimity made it impossible to tell.

Masa never forgot us, even years after we left the country. Gregory visited in 2003, shortly before Masa's death. When he went to see the old man, Masa recalled every one of our family members by name and wanted to know what each was doing.

....

My 2009 memoir was a love letter punctuated by occasional critique. If I revisit that balance today, I come up with the same love and admiration—and the same criticisms. But, as I say, the world and Cuba have changed and so have I. I know more today than I did then, am less willing to follow certain ideological lines out of an unquestioning loyalty. I am able to trace some problems to allegiances that might have been necessary when they were struck but have since been proven problematic. Others seem frankly absurd to me now. Most importantly, I have learned that a failure to consider the issue of power distorts a process from its inception.

Which is not to say that the Cuban Revolution failed. Only that it was not allowed to develop into the Revolution many of us dreamed. The country depended on sugar and was slow to diversify. The US economic blockade was a problem of monumental proportions, and the United States also kept other countries from trading with Cuba. This blockade continues today; during Obama's tenure there was an opening up, but the Trump administration has once again increased restrictions. In what was once the socialist bloc, residual Stalinist rigidity and a rapid march toward state capitalism were signs of the times. To varying degrees and during different periods, those ills were reproduced on the island.

Still, a tiny country that has been able to break down punitive diplomatic and trade barriers, feed its population, and preserve free education, universal healthcare, and an impressive cultural and artistic life is a success story of some magnitude. Gender and racial equality within the Revolution have had their ups and downs, as has freedom of expression, but Cuba is a far cry from the United States, where political power is bought and sold, violence is on the rise, and an epidemic of unchecked murders by police overwhelmingly victimizes young men of color and transgender people.

Without doubt, the greatest challenge to the success of the Cuban Revolution has been the issue of power. Underdevelopment, poverty, a one-crop economy, six decades of multifaceted aggression from the United States, and the 1989 demise of the socialist bloc have certainly been huge problems. Confronting these and other issues would have made it understandably difficult for the Revolution to take the time to look at the dynamics of power, had it wanted to do so. Still, I believe the failure to examine power reflects a reluctance to share it and has been a serious weakness. It certainly played a role in preventing a gender analysis. The revolutionary leadership has often pointed to the US blockade as the main obstacle to development. There is no doubt it has been a tremendous impediment, costing the Revolution billions of dollars. It has also, I think, been used as an excuse.

Fidel Castro was an exceptional leader. Extremely charismatic, he was curious about everything and brilliant in a multitude of fields. He was also extraordinarily personable. Fidel was the unquestioned force behind the revolutionary movement that took power in 1959, proving himself as astute a political leader as a designer of the strategy that won the war. There have been many other important contributors at all levels of Cuban society, but Fidel personified the Revolution; it was impossible to separate the two. His speeches lasted hours and well into the 1990s were lessons in history, politics, and economics. He had the ability to accurately situate a person's life within the context of what was happening in the world. More times than I can count, I and more than a million others stood spellbound beneath a blistering sun in the Plaza de la Revolución listening to one of his speeches.

This exceptionality centered power in a single figure and the group of men (and some women) who shared his vision. Soon after the war ended, the 26th of July Movement had either absorbed or wrested influence from other progressive forces that took part in the conflict. By the time a movement composed of various strands had consolidated itself as the new Cuban Communist Party in 1965, there was no question as to who was in charge. Cubans called Fidel El Caballo (the horse); they made jokes about him but didn't tolerate outsiders doing so.

Despite rhetoric to the contrary, the Cuban Revolution always exercised power from above. A discourse of people's participation only went so far. In

Cuba, democratic centralism had its own face. Elections to municipal and regional assemblies have been scrupulously honest, but they allow low-level decision making at best. Real power has always resided in the Party's Politburo and Central Committee and, as opposed to other socialist countries, in Cuba the Party is not a mass organization but selective and with a limited membership.

Cuban Communism has its idiosyncrasies. But basic adherence to Leninist principles has mostly gone unquestioned. For example, workers are described as owning their labor, but important decisions in factories and other workplaces are determined by the Party or by a labor movement that answers to the Party. An unwillingness to consider the issue of power itself as a political category has, I believe, made grass-roots power-sharing impossible.

One of the things that has made this so complex has been the Revolution's vulnerability to attack from the United States and the ways in which shifts in the international balance of powers have affected the country. Unity has been necessary to maintain a solid front against the blockade, invasion, and more covert attempts at destabilization, such that one sector or another might urge a reassessment of the ways in which power is exercised. But it has always been easy for the leadership to claim such experimentation too dangerous in the face of ongoing threat. At times this may have been a realistic concern. Undoubtedly it was often an excuse that worked to preserve the status quo.

How did this reality play itself out in my life?

Early on, I simply believed. I was impressed with the Revolution's priorities, which were also mine. I didn't see signs of corruption. Or, when I did, they appeared as anomalies, and investigation and punishment were swift. Party membership was selective, and members were held to the highest standards, expected to make the greatest sacrifices. I still know some Party members who live in inadequate housing or drive broken-down cars. From the moment the People's Assembly held its first elections, candidates proposed their ideas with minimal fanfare and schoolchildren protected the dignity of the ballot boxes. Much seemed simpler when I lived in the country.

I remember the first time I seriously questioned the Cuban Party. In the mid-1970s it claimed that the Cambodian genocide was an invention of Western journalists. When I discovered the terrible reality, it shattered my absolute confidence in the Revolution as a force that invariably stood for truth. From that moment on, I learned to challenge official rhetoric. And I use "learned" intentionally. One doesn't easily question a force that has so obviously created good; it's something that must be learned. Not everyone appreciates such

Mother and son, Havana (photo by Margaret Randall).

confrontation. Many on the US left resented those of us who asked the hard questions. They called it "airing our dirty laundry in public" and claimed it provided ammunition to the enemy.

And this only got worse after I left Cuba. In my 2009 memoir I vigorously challenged the 1989 Ochoa hearings and executions; the hearings read like show trials and I felt the executions were a shameful moment in the Revolution's history.[5] I didn't pretend to know whether Ochoa had been involved in drug smuggling or, if so, what his involvement may have been. But I was sure that if it existed it had been approved at the highest levels of Cuban leadership. I also felt that Ochoa's years of service in Cuba, Angola, Nicaragua, and elsewhere should have been considered, rather than condemning him for one presumed misstep. Again, criticism of my criticism mostly came from outside the country, among some on the US left. Inside the country many shared my concerns but opted for silence. And in 2015, when my memoir came out in Spanish from a Cuban publishing house, it was never suggested that I delete my opinions in that regard.[6]

....

I won't say there is no innovation around the issue of power within the Cuban Revolution. Alongside what I consider to be an obsolete power structure, there are practices that astonish. One is the nationwide discussion and input into the creation of major laws. Drafts of important legislation are produced by the Party, published in millions of copies, discussed at workplaces, block committees, mass organizations, and schools throughout the country, and the results of those discussions sent back up to the originating body. Many changes suggested by ordinary citizens are incorporated into the law's final version.

As I write, at the end of 2018, the process is being applied to an overhaul of the Cuban Constitution. A year-long process of discussion was held in workplaces, schools, neighborhoods, and military units. More than two hundred modifications were sent to the body preparing the final version. One change many of us hoped to see was the legalization of marriage equality. But only a third of the population is in favor of such a change, and the Party decided to eliminate it from the final document; it will have to be revisited later. Still, my friends tell me these constitutional discussions have been complex, exciting, and productive, suggesting the possibility of many improvements. It is clear to me that the stalwart group of citizens who have remained in their homeland and continue to believe in revolutionary change have not given up on developing new ways of exercising power in the spaces available to them.

And I want to take a moment to speak about those who have stayed, even when it's meant privation, intolerance, and repression directed at them from time to time. I don't begrudge anyone's right to live where they wish. I'm glad the Revolution was able to overcome its adolescent attitude of crassly insulting those who chose to emigrate. But there is something fearless and wonderful about those who have no intention of going anywhere, who continue to put up with scarcities and hardships of various sorts because they believe in the Revolution and know the struggle goes beyond their lifetimes to embrace the lives of their children and grandchildren. Che Guevara famously said the war was the easy part; changing society would be the real challenge.

One of my first deep Cuban friendships was with Martín, a sociologist who has devoted his life to understanding his country and helping to shape its promise of social change. I no longer remember when or how we met; it's as if we have always known one another. We developed one of those relationships that produces glee even in serious situations. I became the "fall guy" to his raucous laughter. Small of physical stature and gentle of nature, Martín headed the nation's Academy of Sciences through the years, was the country's representative to UNESCO, and eventually ended up in a small but vital interdisciplinary working group attached to the Central Committee of the Party, established to study problems and design policies to solve them. It looks at such diverse issues as alcoholism, diabetes, emigration, an aging population, and climate change. He remains an authentic Party member: passionate, committed, exhausted.

On each of my return visits to the island, I'd call Martín and we'd make time to see one another. Because his workday knows no limits, we'd often have to get together past midnight. I'd adjust my schedule to fit his. I can always depend on his assessment of what's happening, and I also just love spending time with my friend. Now I remember a particularly poignant meeting sometime in the 1990s. Martín picked me up at my hotel in his battered old Lada[7] and we drove to a park in Miramar where imposing Laureles de la India rise out of masses of aboveground roots like great ghostly beings in moon-laced shadows. Martín parked the car, turned to me, and burst into tears.

I reached out and held him in silence until he was able to speak. It took him a while but, when he did, I immediately understood his pain. His only son had immigrated to Miami a few months before, lured by his mother, Martín's ex-wife. A few years earlier his Party affiliation would have discouraged him from contact but by then policy was less rigid. I spent the next hour or so telling Martín that whatever he did he mustn't cut ties with his son. "Keep the lines of communication open," I begged. "Keep on showing you love him. Ideologies come and go, but this is your son."

It hasn't been easy, but Martín has kept in touch as much as he's been able, communicating by telephone and even managing to visit on the rare occasions when he's been able to get a US visa. He's become a grandfather. More than a decade has passed, and he's often thanked me for encouraging him to put feelings before arbitrary Party considerations. The last time we saw one another, Martín was still driving the same old Lada, exhaust fumes now invading its interior. He too is broken, bent from years of overwork without even a decent desk chair that might relieve his overstressed back. He is in line for a hernia operation but waits patiently while more urgent cases receive attention. His confidence in the Revolution has never wavered, and the most important thing in his life is to keep doing his part.

Other friends are Silvia and Ambrosio. Now in their eighties, they were our neighbors in the Vedado apartment house where we lived. They still live on its top floor. Ambrosio is one of his generation's finest literary minds, an astute cultural critic whose analysis is valued throughout Cuba and beyond. Silvia is a librarian. Six decades ago she founded the Casa de las Américas library and, long retired, continues to volunteer there several days a week.

Back when we were neighbors, Silvia and I often did our CDR patrol together, walking early morning streets, conversing in low tones while trying to protect ourselves against a chill wind blowing in from the sea. We were supposed to be defending those streets and the lives of those who inhabited them. We didn't carry guns, and our only distinguishing feature was the cloth arm band each of us wore. This sort of guard duty was clearly more symbolic than anything else, but it gave us a sense of ownership: of our physical space and of the Revolution itself.

On a recent visit I brought Silvia a blue scarf I'd purchased in Mexico with her in mind. It is elegant and of an unusual hue, and I thought it would accentuate her dignified carriage and ready smile. Silvia liked the gift, then said she wanted to show me something. She brought out a worn, light-brown woolen shawl and asked if I remembered it. I didn't. "You gave this to me one night when we were patrolling the neighborhood," she said. "I was cold, and you put it around my shoulders. You never did want it back. I've kept it all these years." I tried to remember and couldn't. But the friendship it represents weathers all change.

....

On an even more recent visit I discovered something that surprised me. If the Cuban Party couldn't change with the times, many of its members have been abandoning it. Some of my friends have resigned. Others simply drifted away. Still others, of younger generations, show no interest in joining. When I asked one young man I met if he is a member, he said, "Yes . . . but please don't think I'm dogmatic." He seemed almost embarrassed.

This would have been unheard of when I lived in Cuba. In the 1970s and for several decades thereafter, Party membership was an honor, something to which all revolutionaries aspired. I find it interesting that these friends, revolutionaries all, realize they may have to look within themselves, to each other, and to more innovative models for direction if they want to respond to the urgent questions of our times. One of the places where profound discussion takes place these days is in literature and the arts. Cuba's official press has rarely presented more than the party line, while poetry and novels play the role many hoped the media would fulfill.

I should also say that I myself have no easy answer to the complex issue of power. I am clear that the likelihood of its abuse in traditional governance is huge. We need new ways of designing our political and social relationships, new ways of looking at power and exercising it, and not only in Cuba. For a while some of us thought the Zapatistas in southern Mexico were waging an experiment that envisioned power in new ways—or, more accurately, old ways because they came from ancient concepts of collective power sharing. Their ideas produced interesting results at the grass-roots level but were never meant to be a state model and disappointed those who imagined they could be. At the same time, it is questionable that the United States enjoys a democracy. Movements like Black Lives Matter and #MeToo have made power abuse visible. Across the globe, revelations of decades of rape and coverup within another patriarchal structure, the Catholic Church, have exposed the misuse of power to a degree that's no longer possible to hide or ignore. The populist governments now sweeping the globe are terrifying. Control is always the name of the game.

The Cuban Revolution was made by young people with great vision and creativity. Inevitably, they aged. By the end of the twentieth century and beginning of the twenty-first century, most of the Cuban leadership was approaching old age, set in its ways and with ideas about life that were often outmoded. The exceptions had been Fidel, Che, Haydée Santamaría, Celia Sánchez,[8] Alfredo Guevara,[9] and a few others: men and women with an exceptional ability to see beyond their time and possessing the belief that people can and must exercise their own creativity. By the turn of the century most of those visionaries were gone. Some managed to leave institutions capable of carrying their ideas forward.[10] At the same time, many mid-level management types were more interested in claiming their small measure of power than in working for the collective.

Today, after sixty years of struggle, with so many setbacks and unmet goals, many Cubans are exhausted. Depending on their class origins, older people who remember what life was like before 1959 may still value a system rooted in greater aspirations of justice, in which necessities and opportunities have been made available across the board. Younger people, who never knew a time before the Revolution, are frustrated with setbacks, unresolved issues, and the slow pace of change. Many have emigrated, most to the United States, where they wonder why healthcare is so hard to come by or life in general doesn't resemble its depiction in Hollywood films.

One of the painful issues when I lived on the island was the gulf—practical as well as political and emotional—between those who stayed and those who chose to leave. An unhealthy, at times hysterical, resentment was aimed at the latter. Mobs would form in front of the houses of those emigrating. People shouted epithets and threw rotten eggs. Those leaving were considered deserters and called *gusanos* (worms). Their homes and property were confiscated. I witnessed many such humiliating demonstrations during the 1980 Mariel exodus.[11] My children and I were deeply affected by those *actos de repudio*, as they were called. We tried to avoid them but didn't feel we could speak up, except for Gregory, who at his university wrote an anonymous article that was posted on a bulletin board to try to calm the hysteria. That ugliness has shamed and haunted us.

In the face of such a phenomenon, it is all the more extraordinary that saner minds on both sides of the divide managed, finally, to reestablish the connection between Cubans living on the island and those in the diaspora. Much credit is due to a number of writers and artists who began meeting one another at international conferences. Journals and anthologies began appearing with work by those on both sides. Group art exhibitions began taking place. Musicians here and there began performing together. What linked these Cubans was so much stronger than what had torn them apart.

Slowly, with a great deal of effort and having to dispense with facile stereotypes, the pioneers launched meetings specifically aimed at healing the terrible rift. They were able to change rigid attitudes and confront the reality: those who stayed and those who left were all Cubans, a single, indissoluble Cuban family. *La isla entera* (the whole island) was the phrase that came into use.

When such important issues can be resolved through listening and seeing "the other" rather than by remaining entrenched in dogma, it bodes well for a relationship. And when we are speaking about a nation rather than individuals, it's immensely important to that nation's future. This ability on the part of Cubans to move in a direction of understanding rather than to stay locked in a stance of pseudo-patriotism on one side and bitterness on the other has been extraordinarily positive.

I have long believed that one of the Cuban Revolution's saving graces is the fact that, despite occasional dogmatic approaches and repressive periods, a great humanity underpins most initiatives. Often the simultaneous existence of parallel visions has meant that the healthier wins out. As Che Guevara famously said, "At the risk of seeming ridiculous, let me say that the true revolutionary is guided by a great feeling of love. It is impossible to think of a genuine revolutionary lacking this quality."

....

One of the unique privileges of living in Cuba during the 1970s was getting to know Haydée Santamaría and, through her, Casa de las Américas. Haydée was one of the great figures of the Revolution, one of two women who took part in its initial battle at Moncada and the only woman who participated in every one of the war's venues: the guerrilla struggle in the mountains, the city underground, and the overseas purchase of arms.[12] She was also an exceptional human being, who would have changed those around her no matter where she'd been born or at what time in history. There are a few men and women like that: absolutely ordinary and absolutely luminous. Their courage, depth, authenticity, and creativity defy place and time. Although she possessed the rare ability to connect with people of vastly different classes and cultures, Haydée was also profoundly Cuban. She couldn't abide hypocrisy, saw with an islander's eyes, had that special mix of salty and sweet one tastes in both *yucca al mojo de ajo* (yucca served in a sauce of lemon juice and garlic) and slow-cooked *ropa vieja* (beef flank cooked in broth for three or four hours with tomato, bell pepper, cumin, and other herbs until separated into strands and very tender).

The war took almost everything Haydée cherished and, although she lived with what was left for another twenty years, many said she was mad: crazed by loss and a ferocious determination to keep going. A frank demeanor and refusal to be co-opted in any way are always signs of strangeness to some. Haydée was small of physical stature and slightly bent, with the protruding breastbone typical of those who suffer from severe asthma and constantly struggle to breathe. She could embark on monologues that wandered for hours, always returning to her point of departure and leaving us realizing she'd taken us on an exceptional journey. She would fix you with her unwavering eyes, listen deeply, and you knew you were seen, understood.

After the war, Fidel gave Haydée a job that surprised many. He asked her to create and run an arts institution capable of breaking through the cultural blockade, as insidious and damaging as its diplomatic, economic, and military counterparts. That institution was Casa de las Américas. Those surprised by Fidel's choice may have wondered why he tapped a woman with a sixth-grade education and no experience dealing with artists and writers rather than one of the country's many prestigious artistic icons. It was, quite simply, a choice of genius.

Haydée educated herself quickly. She understood the idiosyncrasies of artists and artists everywhere adored her. She opened them—us—to new feelings and many discovered the Revolution through contact with her. Casa became one of the preeminent arts institutions in the Spanish-speaking world and exposed the Cuban people to the great artists and writers of the twentieth century.[13] This extraordinary woman also made sure Casa functioned in a truly horizontal way: embracing diversity, making use of interdisciplinarity, and setting the highest standards in every area. When she lived, she welcomed each year's literary-contest jurors by telling them not to make political choices but to judge the entries on artistic merit alone. Since her death, those who have taken her place deliver the same speech.

Haydée and I met on my first trip to Cuba in January 1967. Casa hosted the Encuentro con Rubén Darío and put its special imprint on that gathering of writers who came together to celebrate what would have been the hundredth birthday of the great Nicaraguan modernist poet.[14] The first time we conversed I knew I had found a mentor and a friend. We got to know one another better when I returned in 1968 and even better after I went to live there. In 1970 I was invited to be a judge in the poetry genre at Casa's literary contest. Soon after my arrival I began suffering from asthma, and Haydée initiated me into some of the secrets of dealing with the disease. We shared stories about our children and more than a few extraordinary moments. The night of her wake was one of the most painful of my life. I have written poems, essays, and a book about Haydée.[15] With all that, she remains elusive; words invariably fall short.

But Casa de las Américas is Haydée's enduring legacy and getting to know her also provided me with an ongoing connection to that institution, which—like a half-dozen others—is what I think of when I imagine what real revolution can be. Not the revolution of slogans, or even that of the complicated promise of social change, but the revolution that says no in the face of exclusion, rejects pseudo-solutions and embraces risk, and teaches by example so that each new generation of Casa workers continues to honor democratic principles as it discovers innovative ways to put into practice what its founder envisioned. Almost four decades after Haydée's death, you still feel her presence the moment you pass through the institution's doors.

The women and men who work at Casa encourage and collaborate with each other's work. For sixty years they have sustained a vast publishing program; promoted the visual arts, theater, and music; put out several excellent journals whose unbroken periodicity traces a history of creativity and cultural analysis; created one of the great literary libraries on the continent; and spotlighted younger generations of creative minds. All under the most difficult of economic conditions and all with an energy that has never ceased to amaze me. In 2011 I was once again invited to judge Casa's yearly literary contest, this time in oral history. I have published often in *Revista Casa* and my work with the older generation, those immediate inheritors of Haydée's wisdom, helps keep me grounded in the knowledge that true revolution can survive the terrible detours and disappointments we've faced in recent times.

Within the constraints and difficulties of creating profound social change, the existence of a place such as Casa stretches the possibilities of revolution, makes them bigger, more complex, and daring. This is particularly important in the cultural arena. Today there are Cuban publishers, theater groups, musical ensembles, and museums that, inspired by Casa, move in many exciting directions. They are the country's best insurance against dogma, rigidity, and ossification.[16]

....

Cuba in the 1970s wasn't only Cuba. It was Latin America. An island became a world. During the time I lived in Havana I had important relationships with members of a number of Latin American revolutionary movements, African liberation organizations, and North Vietnamese, Chinese, and even North Korean immigrants. With the latter two, it mostly meant being invited to embassy receptions. With the Vietnamese and Latin Americans, our contacts were closer and much more meaningful.

These relationships were part of the Cuban experience. I couldn't have had them anywhere else. It was a common sight to see young Vietnamese students—always dressed modestly in dark pants and white shirts, the girls with their long black braids—walking Havana's streets. News of their struggles wasn't limited to newspaper articles; we heard about them from the people involved. Gregory's study group at the university included students from Laos, the Soviet Union, Palestine, Namibia, and Guatemala.

The Cuban Revolution took in hundreds of comrades from other countries. Its hospitality went above and beyond. Some took refuge on the island after prisoner exchanges. Some came for guerrilla training. Some arrived for long hospital or rehabilitation stays, healing from torture or battle wounds. These relationships taught me, changed me, provided an insider view I could not have obtained from reading or hearsay.

Particularly important in this respect was Phuc, a gentle man in his early fifties who was head of the Voice of Vietnam, a daily series of twenty-minute shortwave radio segments the Cubans gave the North Vietnamese until the end of the war. These broadcasts allowed the Vietnamese to speak directly to listeners in the United States, and Phuc wanted to grasp US street lingo, a language as accessible as possible to those to whom they were speaking. For this he sought English lessons and, judging my English "the most commonplace" as he put it, chose me as his teacher. Because the phonetics of his name sounded like "fuck" in English, most people called him Fernando.

Three times a week I would go to Phuc's apartment in the massive V-shaped Focsa building just around the corner from where we lived. Our classes lasted an hour or so, and, of course, we talked about what was going on in his country, how the war was progressing, the terrible hardships and creative solutions. Phuc's wife commanded a couple of anti-aircraft guns in Hanoi. I vividly remember one class after a bombing raid by US planes. Phuc sketched his wife's position on a page in his grammar notebook, indicating with relief that the destruction had only reached the far side of the block.

It was Phuc who helped me prepare for my 1974 visit to North Vietnam, during which I traveled the length of the north and spent a few days in the liberated territory of Quang Tri just below the 17th Parallel. I had been invited by the Association of North Vietnamese Women. I had so many questions about what to expect, the weather, what I should ask to see, what he thought I might bring to my hosts. Because his English wasn't as good as I thought, when I asked the latter question, he became confused. He explained there was a marvelous fish sauce, the best of them all, available only on an island off the country's southern coast. I could pick up a bottle at a small specialty shop in Paris.

I followed my student's instructions and delivered the fish sauce to the women who met my plane. They thanked me politely. But when I returned to Cuba, Phuc seemed perplexed. Finally, two or three lessons later, he shyly asked if I had forgotten his fish sauce; it was he who longed for that delicacy! When I told him I'd given it to my hosts he laughed. "Can you imagine," he

Quang Tri, just below the 17th Parallel, South Vietnam, 1974 (photo by Margaret Randall).

said, "that guerrillas capable of digging hundreds of miles of tunnels beneath US military bases, who ride along overgrown jungle paths with 100-pound loads on their bicycles, can't manage to get their hands on fish sauce produced in the South?" No, he had been waiting for the gift he thought I'd promised him.

Another important work trip I made while living in Cuba was to Peru in the fall of 1973. The Pinochet coup had just overthrown Chile's Popular Unity government, and refugees were streaming across the border that separated the two countries. In Peru, a military man with socialist leanings named Juan Velasco Alvarado was president.[17] The new government invited experts to help determine what needed to be done in order to promote effective social change and I was asked by the United Nations' International Labor Office to work for three months at a research center. I was based in Lima but traveled the country interviewing women, listening to their needs and making recommendations.

Velasco Alvarado's tenure was cut short when rightists began resisting the changes he was making, and the president himself was taken ill. In Latin American history that experience hasn't received the attention it deserves.

Most Communists only trusted Marxist experiments, socialists favored those that followed democratic socialism, liberation theologians were interested in initiatives organized through the Christian base communities, and indigenous movements cultivated ancient traditions. Crossover experiences or those that couldn't be so neatly catalogued didn't always get their due. Sectarianism has long been a scourge on the left.

Peru is a beautiful country with ancient cultures alive in its Inca and other ruins, along with breathtaking designs like the Nazca Lines that you can only see from the sky. But what surfaces in my memory are some of the people I met. Alba Vanni rescued me from a depressing room at the boarding house where I landed and invited me to come to live in her small apartment during those three months; she became a lifelong friend. Hilda Gadea and I met up in Lima a few days after my arrival. We were trying to get across the city to a press conference given by Chilean refugees, but the streets were blocked by throngs of the devout celebrating the purple-draped Cristo Morado. Hilda said this demonstrated that no Latin American revolution would be successful without the support of the Church. Soon that brilliant woman would be dead of cancer, but I have often revisited her prediction. Today a resurgence of evangelical influence accompanies and promotes authoritarian regimes. The important anthropologist Stefano Varese accompanied me to the Amazon jungle; he too became a mentor and friend. We reconnected in Cuba in 2011 when both of us were invited to judge the Casa de las Américas literary contest. Zenildo Barreto was a Brazilian revolutionary making his way back home after years of exile in Europe; we too developed an important friendship. I've forgotten the names of some of the other men and women I got to know in Peru, but their faces remain.

Most of the revolutionaries I met in Cuba were Latin Americans. In 1973 I already knew the United Nations would declare 1975 the Year of the Woman. I had gotten to know some of the Nicaraguans who told me about their long struggle. I thought if I wrote a book about a woman in the Sandinista National Liberation Front (FSLN, in its Spanish acronym), it might be a way of introducing the world to what was going on in that Central American country.

My Nicaraguan friends liked the idea and suggested I interview Doris Tijerino, one of the organization's first female combatants, who was in Cuba at the time. She had come for military training but, discovering she was pregnant, had to delay taking the course. Doris and I ended up talking every day for the better part of a year. Her life was fascinating and would become tragically dramatic about halfway through our collaboration when she received news that the comrade whose child she was carrying had been captured and assassinated.[18] Stoically, Doris continued telling me her story.

I entered my book in the oral history category of the following year's Casa de las Américas contest, but it didn't win. Later it was published in Mexico.[19] Doris had given birth by then and had slipped back into her country to rejoin the struggle but was captured in a matter of days. My mother dropped everything in order to translate the book into English; we hoped an edition in that language would draw international attention to her case and prevent the Guard from killing her. The FSLN had a better plan, though. It staged a major operation, taking dozens of hostages it was able to exchange for prisoners, Doris among the latter.

When I think back to some of the revolutionaries I knew—just as was true of the New York artists and Mexican writers and intellectuals who had such a profound impact on my life—I realize what a privilege it was to have been able to interact with men and women who wanted nothing less than to change the world. They challenged and stimulated me. They also taught me that great things are done by ordinary people with the courage to move beyond conventional limitations.

Carlos Fonseca, one of the founders of FSLN, visited our apartment from time to time. He was tall for a Central American, with piercing myopic blue eyes and thick glasses. He was also extremely serious and seemed interested in one thing only: his country's history. I remember an afternoon when he showed up with his son and daughter, who sat politely on our couch while their father shared with me his excitement at a letter that he'd just discovered at Havana's José Martí library.

The letter had been written by Rigoberto López Pérez, the young revolutionary who assassinated longtime Nicaraguan dictator Anastasio Somoza García on September 21, 1956. López Pérez was gunned down by Somoza García's personal guard seconds after his brave action. Carlos was ecstatic at having found this document, written by the young man to his mother the night before he carried out his plan. López Pérez clearly knew he would die in the assassination attempt and wrote his farewell letter in the past tense, closing with the phrase "Your son who loved you very much." It was this detail that moved Carlos so.

José Benito Escobar, whom I knew as Alvaro, became a close friend. Like Carlos and so many others, he died before the Sandinistas triumphed in July 1979. My last image of him was struggling up the nine flights to our apartment—the elevator was broken as was often the case—with two mattresses balanced on his head. Our children's beds were in bad shape, and he'd gotten those mattresses at a shop for foreigners to which he had access. Knowing he would soon be returning to Nicaragua, they were his farewell gift.

After the 1979 victory, the revolutionary union movement was named for José Benito. When I went to live in Nicaragua, I visited a woman named Doña Leandra in Estelí. I had been told that José Benito was hiding in her home the day he died. She took me a few blocks away to where he'd been gunned down. As I prepared to take pictures, a group of neighborhood children clustered around the commemorative cross that marked the spot. Doña Leandra told me that José Benito had bought an ice cream cone for her son just before he was called to the place where he met his death. She later found it melted on the table beside the boy's bed.

For a while Jaime Wheelock and his first wife, Gladys Zalaquett, stayed near us at the Hotel Nacional. Jaime is an economist and was a member of the FSLN's National Directorate who later oversaw the Sandinista Revolution's program of land reform. Gladys is Chilean. She and I remain good friends to this day. I remember asking Jaime why he'd chosen such an English-sounding war name. He laughed and told me it was the one he'd been given at birth. For whatever reason, he never used an alias. One day Jaime and Gladys found a stray kitten and brought it to our kids. They carefully clipped its nails, but Ana was afraid of it and they had to find the small furry bundle another home.

With a Nicaraguan comrade I knew only as Mauro, I made the rounds of Cuban workplaces and schools to publicize the Sandinista cause. When I arrived in Nicaragua just after the victory I wondered if he had survived. I didn't know his real name, so it wasn't easy to ask around. In the fall of 1979 Carlos Fonseca's body was brought down from the mountainous region where he died to Managua for burial. I spent the night before at the wake. Suddenly I felt someone embrace me from behind. He put his hands over my eyes and asked, "Guess who?" It was Mauro, whose real name was Jacinto Suárez. Several years later he would play a role in the FSLN's brief repression of homosexuals. It was something about which he would come to feel profoundly ashamed.

The Ortega brothers—Humberto and Daniel—also occasionally came to visit our Havana apartment. Daniel was a man of few words. I could not have imagined that decades later he and his wife, Rosario Murillo, would turn what began as a beautiful revolutionary experiment into a vicious autocracy. After I moved to Nicaragua, I worked with Rosario at the Sandinista Cultural Workers Association for close to a year. I have never observed a more mean-spirited

Where José Benito
died, Estelí, Nicaragua,
1989 (photo by
Margaret Randall).

person. She seemed to enjoy humiliating colleagues and strangers alike. Her behavior foreshadowed what was to come when Ortega won Nicaragua's 2007 presidential election and soon after named her vice president. The couple's cold and calculating criminality was already evident in 1998, when her daughter Zoilamérica publicly accused Daniel of having sexually abused her for nineteen years, starting at the age of eleven. Rosario did not hesitate to side with her husband, effectively cutting her daughter out of the family.[20]

I got to know several Brazilian revolutionaries, some also in Cuba as a result of the prisoner exchanges of those years. One was Fernando Gabeira, who had played a role in kidnapping US ambassador Charles Burke Elbrick in 1969. The operation was successful and Gabeira's organization, the October 8th Revolutionary Movement (MR-8), obtained the release of fifteen political prisoners in exchange for the ambassador's life. I remember Gabeira being quite critical of the title of a poem I'd written at the time. I called it "I Am Attica." He felt it was presumptuous of me to imagine myself as one of the Attica inmates. I deeply identified with the protest of those brave men and kept my title. Gabeira eventually returned to his native Brazil where he successfully ran for parliament in 1995. Later in life he became a kind of guru of one of the New Age movements that began gaining so many fanatics in all our countries.

Some of these friendships were characterized by a kind of poignancy I find hard to revisit in these very different times. I got to know a woman combatant from Bolivia. She was always embroidering, like others might knit or engage in some other handicraft while conversing. Someone had sent me a length of denim I'd made into a skirt. I asked this woman—whose name I no longer remember—if she would embroider a quetzal bird above the hem. She was happy to oblige but was called back to the front before she could finish it. For years I wore that skirt with its unfinished bird and wondered if my friend was still alive.

In Cuba I knew revolutionaries from Nicaragua, the Dominican Republic, Chile, Guatemala, Puerto Rico, Angola, and Laos. Uruguayan Tupamaros could be seen in Cuba then; their heroic and highly creative actions were well known and deeply admired. Cuban construction workers involved in the micro brigades used the Tupamaro T on their helmets as a way of honoring those comrades who seemed magical in their ability to avoid capture—until they no longer could.

One of my closest friends was Roque Dalton from El Salvador. I'd met the poet years before, when he showed up at our 1964 Encuentro de Poetas in

Mexico. He and his family went to live in Cuba around the same time we did. His sons were close in age to Gregory, and one of them had a crush on Sarah. Roque and I were poetry judges together at the Casa de las Américas literary contest of 1970.[21] He also helped me confront the difficult task of translating a few poems from César Vallejo's *Poemas humanos*. I had translated during the *El Corno* years, but working on Vallejo was my introduction to a deeper level of the art.

Roque returned to his country to fight and was murdered by members of his own revolutionary organization, the Ejército Revolucionario del Pueblo, on May 10, 1975. I remember getting the call from my good friend, the Mexican poet Thelma Nava. She wanted to know if it was true. Perhaps we had access to more accurate information in Cuba. I immediately called Aida, Roque's wife—suddenly widowed. I couldn't tell from her response if I was the first to give her the terrible news. Roque was one of the great poets of his generation. A few years back I had breakfast with his son Jorge in El Salvador, and we reminisced about his father's time in Cuba. Another son, Roque Jr., also died fighting for his country's liberation. His body was never recovered.

Robert and I separated five years after our arrival in Cuba, and a year or so later he returned to the United States. During my last few years in the country I lived with the poet and musician Antonio Castro. Born in Colombia, while still young he had migrated with his family to Venezuela; a younger brother died of hunger on that march. Antonio had joined the Venezuelan Movement of the Revolutionary Left (MIR),[22] spent time in prison, had been released, and then came to Cuba to care for another member of that organization, Domingo León. Domingo had been paralyzed from the waist down in a guerrilla operation. Antonio tended to his wounds and did much else to make his life as comfortable as possible. He also filled our home with music—singing and playing the *cuatro*, a four-stringed rhythm instrument popular in both Venezuela and Colombia. He and I made many trips together, reading poetry in factories, schools, and peasant communities.

....

ANTONIO'S RICE

It was plain white rice, scant ration of salt
to move us on. Cuba, the revolution's glory years
and still we had five pounds a month, a lot

Poets at metallurgical factory, Manzanillo, 1978. Left to right, in forefront: Bladimir Zamora, Antonio Castro, the author, and Angel Peña (attribution unknown).

you'll say, but think of it there on the plate
with nothing adorning its size.

He served it up in little mounds, formed by
filling one light green plastic coffee cup
then inverting its equity before each patient fork.
An egg or some *butifarra* (hot dog–like sausage,
occasional treat) if things were good,

a ladle full of split pea soup if they were not.
How we joked about those split peas,
chícharos in every possible disguise.
Boil and throw the water out, boil again
and throw out the water, and again and again

until the punch line telling you to throw out
the peas. And also the pot.
Carmen whispered that version one early dawn

as we patrolled the block, arms swinging in unison,
collars raised against cold sea air.

Women keeping our neighborhood safe against crime,
invasion, or loneliness,
whatever threatened that nation
of spent cooks. Tomato sauce without tomatoes.
Marmalade made from boiling the mango skins.

Those hours the recipes came—an endless volley
against the dark sea wall, back and forth
between neighbors struggling to stay awake.
Antonio's rice was the stalwart,
the sure thing,
guaranteed to bring that beautiful fairness
into our home.

Toward the end of my time in Cuba, I worked closely with comrades from
the Chilean MIR, an armed struggle organization that had not been part of
the coalition that put Salvador Allende in office but had supported its short-
lived government.[23] Some of them were women who had survived torture in
Pinochet's prisons, and they wanted my help in writing a book that would
describe how they'd managed to do so. It was important and meaningful
work. Soon, though, we realized that the testimonies gave too much away.
Why would we reveal techniques that could still be useful in the long struggle
ahead? The project was scrapped but I'll always remember some of the friendships it gave me.

These relationships and others were part of the Cuban experience. Because
of the Revolution's extraordinary solidarity with a range of liberation movements, I came to know people I would otherwise never have met. I learned
firsthand about their struggles and about a sort of sacrifice that seems unreal
today. I was also continuously discovering the numerous ways in which Cuba
extended solidarity to people around the world: not only by receiving revolutionaries but also by taking in thousands of refugees when projects failed, for
example, after the Chilean coup of 1973. Cuba gave them housing and work,
educated their children, and tried to heal their emotional as well as physical
wounds.

In 1975 hundreds of Cubans went to fight in Angola and Namibia, where
they helped secure those nations' freedom and put an end to South African

apartheid. Because Cuba had been settled by African slaves, it considered that great gesture the repayment of a centuries-long debt. People begged to go and resented it if judged unfit. In more recent years, legions of Cuban doctors, teachers, and others have deployed throughout the world, often in conditions in which a country's own professionals refuse to work.

I have never known another country, especially one as small and poor as Cuba, that does more for those who need its help. The Cuban Revolution sees this as an important part of its own program of social change. This has been true even when the Cuban people themselves might not be enthusiastic about a particular gesture of generosity, such as when the Party decided to send a shipload of sugar to Chile at a time when sugar rations on the island were severely limited. I finally wrote the story of that multifaceted aid in my book *Exporting Revolution: Cuba's Global Solidarity.*[24]

....

During my last two years in Cuba I decided I wanted to learn photography. My desire may have had something to do with my search for a language that was neither English, my native tongue, which, during my years in Latin America, I could rarely share with those closest to me, nor Spanish, a language I spoke with family and friends but one in which I had never been able to write poetry. I chose as my mentor a fine Cuban photographer, Ramón Martínez Grandal. He was loud and opinionated, gentle and loyal, and an exceptional teacher.

Our apartment had once had a maid's room and bath, and it was the latter that we turned into our makeshift darkroom. There was no door, so we hung a sheet and worked late at night when the lights of the city were dim. We had no room for much in that tiny cubicle and there was no running water. We washed our prints in the corrugated stone wash tub on our service porch. That is, when we had water.

And water wasn't all we lacked. In the Havana of those years it wasn't possible to walk into a store and buy yellow envelopes of powders to which one only need add the liquid to make developer or fixer. We found our raw chemicals at compound pharmacies. Once in a while we were lucky enough to locate a gallon amber bottle in which to store developer; when we did, we cherished it. It was impossible to come by film or photographic paper, and while others asked visitors for worn Levi's or deodorant, I begged them to bring me paper. A friend at the Cuban film industry gave us the tail ends of 35-millimeter newsreel film we cut into rolls. I also remember going out to

Photographers, left to right: Grandal, Macías, the author with baby Kelly, Tito Alvarez, Gilda, Rigoberto Rodríguez and wife, Leticia, Havana, 1978 (family snapshot, attribution unknown).

shoot without film in my camera and coming back to tell Grandal about the pictures I'd "taken."

Soon we were a small group shooting and printing and washing and drying our images. Rigoberto Rodríguez, a man we referred to simply as Macías, and an older man named Tito Alvarez frequented the apartment. Raul Corrales came around from time to time; his picture of a young rebel soldier asleep on a cot in the elegant home of a bourgeois family that had abandoned the island remains one of my favorites from those years. The soldier's semiautomatic rifle sits atop a piece of period furniture, a classical painting in an ornate frame hanging above it. Grandal's wife, Gilda, apprenticed with me and became a fine photographer in her own right.

I've always learned best by watching. Standing beside my mentor, I quickly acquired the rudimentary skills I needed to make my pictures. When we had paper, after a few hours' work I'd lay my prints out to dry on our large dining room table. Grandal would study and critique them. He was surprised I learned as fast as I did. When I took off for Nicaragua, he asked if I wanted to send my undeveloped rolls back to him and said he would prepare my negatives. He told me he didn't want me to ruin any of my unrepeatable images. I was incensed that he didn't believe I would be able to do the work myself and rejected his offer.

Years after I left Cuba, Grandal, Gilda, and their daughter Kelly emigrated from Cuba to Venezuela, briefly back to Cuba, and then to Caracas again. Grandal was always restless. When Venezuela became too violent, they moved to Miami, where they had to begin yet another life, this one with a new language in the mix. Theirs was the lot of most immigrants: new horizons always promised better things to come and unforeseen problems invariably arose.

The Cubans never stopped valuing Grandal's art and offered him frequent shows. I always wondered why the family hadn't stayed on the island, but there's no accounting for the things that made that impossible for them. Grandal died in that Florida city in September 2017. I will always be grateful for what I learned at his side.

....

Because I am a poet, the cultural milieu is what I know best—in Cuba and everywhere I've lived. From the beginning, the Cuban Revolution made culture and the arts priorities. Following the literacy campaign, publishing was subsidized, and books can still be purchased for pennies. Concerts, theatrical performances, art exhibitions, and poetry readings are free and attended by those from every region of the country and all walks of life. Young people are also encouraged to become artists; art and music schools exist in every province. Cuba's revolutionary process encouraged explosions of creativity in many genres. Despite periods of repression, creation rather than censorship was what characterized the period in which I lived in the country.

It is true that the arts have suffered periods of repression in revolutionary Cuba. Early measures against homosexuals decimated important theater groups. Books by writers considered "deviant" or who differed with the Revolution's ideology weren't published for a while. The worst of this repression took place in the early 1970s, a time since referred to as *El quinquenio gris* (the five gray years). Retrograde minds managed to take control of culture and many creative people were their victims.

The incident most publicized outside the country at the time was the arrest, so-called confession, and subsequent emigration of dissident poet Heberto Padilla.[25] The "Padilla affair," as it came to be known, elicited a variety of responses from the international intellectual community. A group of well-known writers initially condemned it, then several decided they didn't really know enough about the circumstances involved and changed their minds. I initially supported the Revolution's actions against Padilla but have since come to believe they were a mistake.

Just as in the era of Prohibition in the United States, when society forbids a practice or censors a person or body of work, it ultimately succeeds in creating curiosity, interest, and fabricated need beyond the impact that practice or work would have garnered without the added attention. Padilla was a good but far from extraordinary poet who gained an extra measure of fame out of the contrived turmoil. One more flash point for the right's exaggerated defense and the left's exaggerated attack.

In 1976 the Revolution put an end to the *quinquenio gris* by establishing a Ministry of Culture and putting Armando Hart in charge. Hart was a man of great learning and sensitivity. He wasted no time rehabilitating those who had suffered and supporting all the arts. From then to the present, despite occasional ups and downs, there has been a palpable freedom of artistic expression in Cuba. Abel Prieto succeeded Hart, continuing his policies. Wrongs had been righted, but no public discussion of the repression had yet taken place.

In 2007 a series of coincidences caused a number of poets to wonder if another repressive period might be forthcoming. Concerned, they went to see Prieto. He assured them this wasn't the case, but they demanded public forums in which those previously affected could tell their stories. Writers, critics, visual artists, musicians, architects, and others analyzed the 1970s repression: how it had happened and why it must not be allowed to happen again. I and many others have written about this important exploration.[26]

Like many Cubans, I suffered repression during my last years in the country. Perhaps because I was a foreigner, the contours of what happened to me were blurred. I was fired from my job but continued to receive my salary. Some venues ignored me while others published what I wrote. I went from official to official, unsuccessfully trying to find out why I was being targeted. Some friends avoided our apartment and others continued to come around. Embarrassment and fear made it hard to talk about any of this; much later I learned that others had suffered similarly, but at the time I felt isolated and alone. Gregory, old enough to understand what I was going through, begged me to leave the country, something I refused to do until I received an explanation for what had happened to me. When I did, I moved on to Nicaragua.

Only very recently, forty years after this event, have I come to know the details of what was at stake for some of my friends back then. I will end this chapter by describing what I learned in the spring of 2018. The scene is Matanzas, a city some two hours east of Havana. Each February a big book fair takes place in the country's capital. Then, over the next few months, it moves eastward from province to province, until every major Cuban city experiences its local celebration of books and authors, foreign as well as native. Cubans continue to be avid readers, and these weeklong events are exuberant. Matanzas hosts the first of these provincial fairs.

In March 2018 my son and I were invited to be guests at the Matanzas Book Fair. My Cuban memoir had been published the year before and Gregory's appeared that year, both from publishing houses in the province. Those responsible for the editions are among Cuba's most steadfast preservers of artistic integrity. Today their work receives major national awards and they make a broad range of authors available to a Cuban readership. But they also defended freedom of expression back when that was much more difficult. I am proud to count them among my close friends.

One afternoon a panel discussion was announced at a local café. Gregory and I were both scheduled to participate. When we arrived, the place was full. The other participants were novelist and critic Arturo Arango and poet Víctor Rodríguez Núñez, both of whom had been among the young writers who'd frequented my apartment in the 1970s when they were just beginning their university careers. We have remained close all these years. Arturo lives in Cuba, where he has become a cultural reference. Years ago, Víctor went to the United States for his masters and doctoral degrees and ended up teaching at Kenyon College in Ohio. He divides his time between the United States and Cuba, maintaining an apartment in Old Havana. He has become an internationally known poet, winning some of the most coveted literary prizes in the Spanish language.

In the 1970s Víctor and Arturo were young and just starting out. They were part of a tightly knit group that for several years gathered almost nightly at our home. Others in that group included Norberto Codina, Bladimir Zamora, Alex Fleites, and Leonardo Padura, many of whom are well-known Cuban writers today. There they met some of the great thinkers and writers who came and went, among them Nicaraguan Ernesto Cardenal; Salvadorans Roque Dalton and Claribel Alegría; Argentineans Julio Cortázar and Juan Gelman; Uruguayans Mario Benedetti, Eduardo Galeano, and Pablo Carlevaro; Mexicans Efraín Huerta, Thelma Nava, Arnaldo Orfila, and Laurette Séjourné; and many others whose names I no longer remember.

Our discussions ranged far and wide. We established a Saturday morning writing workshop that met in a corner of the University of Havana campus we called *El rincón de los cabezones* because it was bordered by statues of illustrious figures with oversized heads. After Roque's death we named our workshop El Taller Roque Dalton. There, and also at the nightly salons in my apartment we read to one another, criticized each other's work, and grew. Often singer/songwriters from the incipient *Nueva trova* (New Song Movement) enlivened those evenings with their music.

Those were memorable times, and they shaped everyone involved. After the repression hit, Arturo and Víctor never failed to show up. But it was only at that panel in Matanzas, in March 2018, that I learned the backstory of their unbroken friendship and support. The subject of the panel was something like "Creative Process," and when the Cuban writers began to speak, they revealed that the head of their Union of Young Communists chapter at the university had called them in one day and told them they must not continue to visit me. I'm not sure what the accusation was, but I was obviously considered persona non grata and contact with me could be dangerous. It may have been my feminism and independence of thought, or that some of the writers and political people I hosted held views that differed from Cuba's political line.[27]

Whatever the reason, Arturo and Víctor said the directive was clear. And the implication of disobeying as well. They might have been expelled from the Young Communists—a disgrace at the time—or even from the university. They risked forfeiting their careers. I don't know if those young students said they were going to continue to visit me, or simply did so. They can't remember either. I never knew of the dilemma until that panel. Neither of them was ousted from either the Union of Young Communists or, of course, the university. But I am sure more submissive young men would have given in to the demand. Arturo and Víctor's decision was rewarded by what they have often said was the valuable education they got at my home from contact with a broad range of creative minds—in fact, some of the greatest creative minds of those times. It was also rewarded, of course, by our lifelong friendship.

The Cuban Revolution has weathered shameful repressive periods and come out on the side of freedom. It hasn't been an easy or straightforward journey and the power struggles have taken their toll. It's required a great deal of courage on the part of those I think of as the true revolutionaries to stand up to official pressure and mediocrity.

Now these stories could be told, and they were being told at a public session with an audience of mostly young people, unaware of what their older colleagues had to go through to create a world where difference is honored. My cheeks were wet with tears when that panel ended. So were Gregory's.

....

My life took one more significant turn before I left Cuba for good. During my years on the island I had lived without a passport; I was a woman without a country, so to speak. When I needed to travel, I'd done so on a provisional Cuban travel document. When they invited me to Nicaragua, the Sandinistas offered me a Nicaraguan passport. I was about to accept it when I noticed a small article in the Cuban newspaper: a Mexican ambassador by the name of Gonzalo Martínez Corbalá had just presented his credentials to the Cuban authorities.

A few years before, I had gone to see the previous Mexican ambassador in an attempt to get my passport back. By then all participants of 1968 who had survived were out of prison, home from exile, and some even held government positions. I thought it was time for me to clear up my situation. That ambassador mocked the story of how I'd gotten out of Mexico and refused to help. But now a new ambassador had taken his place, and I recognized his name.

Martínez Corbalá had been one of two ambassadors who'd acted with great courage during the Pinochet takeover in Chile. The other was from Sweden. Both men had received hundreds of Chilean revolutionaries in their embassies and, as each was given safe passage to a country that would take him or her in, they'd accompanied them to the airport to make sure they got out safely. The names of these men were writ large in the resistance of those years.

I called the new ambassador's office and asked for an appointment. He received me the following morning. When I told him my story, he not only believed me but also said there was no reason why I shouldn't have my rightful document back. He instructed me to come back the next day with passport photos and pick it up. And so, when I left Cuba for Nicaragua, I was able to do so with a legal Mexican passport, the one that had been taken from me so many years before.

In 2017 I got the news that Martínez Corbalá had died. Although our personal contact had been brief, he'd played a decisive role in my life. I mourned him like a friend.

....

WHEN JUSTICE FELT AT HOME

Something has changed.
Only old friends,

those who shared split peas
and white rice
on sweltering Havana nights
still call me *compañera*:
sweet designation
meaning comrade or friend
lover or familiar
in those luminous days
when justice felt at home
in our desire.

Now, more often than not,
it's *señora*:
regression to a prehistory
when married or single
young or old
mattered most.

Still, compañera and compañero
are indelibly embossed
on the swaying trunks of Royal Palms,
in Sierra Maestra granite
and along the dissembling coastline
of an Island that still shouts freedom
into gale-force winds.

Chapter Eight

VOLCANO

Nicaragua, 1980–1984

I witnessed and was involved in the realization of great deeds. I lived
through the gestation and birth of a revolution brought by the flesh,
blood, and will of a nation. I watched masses of people celebrate
the end of a forty-five-year dictatorship. I felt the thrilling release of
energy that comes from daring to defy fear and the survival instinct,
in the name of a goal that transcends self-interest. I cried a lot, but
I laughed a lot too. I discovered the joy that comes from surrender-
ing the "I" and embracing the "we." These days when cynicism
abounds, when we easily become dismayed, lose faith, and renounce
dreams, I write down these memories in defense of the kind of happiness that makes life—and even death—worthwhile.
—GIOCONDA BELLI, *THE COUNTRY UNDER MY SKIN*

About twenty kilometers south of Managua, the Masaya volcano reaches for
the sky. It is one of nineteen that dot the map of the Central American country, several of which erupt from time to time and then return to dormancy,
waiting in silence before unexpectedly becoming active once more.

Among Masaya's craters, Santiago is the most turbulent. During my first
weeks in the country I went there several times, compelled by my fascination
with that open wound in the earth. Jaime, the driver I'd been assigned by the
Ministry of Culture, and I would wind our way up the narrow road through
Nicaragua's first officially designated national park. Reality hardly lived up to
the designation since there was little if any visible improvement other than a
restroom that seemed never to have been cleaned and a rickety fence meant to
prevent visitors from climbing down into the crater's mouth.

Volcanoes came to symbolize Central America for me: a dramatic, sometimes violent string of cones running the length of that narrow strip of land linking North and South America. Their turbulence reminded me of the region's history of social and political turmoil, much of it the result of US interference and people's response to that interference. And, indeed, during my years in Nicaragua I heard many stories of ominous rumblings or blankets of black dust descending upon a city overnight and disrupting people's lives.

I was mesmerized by the bright orange sea of fiery magma tossing and turning in Santiago's depths. It was like gazing into Earth's ever-changing interior: fire heaving and swelling hundreds of feet below the rim. I'd heard stories of Sandinista prisoners having been thrown into that crater. I could only hope they'd been dead by the time they were dragged from the dictatorship's torture chambers and their bodies dropped from helicopters or planes.

Yet when I returned to Nicaragua with my wife, Barbara, in 1992 and took her out to see the mass of swirling magma that had so intrigued me when I'd lived there, Santiago was sleeping profoundly. Only a crust of bleak earth met us when we reached the volcano's lip.

....

Although closer in real time, I am finding it much more difficult to write about my years in Nicaragua than about those in New York, Mexico, Cuba, or even my childhood and adolescence. I remember generalities but few details. It may be that the posttraumatic stress I still experience as a result of the beginning of the Contra war has erased some recall. For years I dreamed about young rebels in their simple pine coffins. One of the first things I did when I got to Nicaragua was help dig up and move the bodies of combatants hastily buried without coffins during the war's last months and transfer them to proper graves. One of the last things I did before leaving the country was photograph the bodies of young combatants killed in the Contra war. It's taken me months to overcome what presented itself as a sort of writer's block and pen the following observations of my years with the Sandinistas.

It helped to begin with the images that engraved themselves on my eyes: Managua's main thoroughfares, called *pistas*, that were made of hexagonal paving stones. The rebels, when they brought the war to the cities, dug up those pavers and used them to build barricades. In the late afternoons, thousands of swallows lifted off those *pistas*, a sight of which I never tired.

Taste is another reference. I came to associate my years there with the country's large, flat tamales—moist corn masa with a bit of pork wrapped in banana leaves—and a gritty maiz-based drink served in carved wooden gourds. Nicaragua is corn country, much as wheat defines more northern lands. When, early in the Revolution, in one of its several efforts to hurt the country economically, the United States cut off its shipments of wheat, the Ministry of Culture launched an effective campaign to raise people's appreciation of corn. The slogan we used was *El maíz: Nuestra raíz!* (Corn is our tradition!). I remember we produced a cookbook with hundreds of recipes based on using the native grain.

Curiously, when I evoke my first months in the Central American country my memories surface in present tense, a living continuum. This is typical of places in which culture is deeply embedded in everyday life. Nicaragua's Christian culture is decidedly Marianist, the Virgin Mary as familiar as a mother.[1] It is early December and I am making the rounds of my neighborhood, visiting the small altars in honor of the Virgin. In several of her representations she is wearing the red and black Sandinista neckerchief, displaying a religious/political syncretism unique to that place and time. Or perhaps I am attending Sunday Mass at one of the city's liberation theology parishes; the congregation is belting out Carlos Mejía Godoy's *Misa Campesina* (Peasant Mass). Everyone knows the words.[2]

....

Nicaragua's Somoza dictatorship was one of several on the continent in which corruption and terror had become deeply entrenched. The Somoza family had burdened the country with a dynasty of tyrants for several generations, all funded and supported by a succession of US administrations. The United States had even imposed one of its own citizens as president of the Central American country (William Walker, 1856–1857). Franklin Roosevelt had famously said of Somoza García, father of the final Somoza, that "he may be a son of a bitch but he's our son of a bitch." During Anastasio Somoza's last years, simply being young meant one was likely to be captured, imprisoned, and tortured—or worse. As the Sandinistas organized and consolidated their struggle, Nicaraguans from all walks of life joined them.

In Cuba we followed the Sandinistas' final offensive like we were keeping track of family. On July 19, 1979, Cubans rejoiced as if the victory was theirs. All my Nicaraguan friends had long since left the island and gone home to fight. Some had died before they could see success, but I imagined

Young girl with nail file, pen, and rifle, "Somewhere in Nicaragua," 1979 (photo by Margaret Randall).

others taking part in the progressive occupations of cities and towns as they completed the last months of fighting and marched jubilantly into Managua. When Somoza and his circle fled, it felt like a repeat of Batista's escape from Cuba twenty years before. In the television coverage, I searched for familiar faces.

It wasn't long before Daisy Zamora called. She was in Havana and wanted to know if she could come to see me. A poet who had taken an active part in the struggle and been the voice of its clandestine radio during the war's final months, Daisy was fair-skinned with a wealth of honey-colored hair and piercing blue eyes. Following the victory, she had been named vice minister of culture and came bearing an invitation from the minister, my old friend Ernesto Cardenal. He asked me to travel to Nicaragua to interview some of the women who had played such a prominent role in the war. He hoped I would find the inspiration to write a book like the one I had produced about Cuban women a decade earlier.

Conscious of the importance of recording the stories of ordinary protagonists, Cardenal also asked if I would be willing to give a brief course on how to do oral history. He said those taking the course would include trained academics and people with doctoral degrees as well as those who hadn't completed a primary school education. Ernesto believed in everyone's innate capacity to involve themselves in the work of telling their stories. Creating a different society depended on that. He paid little attention to conventional educational considerations.

I traveled to Nicaragua at the end of 1979 and spent three months doing the field work for what would become *Sandino's Daughters*.[3] My apprenticeship with Grandal, the brilliant Cuban photographer who had taught me the art, had barely been three months long at that point. I garnered my meager skills and was able to borrow a small darkroom belonging to the elderly man who was the photographer for the Ministry of Culture; my shift began around midnight when he went home to bed. From then on, it was trial and error on the ground.

The Ministry also gave me a jeep and driver and I went all over, from the war-torn western part of the country to the Atlantic Coast, which looked more like the English Caribbean. Its inhabitants spoke English or Miskito. Things seemed very relaxed yet intensely alive during these months immediately following victory. The emphasis was on getting things done. There was enormous excitement and I had extraordinary access everywhere I went.

OUR JOB WAS TO MOVE THEIR BODIES
FOR DAISY ZAMORA

1
Sometimes in the high noon heat of an August day,
monsoon rains coax millennia
of discreet scents
to the surface of my desert home.

Through layers of ancient cook pot smoke
smell of bone dreams and builds
bedrock to today's exhaling sage
and I catch that purging pungency.

Nineteen seventy-nine and the war was won
or so we thought.
Along shell-pocked roads and small backyards
fallen revolutionaries outgrew their shallow graves.

Our job was to move their bodies
to proper sites, cemeteries
where a nation of lovers
could mourn them in gratitude.

What remained of red and black, one arm
of a checked shirt, a single shoe
or blood-caked pair of pants
now forever sizes large.
A skull came free in my hands.
Thin book of poems without a cover.

It was the stench that trapped us
where we worked,
invaded willing shovels
entered living nostrils
beneath protective safety masks.
I wondered how long before earth would calm
the clinging color of death.

But today I mourn a greater loss: pure scent
they fought for dunged by imposters,
murdered by power where every hack speech
every greed-spliced lie spits in the gaping sockets
of men and women
whose last sad fumes still gag my memory.

2
Faint olfactory waves at Rome's arenas
where clawed gladiator flesh
screams bloodied concession for the ages.
Unmistakable stench of human burning
no neighbor German farmer dared challenge.

Defining scent of death trapped on the surface
of an old black and white photo,
sight fading to smell when senses cross clean lines,
explode nerve endings,
render every explanation meaningless,
too messy to fold and file in neat drawers.

One unexpected unforgiving moment
always escapes the polished surface
of *we must never forget*
or *let's put it behind us and start again.*
Its rising mist menaces us where we stand.

I interviewed Gladys Báez, one of the first women and few survivors of the early years of the Sandinista National Liberation Front (FSLN). Gloria Carrión and I became friends, and I sometimes accompanied her as she traveled in representation of the Luisa Amanda Espinosa Association of Nicaraguan Women. The group was named for a young girl from the countryside who had been killed in action before her twenty-second birthday. Lea Guido, a sophisticated feminist, was the new government's minister of social welfare. Women in leadership seemed much more visible than they'd been in Cuba following that country's revolutionary war.

I chased Commander Dora María Téllez from city to city, finally catching up with her one night at an old house in León. Dora María and her high command—consisting of five women and two men—had liberated the city of

León, creating the rebels' first free territory. I was told the commander could give me a half hour; we ended up talking for seven. Or she talked and I listened. The room was high-ceilinged and dark, and I had no flash attachment for my camera. I ended up opening my lens as wide as I could and shooting blindly, then pushing the film in the developing process. I couldn't remember how many extra minutes Grandal had instructed me to leave film in the canister for every additional hundred ASA[4] I wanted to achieve. So, I went to bed that night hoping to dream the solution to my problem. Luck or the power of the dream was on my side. When I woke the next morning, I had my answer. Several dramatically lit portraits from that interview are among my most evocative taken during those initial months. Sometimes my successes were accidents, sometimes a product of training and skill, occasionally the result of magical thinking.

I didn't limit myself to the already legendary female figures but sought out ordinary women and girls whose courage and determination had contributed to the victory of this second people's revolution on the continent.[5] I found a number of mothers and daughters who had acted in concert. I wanted to know what made protected young society women able to take up arms. I discovered that women in general had been more willing to participate in support work than men: perhaps because the men had to hold down jobs, perhaps because women were able to use their gender in ways that didn't provoke suspicion, or simply because they were more committed—in some deep sense they may have felt that liberating their country was also a way of liberating themselves.

Market women hid arms and ammunition in the bottoms of vegetable crates. Nuns took combatants into their convents. Young women just out of private Catholic schools made the leap from social justice charity work to armed struggle. I interviewed a mother and daughter duo who hadn't been aware of one another's participation until both were captured and found themselves sharing the same prison cell.

Two important differences marked the Nicaraguan Revolution in contrast with Cuba's. Twenty years had passed between the Cuban victory of 1959 and the FSLN's in 1979. During those twenty years, the Second Wave of feminism had swept the Western world and many Nicaraguan women considered themselves feminists; it was no longer a dirty word. And the Catholic Church had experienced its own profound changes with Vatican II and the resultant wave of liberation theology. Many of the men and women who went to war in Nicaragua came out of a renovated Christian movement, one that proclaimed a "church of the poor" and understood Christianity as being about justice and meeting human need here on Earth rather than waiting for some promised reward in the hereafter. Nicaragua's faithful saw no contradiction between their religious faith and profound social change.

Many men and women from other countries went to fight in Nicaragua. The Sandinistas welcomed their solidarity. Some of these fighters stayed on after the war was won, occupying positions in which they contributed different sorts of expertise. There was an internationalism palpable in those first years reminiscent of the brigades that had fought in Spain. Except that in Nicaragua, they saw victory rather than defeat.

At the Ministry of Culture, based in a beautiful old house that had once belonged to Somoza's mistress and was one of many requisitioned by the Revolution, I gave that short course in oral history, or *testimonio* as it was called in the Latin America of those years. I covered everything from how to work a tape recorder—the clunky old variety we used back then—to the ethics of telling another person's story: Who owned that story? Who should control it and how could the oral historian involve the informant in the process? How can we weave a nation's narratives from the disparate lives of individuals? I myself had barely begun a journey through oral history that would eventually result in a dozen books. My course was rudimentary but appreciated. It surprised me that a Costa Rican publisher collected my lectures into a booklet, that they were later translated into English and released in Canada, and that those booklets, simple though they were, became references for many.[6]

I remember Ernesto one afternoon gathering those who worked at the Ministry beneath one of the immense laurel trees that shaded the grounds. He had just returned from an official visit to Libya and wanted to share his experiences. He told us he had perceived a dangerous fundamentalism in that country as well as working-class people struggling for change. He could see that fundamentalism within every religious denomination—Catholics, Jews, Muslims, Hindus, Buddhists, Protestants—represented an increasing threat to the world, and that this was the way in which class struggle was manifesting itself within the major religions. I've often thought, since, how prophetic that observation was.

And then I returned to Cuba. Throughout much of 1980 I worked with the material I had collected, shaping the book that would eventually be published in half a dozen languages and remains my most popular title to date.

Nicaragua attracted me for several reasons. I've long been moved by countries with strong indigenous cultures. There is a continuity and artistic richness that are lacking where native life has been erased. Cuba's indigenous people had been decimated soon after the Spanish Conquest, while in Nicaragua the Miskito, Sumo, and Rama people retain a vital presence along the Atlantic Coast; their belief systems, culture, and art permeate life in general.

The Central American country is also a nation of poets; its love of poetry is exuberant and extends to social groups that in most places have never been exposed to the genre. And this engagement with poetry infused the Revolution. I have a photograph I took on the anniversary of Rubén Darío's birth in the small community that now bears his name, Ciudad Darío. Beginning in 1979, an outdoor reading is held there on that date each year. In my photo hundreds of farmers and field hands are sitting on a wall, listening raptly as local and internationally known poets read.

During the years I spent in the country, scenes like that repeated themselves in all sorts of venues. And the designation "poet" was one of honor. Cardenal, for example, who might have been addressed as minister because of his government position or Father because he was a priest, preferred the title of poet: Poeta Cardenal.

The humanism that came out of progressive Christianity, and the fact that a feminist consciousness was so much more advanced, also made me curious to know how these two important influences might shape the Sandinista Revolution differently from the more traditional Marxist orientation that had consolidated itself in Cuba. Social change in Nicaragua was much less materialistically based. It drew on the nationalism of Sandino, the humanism of Vatican II, and a series of ideas that emerged from the struggle itself. My friendship with Sandinistas on the island had also imbued me with a love for their country.

In Cuba the repression had worn me down. I continued to love and support the Cuban Revolution, but once I'd received an explanation and as much of an apology as I was going to get, I felt it was time to move on. In most families it's the children who grow up and leave home. In ours, I was the one who left. Ana was only ten at the time, so I insisted she accompany me to Managua. I gave the other three a choice: they could come with me or remain. Ximena wanted to finish high school. When she did, she joined

Poetry reading, Ciudad Darío, 1981 (photo by Margaret Randall).

Ana and me. Gregory and Sarah, both at the university by then, opted to stay behind.

At the end of December 1980, I was on my way to a new life in a very different place.

....

My plans had been to go to work at the women's organization, where Gloria Carrión had assured me a job would be waiting. But by the end of 1980 serious economic problems were already plaguing the Sandinista Revolution. Cutbacks to funding for the mass organizations meant all work at them had to be voluntary now, and my promised salary was no longer available.

Ernesto came to the rescue by offering me a job at the Ministry of Culture. I worked there for a year. I attended to foreign visitors, most of them artists. My supervisor was a rather stodgy woman, all competence and little imagination. I no longer remember her name. Most of my innovative ideas went unheard; she had a proper but staid sense of how to entertain those guests.

In that job I spent time with US American singer/songwriter Joan Baez, German novelist Günter Grass, English writer Graham Greene, Soviet poet Yevgeny Yevtushenko, Argentinean singer and performer Mercedes Sosa, Bolivian activist Domitila de Chungara, and others.

I remember a difficult conversation with Baez, whose music I loved. She told me she felt the North Vietnamese had "taken advantage" of her. I had a very different perception of the Vietnamese people and was shocked that she hadn't understood their need to garner support where they could find it. I spent a day driving around Managua with a copy of Günter Grass's *The Tin Drum* on the dashboard of my car, trying to skim the novel before meeting Grass's plane. Mercedes Sosa told her Managua audience that her daughter was giving birth to her first grandchild in Buenos Aires, but she hadn't canceled her trip because she wanted to accompany the victorious Nicaraguan people.

Yevtushenko and Allen Ginsberg gave a powerful reading. I remember Roberto Vargas, also a poet and then Nicaragua's consul in San Francisco, translating Ginsberg's poems. When Allen repeated a refrain that went "He sucked my cock / he sucked my cock / he sucked my cock," Roberto couldn't bring himself to translate in the first person. He looked down at the floor as he changed the line to multiples of "He says he sucked my cock."

Everyone wanted to come to Nicaragua then. Luminaries from around the world showed up, eager to experience for themselves a revolution that seemed independent, innovative, and bursting with energy. Writers as different from one another as Salman Rushdie, Claribel Alegría, and Julio Cortázar wrote their impressions. A young US American hydraulic engineer named Ben Linder rode his unicycle into villages and towns, put on one-man circus acts, and built a series of small hydroelectric dams that brought electricity to communities that had never known that bounty. He was savagely murdered by the Contra, but others continued his work. US muralists Miranda Bergman and Marilyn Lindstrom were among dozens who traveled to the country to paint its walls in brilliant color. When they made their mural at Managua's children's library, I brought some of my photographs of locals so they could get a sense for the faces. Thousands of people from many countries contributed their skills to a project they saw as unique.

The beautiful National Theater in the center of Managua had been spared in the 1972 earthquake; it stood in all its glory surrounded by acres of rubble, shells of semidestroyed buildings inhabited by homeless people and their makeshift enterprises. The Ministry of Culture filled that theater for every performance by local performers as well as the many internationally known artists eager to visit the new Revolution. Several rows of the best seats were always saved for the street kids who inhabited that vast area that came to be known as *las ruinas*, the ruins, devastation Somoza had never bothered to rebuild.

At the Ministry of Culture, I was able to appreciate the work Cardenal and others were doing to revitalize Nicaragua's native crafts: pottery, hand-woven hammocks, carved wood, and little figures of birds and animals made of a soft pale pinkish soapstone. A lot of thought was given to the ways in which those craftspeople could make a living from their wares. The Ministry took on the task of supporting the country's artists, creating markets for their work and promoting cultural activities in general. Orchestras, publishing houses, literary journals, theater and dance groups, art schools, even local small-town marching bands and circuses all received attention. Artistic events were free and attracted large audiences.

One of Ernesto's pet projects was the series of poetry workshops he established throughout the country: on farms, in factories, at schools and military units. He wrote a ten-point list of procedures to be followed when creating a poem: write about what you know, always use particular names of things—such as "palm" or "willow" rather than simply "tree"; call birds and plants by their names—and read a text out loud to listen to its music. These rules were simple but effective. Some writers thought the list arbitrary. They believed Ernesto was imposing his own style and made fun of his methodology. But the poet priest turned minister of culture was developing a broad poetic movement. His methods produced many fine writers throughout the country. I believe he created a poetry revolution.

....

My youngest daughter, Ana, was ten when I uprooted her from her Cuban life and took her to Managua. She was shocked at seeing beggars in the street and frightened the first time she was invited to attend a Catholic Mass, a customary part of the celebration when young girls turned sixteen. Religion in Cuba had been seen as retrograde, even counterrevolutionary. In Nicaragua it was firmly embedded in everyday life. With her youth and smarts, Ana soon made friends and became part of the local scene.

My second youngest, Ximena, wanted to finish high school in Havana but joined us there a year later. From a society that was safe and organized, with children as its most precious members, my daughters soon found themselves facing the uncertainty of impending war. Ana's first year of school was fairly stable, but by the time her sister arrived classes more often than not were suspended because of the threat of imminent attack.

Both girls joined militia units. Ximena's actually saw some action when hers went to pick coffee in the northern part of the country and she happened to be doing guard duty the night a small group of counterrevolutionaries invaded the fields where they were working. She fired a couple of shots into the air and they ran off. But the terror stayed with her for years.

Ana was twelve when her all-women battalion, which included members of all ages, went off for a week of military practice. I remember that Daniel Ortega's and Rosario Murillo's daughter Zoilamérica was in the same battalion; she might have been fifteen or sixteen at the time. Another mother and I commented, even back then, that the girl seemed troubled. We had no way of understanding what we intuited in her; incest and other varieties of sexual abuse weren't even acknowledged at the time. Years later, when Zoilamérica denounced her stepfather's abuse, that mother and I would talk again, remembering the impression she'd given as a teenager.

....

ALL LAST WEEK
FOR MY DAUGHTER ANA

All last week you preened before the mirror
viewing emerging breasts, then covering them
with gauze-thin blouse
and grinning: getting bigger, huh?

The week before you wore army fatigues
leveling breasts and teenage freckles,
tawny fuzz along your legs. A woman. Beginning.

Today you don fatigues again.
Today you pack knapsack and canteen,
lace boots over heavy socks
and answer the call Reagan and Haig
have slung at your 12 years.

Yours and so many others
—kids 14, 15, 18, so many others who will go
and some of them stay, their mothers

shouting before the Honduran Embassy:
"Give us our sons' bodies back,
give us back their bodies!" At least that.

All last week you preened before the mirror,
moving loose to new rhythms
long weekend nights. Junior High math. Sunday beach.
Today you go off
to the staccato of continuous news dispatches.
And I, in my trench, carry your young breasts
in my proud and lonely eyes.

All the country's children were being asked to do things far beyond their years. In this context, their sexuality was also being stretched beyond that which might have been age-appropriate. I tried to keep tabs on my daughters. I asked them to be honest with me about who they were dating and what they were doing, but they lied just as I had lied to my parents about sleeping out on the desert. And just as my mother had taken me at my word, I believed theirs. Years later they berated me for not having known that they were experiencing confusion and pain in many of their relationships.

....

The atmosphere generated by the delirium of the new society favored casual sexual encounters among adults as well. But it may not be enough to simply describe such encounters as casual. All social revolutions (French, Russian, Mexican, Chinese, Vietnamese, Cuban, Chilean, Nicaraguan) liberated people not only economically but also culturally and emotionally. This liberation manifested itself sexually as well as in other ways. Women as well as men experienced and reveled in a new sense of freedom. They naturally did so in the context of their prior social conditioning. In patriarchal societies men brought their misogynist habits to the explosion of joy.

The FSLN's guerrilla commanders in their smart olive drabs were drunk with victory. They thought they had a right to bed any woman they wanted. Many women concurred and, as time went by, the threat of ongoing death in battle created new and more urgent reasons for acting on immediate desire rather than waiting out the journey of getting to know a prospective lover. As is always the case, though, these sexual liaisons took place on the men's terms. Women often found themselves used but playing along.

I was mostly caught up in the day-to-day demands of trying to shape a more just society and of resisting US intervention. After a year at the Ministry of Culture, I went to work at DEPEP, an FSLN department that dealt with ideology in the media, transforming radio, newspapers, and television. I worked under the poet Gioconda Belli who, in turn, took orders from Carlos Núñez, one of the nine members of the National Directorate and one of two or three in that leadership body who was not a freewheeling womanizer. Another person in our department, Rita from the Dominican Republic, had come to Nicaragua to participate in the war and stayed on. She was an opera buff and flooded the office with the sound of arias from a tape recorder sitting at the corner of her desk.

Our work was intensely interesting. We were charged with reshaping the values endemic to conventional mass communication, values expressed in everything from sitcoms to the news. It wasn't enough that boy-meets-girl programming now featured the young revolutionary soldier who falls in love with the rural schoolteacher. The values themselves needed to change to reflect those of the Revolution. Our job wasn't to impose those new values from above but to get script writers, directors, and actors to come to them out of their own convictions.

Under the pseudonym Ana Herrera,[7] I wrote a series of columns for the Sandinista newspaper, *Barricada*. This was the only time I assumed a Latin American identity in print. I never knew how many readers, if any, suspected my national origin. In those columns I promoted what I considered revolutionary values, many of them feminist in nature. I was proud of those texts and they received quite a few compliments.

I worked hard and learned a lot. We had some successes. We also encountered entrenched social mores that shouldn't have surprised me but did. A member of the conservative Catholic hierarchy was discovered at the home of his female lover and a photographer from the Sandinista press stationed himself outside the woman's house. Through trickery, the man was forced out wearing only a towel. When the waiting photographer snapped a picture, which was published in the following day's paper, we thought we had achieved some sort of coup. Instead of shaming the priest, however, the disclosure backfired. People were incensed, not at the clergyman but at those of us who published the photo. "Men will be men" was the general consensus, even regarding a man of the cloth.

As in other processes of social change before it, the Sandinista Revolution talked a good line but never really questioned traditional male/female

Washerwomen posing before a wall with lines from a Leonel Rugama poem, Tipitapa, 1979 (photo by Margaret Randall).

relationships or power abuse in general. Most of the male commanders assumed the right to make the important decisions. These went beyond political policy and might include shifting underlings when they challenged the official line or sleeping with anyone they wished. From there it wasn't much of a leap to some of them taking possession of land, houses, and cars. Just before they were voted out of office, the infamous piñata referred to a shameful takeover of private property by some in leadership positions. Offenders may have been few in comparison with the vast majority of honest revolutionary leaders, but their actions tarnished the Sandinista image. The FSLN also had more women commanders than previous revolutions and most of them were every bit as honest and transparent as some of their male counterparts were playboys, albeit playboys in uniform. The prominence of these women made the contradictions all the more obvious and disappointing.

And here I want to say something about power itself. In revolutionary processes it often seems as if all those who died young, often before victory, were without blemish. Time allows the survivors to indulge in the temptations power bestows. This applies to women as well as men, but where the men are concerned it often means entrenchment in traditional patriarchal attitudes and behaviors. Who knows how the martyrs would have evolved, had they lived. The truth is, they are frozen in their heroism. My son, referring to his generation of activists, once said, "If we'd won, we would be heroes, with statues and streets named for the most outstanding. Because we lost, a great deal of heroism has been forgotten."

Nicaragua's first decade of Sandinista governance showcased this phenomenon all too well. We continue to revere the heroic dead even though we have no way of knowing how they might have acted had they lived. And we criticize those who became corrupted, sometimes forgetting their earlier abnegation and sacrifice. Social change is made by human beings after all, with all the complexity we humans possess.

The Sandinista Revolution, like the Cuban Revolution before it, emerged in an explosion of exuberance, passion for justice, and creativity. I was immensely fortunate to be able to share something of its birth, and my years in the country gave me a great deal. As that initial period gave way to political and social consolidation, though, the conniving and positioning inherent to capitalist relationships also became more evident. Daniel Ortega's wife, Rosario Murillo, headed the Sandinista Cultural Workers Association. She was bitterly jealous of Ernesto Cardenal and did everything possible to undercut his position as minister of culture. Fiefdoms were replacing logical divisions of labor within the collective project.

As I mentioned before, I wasn't surprised several years later when Rosario's daughter Zoilamérica Narváez publicly denounced her stepfather for having raped her for nineteen years, and Rosario defended Ortega, abandoning her daughter and isolating her from her family. The abuse had started when Zoilamérica was eleven. Ortega not only had pursued her relentlessly but also had told her that submitting to his will was her revolutionary duty. This was an egregious example of power abuse. Ortega was Zoilamérica's stepfather, the leader of her political party, and president of her country. He couldn't have represented a more authoritative figure in her life.

The Sandinistas, even today and in their return to government, have promoted policies aimed at raising people out of poverty, providing them with healthcare and education, and otherwise improving life for the majority. For this reason, much of the left, both in Nicaragua and outside the country, defends them. At the same time, sectors of that same left have refused to acknowledge any connection between Ortega's long-term sexual abuse of his stepdaughter and his ability to lead or govern. If they believe her at all, they see the abuse as personal and irrelevant to public life. This was true in 1998, when she went public with her story and remains true today.

I remember a particularly telling conversation that took place years later. A small gathering in Albuquerque included several women and a man whose leftist credentials seemed impeccable. The subject of Zoilamérica's ordeal came up, and the man said that he believed her because "after all, her ex-husband Alejandro Bendaña had stood beside her at her press conference and confirmed her story." We looked at the guy in shock and then anger, outraged by his willingness to believe a woman only when a man confirms her words.

As I write, the Ortega/Murillo duo has taken possession of the country, turning revolution into tyranny. Social projects remain, but pale in the context of generalized political abuse. Over a period of years Daniel carefully orchestrated his way to the presidency, systematically eliminating anyone who stood in his way. Then he named his wife as vice president. They have met increased public protest with greater and greater repression, killing hundreds of civilians, imprisoning and torturing opponents, getting teachers who support the protest and medical personnel who treat wounded protesters fired from their jobs, and forcing many authentic Sandinistas into exile. Still, sectors of the US left continue to support the Ortega/Murillo government, claiming the real villain is the United States.

This inability or unwillingness to consider rape on a par with other crimes is inexplicable to me. I don't doubt that the United States is doing everything in its power to undermine what's left of the Sandinista Revolution. It has always stood against progressive movements in Latin America and played an important role in destroying the Sandinista project. But it seems to me one can protest both covert action on the part of the United States and Ortega's power abuse. One doesn't negate the other. Of course, doing so would imply an understanding of woman abuse as criminal, a position most people of all political persuasions are still reluctant to embrace.

I first met Daniel Ortega when I lived in Cuba. We had an old ditto machine at our apartment, on which we reproduced poems for our weekly writing workshop, and we offered it to others who needed to run off texts of one sort or another. Daniel would show up in pressed Levi's and a white T-shirt. He was quiet, almost shy. Modest is the word I would use to describe the impression he gave. I would bring him a cup of coffee if I had some to spare and leave him to his work. I could not have imagined that not that many years later he would become a member of the National Directorate that took control of Nicaragua when the war ended, much less that his criminal relationship to his stepdaughter would be revealed or that he and his wife would become autocrats.

This might be the place to speak of Tomás Borge, one of the three founders of the FSLN, another member of its National Directorate, and, at the end of the war, a man revered by almost everyone. He embodied the contradictions that typified so many of the male Sandinista leaders during the years I lived there, indeed so many powerful men in a variety of movements and institutions worldwide.

On the one hand, Tomás was a mythic figure. In one of several imprisonments he had survived a hunger strike that took him to the very threshold of death. Shortly after victory he faced the Somocista prison guard who had tortured and murdered his first wife. The man had been taken prisoner by the Sandinistas when they claimed victory. He cowered before Tomás's small, compact figure, expecting to receive a death sentence for his crime. But the Sandinistas had done away with capital punishment early on. Tomás looked him in the eye and pardoned him instead.

Sometimes I had the occasion to work with Tomás and certainly recognized his brilliance. I wrote a couple of his speeches. One in particular I remember focused on racism in the United States and the importance of guarding against that in Nicaragua. When he spoke with groups of English-speaking visitors, I was often called upon to translate and learned to anticipate his discourse to the point where I came very close to being able to do simultaneous interpretation. I also rendered a beautiful book-length poem he wrote into English; it was called *Carlos, the Dawn Is No Longer beyond Our Reach.*[8]

On the other hand, Tomás's misogyny was legendary. He absolutely believed he had the right to seduce any woman or girl who caught his fancy. In the Nicaragua of those days it went unchallenged, at least publicly. He once asked me to leave a party with him to visit the home of a family mourning their young son who had been killed by the Contras. I accompanied him to the impoverished house where mourners surrounded an open casket in which the body of a teenage boy lay broken and inert. We sat a while with the grieving parents. I felt out of place in my party garb, but glad to be able to show my solidarity.

Then Tomás announced we'd be going to a protocol house where he obviously expected we'd have sex. When I refused, he seemed shocked. He wasn't accustomed to rejection. I knew a young girl—she couldn't have been more than fourteen or fifteen—to whom he sent a beautiful dress prior to taking her out and trying to seduce her into bed. He hoped to see her in that dress, an object of his momentary desire decked out in a style he'd chosen. She was flattered by the gift but managed to escape his expectations. His sense of ownership of the female sex seemed to have no limits.

A certain tendency toward deception also ran through other aspects of Tomás's life. At one point he received some public criticism for living in a mansion abandoned by the country's fleeing bourgeoisie. In response he left the house, ordering it be turned into a daycare center, a gesture for which he was widely applauded. Then he moved into what appeared to be a small dwelling in a working-class neighborhood in downtown Managua. Several US guests and I were invited to dinner there one night and ate in a cramped room in which the table filled almost the entire space. Later, though, I learned that this house was one of a whole series, eight or ten such cookie-cutter homes surrounding a park. All of it was hidden behind a wall several city blocks square, and Tomás had requisitioned the compound to lodge not only himself and his family but also his personal guard and other staff. What looked modest if you entered only one of the dwellings was in fact a fiefdom. Who knew where those homes' original inhabitants had been forced to move.

Tomás had been one of the three original founders of the FSLN. During much of its decade in power he was secretary of internal affairs, effectively reorganizing and commanding the national police force. In 1982, he was elected vice president of the Permanent Conference of Political Parties in Latin America, an association of social democratic, socialist, and liberal parties on the continent. When the Sandinistas were voted out of office in 1990, he, like other erstwhile revolutionary leaders, became a wealthy entrepreneur. At his request, in 2007 he was named Nicaragua's ambassador to Peru. He died in 2012 at the age of eighty-one.

There were Sandinista leaders who were models of integrity. There were some who displayed astonishing qualities of sacrifice and determination, made a revolution against seemingly insurmountable odds, and then the power of victory turned them into unrepentant drunks, misogynist and corrupt. Tomás Borge displayed impressive qualities of brilliance, talent, and also male entitlement. Thinking about the complex contradictions he embodied helps me understand that both extremes are often found in a single man. What needs to change is the left's insistence on separating the personal from the political. We must demand respect and accountability in the former as well as in the latter, leaders able to resist old patterns and set holistic examples of power sharing.

....

In Nicaragua, the extraordinary victory of the Sandinistas and their ultimate defeat in the 1990 elections bookended experimentation through which all sorts of issues could be examined. The economy, land reform, religious belief, gender equality, native rights, and other areas provided opportunities for economists, agronomists, liberation theologians, women's rights advocates, preservers of native cultures, and others to put their theories to the test: not only Nicaraguans but also those of us from elsewhere.

The active participation of priests and religious sisters who saw no contradiction between their faith and revolution created an atmosphere of religious freedom that was important to Nicaragua's multiplicity of ideas. The Sandinistas promoted a mixed economy that was more like Vietnam's than Cuba's; state control of major industries such as transportation and utilities coexisted with small businesses that remained in the hands of individuals. Land reform was also not as radical in Nicaragua as it had been in Cuba, allowing for cooperatives and other models of owning and working the land that were generally more successful.

A big challenge for the Sandinistas was how to approach the needs of the country's indigenous peoples—Miskitos, Sumos, and Ramas—who populated the Atlantic coast. Not long after the 1979 victory, counterrevolutionary attacks from across the Honduran border created a zone of vulnerability that prompted the government to move whole communities inland from their traditional territories. This proved to be a costly mistake. People were resistant to abandoning the lands where their ancestors were buried. Dissatisfaction and then rebellion on the part of indigenous leaders produced a dichotomy in which several joined the Contras. Interestingly, powerful native women leaders, such as Myrna Cunningham, Dorotea Wilson, and Hazel Lau, were among those who tried to bridge those differences and design policies that attempted to keep the indigenous peoples in the Sandinista camp.

My question today is how can countries make the transition from state control to a socialism that is truly democratic, allowing for diverse opinions

Mother and daughter, San Pedro Norte, 1983 (photo by Margaret Randall).

and individual creativity? Most of the countries that called themselves socialist have versions of state capitalism. International pressures have proven difficult to resist. We must find ways for people to retain their differences while
working for the common good.

Within the Sandinista movement, strong feminists were able to make the
gender analysis of Nicaraguan society that was so lacking in Cuba. Over the
years I lived in Managua and on several return visits, I spoke with dozens if
not hundreds of Nicaraguan women. I interviewed many for my books. With
others, ongoing friendship and correspondence have enabled me to follow the
ups and downs of their struggles. Almost all credit the FSLN with awakening their sense of self-worth and political agency. Almost all also say that the
male-dominated party eventually limited their ability to push gender equality
as far as they might otherwise have been able.

After the Sandinistas were defeated at the polls and the country fell back
into the hands of bourgeois forces, a strong multiethnic women's movement that
crossed class and even ideological lines continued to delve more deeply into its
analysis of power. International nongovernmental organizations stepped in to
offer the support the FSLN no longer provided. Today education and outreach
and action programs, such as those carried out by Puntos de Encuentro, continue
to spearhead the rights of women, children, families torn apart by war, victims of
domestic violence, and the lesbian, gay, and transgender communities.[9]

The Sandinista Revolution was triumphant in 1979 but defeated in 1990. During that decade, the tensions created by international and internal opposition made the natural evolution of a number of programs difficult. Many of us, myself included, feel that true Sandinism, that which was envisioned by the movement's founders and martyrs, only existed during the first half of that decade. Its last five years saw too much compromise. Too many of the original ideas and efforts had become diluted or been abandoned altogether. After I left the country in 1984, determined revolutionaries continued to try to effect social change through other means. On subsequent visits, I would be able to assess their successes and failures.

On one such visit, in 1992, I was doing the field work for a companion volume to *Sandino's Daughters. Sandino's Daughters Revisited* gives voice to women able to examine not only what the Revolution meant in their lives but also how losing that Revolution affected them. In some ways political defeat had been a negative. In others, no longer being subject to a male-oriented party opened new possibilities for struggle. It was on that 1992 trip that I had an experience that illustrates the complex contradictions between the Cuban and Nicaraguan experiences.

An old friend, the Cuban poet Víctor Rodríguez Núñez, was in Nicaragua at the time. He was working as one of Tomás Borge's personal secretaries. Indeed, it was Víctor who made me aware of some of the ways in which Tomás was not who he pretended to be. Some of the stories were very sad, such as the one in which the commander visited the home of the mother of a martyr and the woman showed him her son's combat diary. It was scrawled in a lined notebook and was one of her most prized possessions. Tomás offered to take the diary to Managua, have it bound in leather, and then return it to her. Many months later Víctor came across it in his personal library. Quietly, he took it back to its rightful owner, who never knew the revolutionary leader she so admired had intended to keep it for himself.

One evening Víctor wrangled an invitation for me to attend an exceptionally interesting gathering at the Cuban embassy in Managua. Three well-known Cuban journalists and three respected journalists from Nicaragua would debate the issue of freedom of the press within their respective revolutions. Other attendees included important Sandinista leaders Sergio Ramírez, Dora María Téllez, Ernesto Cardenal, Milú Vargas, Tomás Borge, and Jaime Wheelock.

Freedom of the press is always a revolutionary goal, but it rarely survives the dangers and demands inherent to the creation of a new society. In Cuba, very early on, any semblance of diversity of opinion was sacrificed to a perceived need for political unity. Conflicting opinions were feared. Cuba's mass media is still homogeneous and boring, presenting the Cuban Communist Party's single point of view. Specialized journals are more diverse, but the word on the street is that the dailies aren't much good for anything but being cut into small squares to stand in for ever-scarce toilet tissue.

In Nicaragua, on the other hand, the effort to retain a multi-opinion press became a point of honor within the FSLN. Three main newspapers represented different ideological positions. *La Prensa*, which during the last years of the war had been a source of news about the struggle, now reflected the views of an oligarchy hoping to regain power. *El Nuevo Diario* published a range of middle-of-the-road opinions. And the FSLN's official newspaper, *Barricada*, spoke for the Revolution.

Emotions ran high at the Cuban embassy gathering that afternoon. The Nicaraguan journalists defended the importance of open discussion. They insisted that a true revolution cannot develop and grow under censorship. The Cuban journalists agreed—in principle. But they justified what they called a lamentable need for censorship by pointing out that their Revolution was still going strong while the Nicaraguan one had been defeated. One could argue that Cuba still had its Revolution but that it had been undeniably undermined by censorship. On the other hand, the Sandinistas promoted a free press, but what difference did that make if the Revolution itself no longer existed? The discussion had no winners.

....

The Sandinistas inherited one of the poorest countries on the continent and began turning it around. They outlawed capital punishment, prohibited denigrating images of women in the media, nationalized major industries, carried out an impressive land reform, waged a year-long literacy crusade, broadened education, and strengthened labor laws. They were successful at eradicating diseases born out of poverty, such as tuberculosis and night blindness, that affected large segments of the population.

The first few years of the Sandinista experiment seemed transparent and promising. But once again the failure to address the issue of power allowed old values to surface. Counterrevolutionary groups in the United States, as well as the Reagan administration itself, spent millions to destroy the Nicaraguan Revolution. Even after the Contragate scandal was exposed, money and arms continued to be funneled to the Central American country.[10]

I knew brilliant women in Nicaragua who had hopes for substantive change. Gloria Carrión and Flor de María Monterrey, who respectively ran the women's organization, told me they wanted to avoid the politics of Cuba's Federation of Cuban Women, always controlled by the Cuban Communist Party. Lea Guido, who had been named minister of public welfare in the first assignment of cabinet positions, began promoting laws that favored women's and children's rights. Daisy Zamora, who was vice minister of culture under Cardenal, brought a feminist vision to the area of culture. An ex-nun named Aminta Granera became Managua's chief of police and immediately set up units trained in dealing with victims of domestic abuse. Doris Tijerino, whose story filled my first book about Nicaragua, was eventually named the country's first female police chief. She later told me that she'd had to make male underlings believe they'd come up with her ideas in order to get them adopted.

As soon as one of these women threatened the power structure, the male-dominated leadership of the FSLN wrested control. Only Dora María Téllez seemed able to impose her powerful personality and intellect. As a military commander, she'd directed the takeover of the city of León, leading to the FSLN's final victory, and it might have been her military acumen that earned her a greater measure of respect. She served as a senator for years, before and after her five-year stint as minister of public health. Téllez stepped down from that position because she believed people should limit their tenure in positions of power. Change is always healthy, she told me. Mónica Baltodano was another woman who had played an outstanding military role, and later held a number of leadership positions, but eventually was relegated as well.

An exceptionally capable lawyer, Milú Vargas, was prominent in those early years. Among other things, she oversaw the creation of a new Constitution. Milú was married to Carlos Núñez, which made her work easier; Carlos remained one of the very few men in Sandinista leadership who had a feminist consciousness. When the time came, and against the expected opposition, he helped create space for Nicaragua's gay and lesbian communities. Tragically, Carlos died much too young, of a deficiency resulting from childhood poverty.

At Managua's Jesuit University, Vidaluz Meneses was offered a dean's position. She didn't want to be a token and refused to accept it, advocating instead for a three-woman panel that included Michele Nájlis and another woman whose name I've forgotten. They were able to force acceptance of their alternative. Vidaluz, who was also a marvelous poet, had a fascinating personal history. She was from a conservative family and had come up through the Christian youth movement. Her father was a general under Somoza, and toward the end of the dictatorship had been appointed Nicaragua's ambassador in Guatemala. There, members of an armed struggle organization made an attempt on his life. He didn't die right away but lingered in a hospital for several weeks. Vidaluz had to fly to his side to accompany him in his agony. Nicaragua offered up many such stories of families in which left and right converged.

There were women like Gladys Báez, early participants in the armed struggle that had brought the Sandinistas to power, who seemed untouchable; but the men eventually found ways of immobilizing them as well. I got to know all these extraordinary women and others. I interviewed many of them for *Sandino's Daughters* and *Sandino's Daughters Revisited*.[11]

While the Catholic Church had played a conservative role in the Cuban Revolution, in Nicaragua only the hierarchy was against the changes being made. Many priests and religious sisters supported the process, often risking their lives to bring it to fruition. I knew Uriel Molina and Antonio Castro, who made their inner-city parishes havens of social action and revolutionary change. Miguel d'Escoto, a member of the Maryknoll order, was the country's long-term secretary of state. Ernesto Cardenal and his brother Fernando were members of the FSLN. Fernando, a Jesuit, was the minister of education who oversaw the successful literacy crusade.

A group of Jesuits, including Fernando, lived down the street in my pleasant Managua neighborhood of Pancasán. They often invited me to communal dinners on Friday nights. A member of that group later transferred to El Salvador where he was one of several in his order murdered by counterrevolutionaries. Many religious men and women gave their lives in the struggles of those years: some when they left their parishes to take up arms, others simply because they supported revolutionary change.

Ernesto was such an outstanding example of the fact that a priest could also be a revolutionary that when Pope John Paul II visited Nicaragua in 1983, he admonished him publicly and restricted his ability to say Mass or exercise other priestly rites. A photograph taken on the airport tarmac circled the world. It was of Ernesto kneeling to kiss the prelate's ring and the pope shaking his finger at him. The Vatican feared religious men and women who refused to bow to its will.[12]

I knew Sister Marta in Matagalpa. She had run guns and hidden fighters during the insurrectional period. Her order eventually sent her to Spain to get her away from the Revolution. Sister Beatríz, who worked at Managua's Centro Valdivieso, remained a staunch advocate for social change throughout the years I lived in Nicaragua. She was a Franciscan sister. Some orders were more progressive than others and supported their members who became involved in the Revolution.

There were also a number of US religious sisters who contributed to the country's process. One of the most outstanding was Mary Hartman, a Sister of St. Agnes who was particularly active in prison reform. She suffered from an autoimmune disease and was so thin as to be almost emaciated but had a limitless energy. I once accompanied her to the big prison at Tipitapa. We brought a wedding cake for a prisoner and his soon-to-be-wife, who were married with Sister Mary as their sponsor. I often accompanied her on some mission in her beat-up old Volkswagen Beetle.

One of my friends was a Maryknoll lay sister named Patricia Hynds. We took to having lunch once a week at a small eatery on the Masaya Highway. I think it was called La Margarita. I still associate the smell of its signature chicken tacos with the talks we had there, as we tried to process the more and more serious situation that engulfed the country and ourselves in the run-up to full-blown Contra war. After Nicaragua Pat went to Peru where she lived during a particularly intense political period. Much later she would leave the lay sisterhood and move to Albuquerque, where we reconnected. We're still good friends.

Another outstanding product of the Church was María López Vigíl, an ex–Dominican Sister who left both Cuba and her order and ended up in Nicaragua. She edited *Envío*, an important publication housed at the Central American University, which was run by progressive Jesuits. María later hosted monthly discussions of current events with protagonists at the center of things who kept us in touch with what was happening. She remains a vital source of information and analysis.

But these were exceptions to an utterly misogynist Church policy that dominated and eventually decimated any real power held by women. Individually, these women had histories that brought them a measure of respect and ideas that enabled them to use what space was available to them. Ultimately, they were contained by a patriarchal system. Individuals couldn't make an ongoing difference when the Revolution's male leadership refused to evaluate the issue of power.

I did field work in Nicaragua for several months immediately following the Sandinista victory of 1979 and lived there from the end of 1980 to the beginning of 1984. Because of prior friendships, I had extraordinary access to movement leaders who went on to occupy important positions in a variety of areas. Aside from the two books I've mentioned, I researched and wrote others—one of interviews with government officials who were writers and another that looked at the role of liberation theology in the Nicaraguan revolutionary process.[13]

I saw amazing men and women at their best, and some at their worst. Like so many others, I witnessed the demise of a movement that had promised profound social change. Its failure was not only due to ongoing interference by the United States, but also to weaknesses on the part of FSLN leaders: avarice, opportunism, corruption. Its death was a loss not only to Nicaragua but also to the continent and to that part of the world that values justice. I ache when I think of my friends who gave their lives, confident they were doing so to make their country a better place. And I rage when I think of the United States, which has never been willing to allow a country in its sphere of influence to construct a future of its choosing.

As the Contra war heated up, life in Nicaragua became more and more agitated. I was working for the FSLN's media department alongside men and women half my age. I had been in Latin America for close to a quarter century by then. I identified with the struggles in which I had participated but also began to long for home. In my late forties, I realized that the work I was doing could be done just as well or better by others. My real calling was writing, and there was no way that I could take that calling in the direction I knew I needed to take it if I continued to work eighteen-hour days.

Hadn't I discovered, way back during my years in New York City, that nothing mattered as much as doing one's own work? Social change was important to me, and I believed that revolution was the way to get there. I don't know if my participation in revolutionary movements can be considered detours, for I always continued to write, and I published dozens of books during my years in Latin America. Just as I have always worked for social justice. Perhaps it was my frustration at the journey not being as direct as I anticipated, perhaps it was my age and exhaustion; whatever the case, I knew I had to begin putting writing once more at the center of my life.

At work one day, sitting at my desk I began to cry. I couldn't stop. After a while my comrades sent me home. I continued to sob for several days. I was falling apart. I asked to see a psychologist and had several sessions with a wise Mexican woman named Tony. She told me I needed to go home. I knew she was right yet felt conflicted to be leaving my friends in a situation of impending war. Gradually it became clear to me that home was where I should be.

At the beginning of 1984 I packed up my things, intending to send them on ahead by ship. Then the United States mined the Corinto Harbor and I had to take only what I could on the plane. Once again, I gave the two daughters living with me their choice of where to go. Ximena opted to move to Mexico where her father lived. Ana chose New York City where Robert had been for a while. She lived briefly with him and his wife, then moved in with his parents, and eventually joined me in New Mexico. In January 1984 I boarded a plane in the intense Nicaraguan heat and disembarked in the winter cold of Albuquerque. Waiting for me at the airport were my parents; my brother, John; and Floyce Alexander, a poet with whom I had established a relationship some months before.

Another chapter of my life was about to begin, one whose contours I could not have imagined.

Chapter Nine

HOME

1984 and Beyond

A woman's memory is trustworthy . . .
I don't want to pretend to be younger;
I earned it.
—ROSANNE CASH, IN AN INTERVIEW WITH
CHRISTIANE AMANPOUR (NOVEMBER 2018)

The homeland
calls out to us in great voices
like the mother to her son
when dinner is served
and he's gone in search
of something to adorn the table.
—ANTONIO CASTRO, A STANZA FROM THE
POEM "PATRIA," NOT COLLECTED IN A BOOK
(TRANSLATION BY THE AUTHOR)

Home turned out to be a rugged trail, sometimes taking me across familiar
terrain, most often—at least through the first decade—hugging the edges of
precipices as it offered up mirages threatening to fade as I approached. I sometimes felt as if I were clinging to the cliffside as I glanced surreptitiously at a
valley dropping thousands of feet below me on the other side.

I was forty-seven years old, a physically and psychologically exhausted
forty-seven. The embrace of home and family was offset by the guilt I felt
at having left my comrades behind in a country careening toward war. Once
again, the beautiful promise of revolution was threatened by the United

Southwest landscape (photo by Margaret Randall).

States' refusal to allow a people the right to make their own future free from imperialist intervention. Once again that meant broken promises, too many friends sacrificed, years lost to a desperation only a trembling handhold above resignation.

I had come home seeking refuge in the aggressor nation that was also my own, one in which landscape, language, and culture—including everyday interactions and humor—were all familiar. My aging parents, brother, and a man I'd met when he'd visited Mexico during the 1968 Student Movement welcomed me home. US American poet Floyce Alexander and I had kept in touch over the ensuing fifteen years and become close during my last months in Nicaragua. I also felt welcomed by the desert landscape so important throughout my life, and by Albuquerque's energized women's community that would open doors in my own psyche I couldn't yet imagine.

Weighing against heart and mind, tipping the scale in the opposite direction and sometimes throwing me into despair, were my homeland's brutal political policies. Ronald Reagan had just been elected to a second term. From my disagreement with every one of his initiatives to the overwhelming confusion I experienced when faced with my country's obscene affluence and abandoned poor, and confronted by a daily barrage of consumer goods, I felt off-balance much of the time. It was hard for me to go into a large supermarket, where I confronted dozens of brands of toothpaste, milk that ran from whole to skim and nondairy varieties, salted or sweet butter, two hundred types of cheese, every cut of meat, and a wealth of out-of-season fruits and vegetables. I'd come from countries where scarcity was the norm, a single brand was all you got, and equal access was the goal. I often asked my father to come with me when I had to go food shopping. His gentle companionship did a lot to ease my reentry.

The therapist I'd seen in Managua had warned me to rest when I got home. She recommended I not get a job right away but give myself a chance to heal. I'm sure my parents would have taken me in for a while. But Floyce and I married briefly, and I went to live with him in his apartment at the University of New Mexico (UNM) Married Student Housing complex where he worked as a manager. A prerequisite for that employment was that he himself not be married, something he didn't tell me. When his boss read the notice of our marriage in the newspaper personals, he lost the job. I began feeling uneasy in an atmosphere of semitruths. Or should I call them lies?

Two years older than I but something of a perennial student, Floyce had been stretching out his doctorate in film studies for quite a while. He was enthralled by Stanley Kubrick, and we watched *A Clockwork Orange* and *The Shining* again and again while he took copious notes. Close viewing, he called it. Kubrick's vision seemed contrived and altogether irrelevant to my state of mind.

At midlife, I couldn't resign myself to relinquishing the independence for which I'd fought so hard and had maintained for so long. My natural inclination was to go to work. But what could I do to support myself? Strange as it may seem, I remember thinking about air-traffic control; where I got the idea that it would be something I would enjoy or be good at, who knows. Perhaps it came from a desire to organize and keep the disparate elements of my life together, flying in some sort of order as it were. I inquired and learned I was too old to be admitted into air-traffic control school.

What skills did I have? I briefly considered a photography lab, but my training was wrong for this country's assembly-line version of photographic reproduction. Neither was this a nation in which paid positions for revolutionaries abounded. Those with experience working to change society weren't in high demand. I no longer lived in Cuba or Nicaragua where people, whenever possible, were given jobs in areas that needed their skill sets. Poets weren't appreciated either.

It soon dawned on me that what I had to share, what might actually allow me to earn a living, would be my life experience shaped into a package I could offer on a university campus. And so, the woman who hadn't graduated from college, who had never thought to list her accomplishments on a curriculum vitae and knew nothing about writing a syllabus, decided to apply for adjunct teaching at UNM.

I already knew I was going to have problems entering the country and, especially as my immigration status became public knowledge, would face a good deal of political opposition. I also found some generous advocates on campus. Universities were hiring adjuncts so as to be able to pay them less, avoid providing benefits, and engage in other exploitative practices. I managed to get a few courses in UNM's American Studies department and Women's Studies program. I learned something about how to navigate campus politics, design a sixteen-week course, and make my incipient way in academia.

Professors at other institutions across the country had read my books—which I learned in certain fields could earn me merits comparable to a degree—and some of them got in touch. Over the next decade I taught at Oberlin, Macalester, the University of Delaware, and, most regularly, Trinity College in Hartford, Connecticut, a school that gave me a visiting professorship for nine years running. These schools hired me despite my vague immigration status, risking possible government reprisals. I will always be grateful for their support.

I invented a course in exploring women's creativity. I wanted my students to look at the obstacles that society and their own conditioning place in the way of women's creative drive. That turned out to be a class that excited me, and I continually refined and improved it. I also taught Latin American literature in translation, and poetry. As with so much else in my life, success on a college campus came at an unexpected time. I loved my students. They taught me as much as I taught them. Teaching turned out to be an ideal reentry to the land I had left so many years before. It put me in touch with young people and the cultures they were creating.

During the nine years I taught in Hartford, Connecticut, I made a precious friendship with imprisoned revolutionary Kathy Boudin.[1] She was at the Bedford Hills Correctional Facility for Women then, serving what seemed as if it would be a life sentence. Despite the routine obstacles the prison system places in the way of human interaction, after we were introduced by mutual friend Ruth Hubbard, I drove down to see Kathy almost weekly. And later, when I taught at the University of Delaware, I made the longer trip north whenever I could. She was released after twenty-two years and we continued our friendship on our own terms; she came to visit us in New Mexico and we would get together when I went to New York. Kathy is a beautiful example of how a person can contribute to society even in the most restrictive conditions. She taught me a great deal about patience and commitment.

....

Floyce and I married and lived together for almost a year. As with so many of the men in my life, we would have been better off remaining friends than becoming romantically involved. We were from different worlds. He was kind and solicitous and tried hard to rise to the needs my complicated transition demanded. He supported me in what for him must have been circumstances resembling outer space, was loyal and decent. But we ultimately spoke languages unintelligible to one another.

One night, Floyce got drunk. We were at a friend's house and several people were present. I'd been talking about an invitation I'd received to go somewhere to work for several months, and I noticed that as I expressed my enthusiasm at the possibility, my new partner finished one beer and poured himself another. I had never been with an alcoholic and, although he didn't become physically abusive, his aggressive language frightened me. I told him the next time he drank, I would leave. It only took him a month or so to repeat himself. The morning following that second drinking bout, he explained he'd only been testing me. I packed my things and moved to my parents' home just as he may have been wondering why his test produced the results it did.

Or maybe not. Maybe the drinking was his way out of a relationship that wasn't right for him either. Soon he was back with the woman to whom he'd been married and from whom he'd divorced before we got together. They were soulmates, helped each other get sober, and remain together to this day. Floyce and I had been detours in one another's lives. I admire his poetry and count him as a friend, someone who did his best to ease a part of my long journey home.

Coming home put me back in touch with a great deal with which I was familiar and also much that was new. The city had changed, but I recognized streets, buildings, angles. A movie theater where I'd lied about my age and

Dad and Mom,
Albuquerque, 1985
(photo by Margaret
Randall).

paid ten cents even after my twelfth birthday. The old community center, where I'd spent such hopeful/miserable hours at those Friday night dances in junior high, was now a shabby building with peeling paint. My grade, middle, and high schools, each of them looking so much smaller than I remembered. The house where I'd grown up at 515 Tulane Drive NE, and the one on Avenida Mañana where my parents lived after I moved away. I reconnected with my brother, Johnny, who had always been important in my life. He and his first wife, Joanna, introduced me to new places of interest in the city where I'd grown up.

I'd never had a credit card and had to establish credit in middle age. My father cosigned for me at first. I'd never used an automatic teller, bought insurance, or owned a home computer. Every modern convenience was a challenge, the consumerist aspect of US society overwhelming.

....

After I'd left Albuquerque, Mother and Dad built their dream home, an adobe in the foothills of the Sandia Mountains. When they bought the land, it was open country, roads unpaved, few neighbors. Later it became quite a wealthy neighborhood, where my parents' house at the edge of national forest land was magically situated but modest when compared with others, all of which had larger floor plans and multicar garages. What had been a retreat on the outskirts of the city became a refuge in the midst of a largely Republican suburb.

One of the first things I did upon my return to Albuquerque was pay a visit to the First National Bank building on the corner of Central Avenue and San Mateo. Fifteen stories high, in my childhood it had been one of Albuquerque's few skyscrapers. I remembered that my friend Alice Garver painted murals on twelve of those floors—she'd skipped the ground and top stories and there was no number thirteen (in deference to the US superstition in which that number is considered unlucky). The murals depicted the history of New Mexico, beginning with Coronado's arrival—I wished she'd begun with the indigenous cultures rather than the Conquest—and progressed upward until the invention and testing of the atomic bomb.

You exited the elevator at each level and stood facing those murals, which were huge and rendered in decisive, richly hued strokes. I wanted to see them again. I must have felt the need to reconnect with Alice's murals as a way of reentering the years I'd lived in Albuquerque as a young woman. But when I got to the building and inquired about them, no one knew what I was talking about. No one working there had ever even heard about any murals. They'd been painted over years before. An artist's first big break and last commission: erased.

Alice died at the age of forty-two, much too young. I no longer lived in Albuquerque but remember my mother telling me she'd been taken to the hospital with a serious illness, was released, and suddenly took a turn for the worse, dying at home. Possible explanations included a virulent case of spinal meningitis or a poisoned water well. Her husband, Jack, also a well-known local painter, came to see us in Mexico the following year. He was drinking heavily and seemed lost. He too died a few years later. Their three children, whom I had known as toddlers, were orphaned early. One of them, Carlos—known as Rag Man when he wandered homeless around the university area years later—was murdered when someone set fire to the old couch he slept on behind my brother's bookstore. I reconnected with his sister Grace as I began to write this memoir.

....

Meanwhile, there was the citizenship issue, central to my being able to remain in the United States. Soon after my arrival, I'd followed Charles Peacock's instructions, gone down to Albuquerque's Federal Building and applied for residency: the ubiquitous green card so coveted by immigrants to this country. Initial formalities were shrouded in a pretense at normality. I was told the process would take a routine sixty or ninety days, and that I would be issued the appropriate papers within that time frame.

When sixty and then ninety and then many more days passed without hearing anything, I realized things weren't going to be easy. I hired a local lawyer, but soon discovered that my situation was beyond the range of his experience. Then I called my old friend Michael Ratner, at that time president of the Center for Constitutional Rights in New York City. The center is a decades-old institution of onsite legal staff and collaborating attorneys that defends progressive peoples in all areas of struggle: worker and voting rights, land issues, prison abuse, antiwar protest, freedom of expression, gender rights, US crimes against foreign countries, and more. My friend didn't hesitate to assure me that the center would take my case.

Michael flew out to New Mexico and accompanied me to the Federal Building. Douglas Brown, the man in charge of immigration at the Albuquerque office, didn't hide his displeasure. The involvement of a high-profile East Coast lawyer clearly annoyed him. Brown refused to invite us into his office, instead standing with us in the waiting area. Michael was soon joined by David Cole, who was just beginning to argue his first cases at the time but who, in the years to come, would become a brilliant constitutional lawyer. We were also joined by an experienced immigration attorney, Michael Maggio, who was based in Washington, DC, but collaborated with the center. My extraordinary legal team helped me ready myself for battle.

In June I was called down to the Federal Building again, ushered into a small room where a dozen or so of my books lay open on a table that also held a tape recorder. Passages were highlighted in yellow magic marker. The polite official interviewed me for several hours, asking what I meant by this or that opinion. All the passages he pointed to concerned US governmental policy in Southeast Asia or Central America. My writing clearly showed my disagreement with those policies. I freely admitted to my opinions and said that, as far as I knew, freedom of expression and dissent existed here, that democracy protected a person's right to disagree.

The interviewing officer was noncommittal. At the end of the taped session he simply said I would be hearing from immigration again. He told me the FBI would pay me a visit, something that never happened (at least not that I noticed) and was probably just to keep me on edge. I continued to live my life, wait, try to adjust to the immense changes I was going through, and maintain my equanimity. My parents gave me a beautiful piece of foothill land adjacent to theirs and lent me the money to build a house. I knew this gesture was a vote of confidence, their way of telling me they believed I would win my case and be allowed to remain in the country. I also knew defeat was a very real possibility.

In October 1985 the deportation order finally arrived. It was an eleven-page document written by the Southwest Regional Immigration and Naturalization Service (INS) director, Alfred Giugni, and ended with these words: "Her writings go far beyond mere dissent, disagreement with, or criticism of the United States or its policies. . . . Your pending application for adjustment of status is hereby DENIED." That sudden switch from third to second person seemed to emphasize the decision. The final word, written in capitals, did too. I was given twenty-eight days to leave the country.

I remember taking that letter from the rural mailbox by the road in front of my new foothills home. There was a blaze of gold topping the chamisa, and the air was alive with light: a typical New Mexico October. The Justice Department's return address prompted me to open the envelope and read its contents standing in the midst of all that beauty. As I pondered the deportation order, I felt determined to disobey it, to stay and fight for myself and others. And to win if I possibly could.[2]

....

IMMIGRATION LAW

When I ask the experts
"how much time do I have"
I don't want an answer in years
or arguments.

I must know if there are hours enough
to mend this relationship,
see a book all the way to its birthing,
stand beside my father
on his journey.

I want to know how many seasons of chamisa
will be yellow and grey-green
and yellow
/light/
again,
how many red cactus flowers
will bloom beside my door.

I do not want to follow language
like a dog with its tail between its legs.

I need time equated with music,
hours rising in bread,
years deep from connections.

The present always holds a tremor of the past.
Give me a handful of future
to rub against my lips.

I was being prosecuted under the ideological exclusion clause of a law called the McCarran-Walter Immigration and Nationality Act. McCarran-Walter had been passed in 1952 over President Truman's veto, and used against prospective immigrants since. More than thirty clauses barred entry to applicants who were members of a Communist, Socialist, or Anarchist Party or to those who had "meaningful relations" with such members. People belonging to fascist parties or having meaningful relationships with their members weren't targeted. Other reasons for being denied entry included having an infectious disease or being a "sexual deviant," the law's term for homosexuals.

The government claimed that my writing went "beyond the good order and happiness of the United States." That verbatim line often brings laughter when I quote it in public. But it is absolutely serious, and it reflects the immigration policy of a country that, in this area at least, is backward and isolationist. The McCarran-Walter clause used against me has also been used against such international figures as Farley Mowat, Dario Fo, Carlos Fuentes, Gabriel García Márquez, and Hortensia de Allende. With my lawyers' help, and with the generous support of thousands of writers, artists, academics, members of the women's community, and others, I prepared myself for a long fight.

Among those who took an active part in my case were writers Adrienne Rich, Audre Lorde, Sonia Sanchez, Kurt Vonnegut, Arthur Miller, Grace Paley, Susan Sherman, Alice Walker, William Styron, and Norman Mailer; singer/songwriters Ronnie Gilbert, Holly Near, and Pat Humphries; historians Gerda Lerner and Howard Zinn; biologists Ruth Hubbard and George Wald; painters Elaine de Kooning and Jane Norling; politicians Barney Frank and Ron Dellums; and cultural icon Jessica Mitford. Institutions such as PEN International and the National Lawyers Guild were active on my behalf. University professors across the country came to my defense. Internationally, such figures as Mario Benedetti, Eduardo Galeano, Carlos Fuentes, and Roberto Fernández Retamar wrote letters saying that keeping me out of the country of my birth was an affront to intellectuals everywhere. Booksellers were particularly supportive; banned writers were at least as much of a concern as banned books. Thousands of ordinary citizens rallied to my cause.

I also had enormous support from my immediate family. My parents did what they could, Mother testifying eloquently in El Paso. My youngest daughter, Ana, the only one of my children living in the United States, was also in El Paso for the trial. Not quite seventeen, she took the stand, demonstrating a passion and maturity beyond her age. My other children and their families—in Paris and Mexico—sent moral support from afar. One of our sorrows during the years of my immigration case was that I could not travel to be at the births of my grandchildren. As finances allowed, their parents brought them to visit Albuquerque. Floyce, from whom I was already separated, nevertheless came to El Paso to show that our marriage had been legitimate.

My legal battle lasted almost five years. My case went to immigration court in El Paso, Texas, in the spring of 1986. That trial took four days, during which Judge Martin Spiegel heard government witnesses who attested to my "links to international communism," having children by several different men, having modeled nude for art classes as a young woman, and later publishing "subversive" literature in *El Corno Emplumado*. The government's strategy was extremely misogynist; many of the opposition's questions were meant to shame me as a woman. Some would have been laughable had they not been serious. The trial was reminiscent of the mid-1950s when McCarthyism was in full force, proving once again that, despite our vows not to allow them to return, repressive periods repeat themselves throughout history.

The government's lead lawyer, Guadalupe González, didn't speak or read Spanish. She asked me why I had gone to Cuba to meet Rubén Darío. The Encuentro con Rubén Darío had not been a meeting with the great Nicaraguan poet, dead for many years by then, but a gathering of poets to study his life and work. We brought our own witnesses: people who attempted to put my years in Cuba and Nicaragua in perspective, spoke about my family ties and contributions to the community. My side of the courtroom was filled with feminists from Las Cruces and several surviving veterans of the 1954 Salt of the Earth miners' strike near Silver City. The government filled its side with bored office workers on their lunch breaks.

Judge Spiegel had flown bombing missions in Vietnam. My lawyers told me that on the wall of his office he had a large framed photograph of a B-52 refueling in midair. In court González asked if it was true that I had worn a ring made of the metal from a downed US bomber. Spiegel may have borne me some animosity because we had been on opposite sides of the American war in Vietnam. He ultimately ruled against me. But he also displayed an interesting fairness. His judgment left the door open for appeal. It may have been that he didn't want the responsibility of giving me a win but didn't believe I deserved to lose. Whereas Giugni's deportation order hadn't found me ineligible for residency but had been based on his discretionary powers to exclude me, Spiegel wrote that in his discretion he would have granted me the right to stay because of family ties and service to the community. He, however, found me ineligible under McCarran-Walter.

For the next several years my case wound its way through the immigration court system. The legality of hiring me during that time was something of a gray area, yet several institutions, most notably Trinity College, put themselves on the line defending my freedom of expression. Others used my situation as an excuse to deny me employment. At one point 194 Trinity professors and staff, including the college president, sent a letter to US Attorney General Richard Thornburgh on my behalf. It had no immediate positive effect but constituted impressive moral support.

The Center for Constitutional Rights established defense committees throughout the country; at the height of our struggle I counted twenty-six. They raised money to fight my case and educated the public about McCarran-Walter, a law few citizens knew anything about. While I waited, I flew back and forth from coast to coast, often making weekly trips to appear on national news programs and talk shows. I appeared at conferences, congresses, sit-ins, read-ins, bowling marathons, house parties, and other events. I wrote thousands of individual thank-you notes to people who contributed anything from $5 to $5,000. Once in Berkeley, California, a stranger pressed a red rose and a $20 bill into my hands. As he did, he told me, "We need bread but roses too."

Whenever the case was out of the news, I was able to go on with my life relatively undisturbed. When a new appeal was announced, or some other facet of the case exploded in the news, public attention was reignited. I was physically attacked by a loner at the University of New Mexico, leading to a campus detective having to sit outside my door each time I held student office hours. I received hate mail threatening me with a variety of ugly assaults, including cutting my vagina end to end and filling it with lye. In the street someone might suddenly shout obscenities at me while others turned to stare. I was vilified, spat upon, and once almost driven off the road.

These attacks were infrequent when compared with the hundreds of demonstrations of support I received: hugs from strangers, encouraging letters, declarations by some of the world's most important writers and artists, a whole fifth-grade class at my old primary school that adopted my case for a year. At one point the students in that class all wrote me letters. One, written by a young boy, said, "Please don't be sad. I know how you feel. I am a Sikh, and everyone hates me too."

The attacks were also mostly spontaneous, made by individuals filled with hate, always ready to pounce when the media makes an easy target available. Some, though, were part of the government's strategy and aimed at creating a deeper fear. One of these took place on an otherwise peaceful afternoon as I was sitting in the waiting room at my gynecologist's office. We were all women awaiting our turn. The door opened, and a man entered, making his way directly to the receptionist's desk. It was Douglas Brown. I recognized him immediately. I couldn't hear the low murmur of his exchange with the receptionist but saw her glance furtively in my direction and then hand him a large unmarked manila envelope. He left with it under his arm. Through the window a few minutes later I watched as he crossed the parking lot, opened the door of his official INS vehicle, and drove away. I had no doubt that he had requisitioned my personal medical records or that the gynecologist had made them available. I didn't stay to see the doctor that day and had to find a new provider.

In August 1989 I was writing at my desk, occasionally looking out the large window with its undisturbed view of my mountains. The telephone rang, and I answered. It was Michael Maggio. He asked me if I was sitting down and I said yes. Then he told me we'd won. At the Court of Immigration Appeals, the last judicial level before my case would have entered the federal court system, a panel of five judges had decided three to two in my favor. David L. Milhollan wrote the favorable decision to which two of the other members subscribed. They not only granted me residency but restored my US citizenship. They found, as I'd claimed, that I had become a Mexican motivated by economic duress and therefore should never have lost my US citizenship. All other issues were rendered irrelevant. Fred W. Vacca wrote a scathing dissent, more or less a rehash of Guadalupe González's argument.

González had traveled to Washington to argue the government's case before the Board of Immigration Appeals. She'd quoted at length from Allan Bloom's right-wing classic *The Closing of the American Mind*. "The danger is that we will dilute the battle between freedom and communism to the level of no-fault auto insurance," González told the board. "The danger is that we will view this case in a context where there is no right or wrong. But there is a right and a wrong. The American Congress has stated that our system of government is right, and it is good, and the Communist system is bad. We *are* an intolerant government. We are intolerant of world communism, and we are intolerant of those individuals, like Randall, who attempt to increase its hold on the world."

There really is no clearer example of the official point of view on this issue, at least the point of view of those within our government—the zealots—who reduce complex social and political thought to pseudo-patriotic gibberish. Like a pendulum swinging back and forth, every so often these shallow reductionist thinkers take control of our major institutions. It's interesting that I won my case at the end of the Reagan years. I've often thought my win might have been more likely during the Carter, Clinton, or Obama administrations. Would such a victory be possible today? This points to the importance of an unbiased, fair-minded judiciary.

I felt numb as I listened to Michael's news. I finally pulled myself together and called my partner, Barbara, at work, notified my parents, contacted my kids. Newspaper reporters and television people were already gathering at our front door. Floral arrangements were delivered. The phone rang incessantly. The government could have appealed but didn't. Soon I would be issued my first US passport since the previous one had been invalidated by that US consul in Mexico City so many years before.

The first time I traveled after winning my case, when I reentered the country my name was still flagged on the immigration agent's computer. When I told her my story, she was sympathetic and said she would remove the flag. The problem seemed resolved, but every ten years when I've had to apply for a new passport, I've been reminded that I am still in the government's crosshairs. On two such occasions I had to appeal to my legislative representative to help me get the document. Once, after a delay of several months, the new passport was sent to me in a large envelope also containing a transcript from my El Paso trial. Once targeted, dissidents may win legal battles but are constantly reminded we are being watched. It is a form of passive harassment.

It was painful to have to go through such a struggle to regain my US citizenship and be able to live in the country where I was born and had family. It was also a privilege. Throughout those five years I never stopped thinking about the hundreds of thousands of immigrants who come to our borders fleeing repressive situations in their countries of origin, cross illegally or even legally, and lack the support I enjoyed. The vast majority are sent away, often to their deaths. I felt I was fighting for them as well as for myself.

I was also conscious of what it meant to be female fighting such a case. During the El Paso trial I was consistently asked questions meant to humiliate my condition as a woman: questions about my marriages or modeling nude that would never have been asked of a man. The government also frequently implied that if I showed remorse for my prior opinions and vowed never to say such things again, I might be forgiven. This idea that if we say we're sorry all will be forgiven is one we women know all too well.

In my late forties, I continued to hold the same values I'd held in early adulthood but wouldn't have expressed myself as I had in my twenties and thirties. I would no longer have written America with three k's or used some of the other cliched expressions in my incipient writer's vocabulary. But I knew enough not to let myself be tricked into saying "I'm sorry." Throughout the years of my case, each morning I'd get up and rededicate myself to defending my right to my opinions, whether or not I would have articulated them then in the same ways.

Today, with Trump's Machiavellian policies, all immigrants are portrayed as criminals, border detention camps are overflowing, and children are being separated from their parents in the ugliest of all efforts to discourage immigration. Three decades ago, I believed my case could help change this country's unjust immigration laws. The truth is, it and others being waged around that time did bring changes to aspects of the law. Some of McCarran-Walter's clauses were overturned. But today Communists and socialists are no longer the enemies. Since September 11, 2001, Muslims are the primary targets of governmental fear and hate. Or anyone stereotyped as Arabic or assumed to be Muslim. Such people are frequently thrown off planes and beaten or murdered by citizens encouraged by governmental rhetoric. The use of immigration law as a political weapon continues. Only its victims have changed.

....

My immigration case wasn't the only issue I had to confront upon my return to the United States. I've mentioned the shock of moving from impending war to a nation of affluence, where the consumer culture seemed to bombard me from all sides. Living for the first time without any of my children was also a big change. During the years of my case I couldn't travel outside the country and was unable to be with them when they began having children of their own. I experienced an intimate loneliness.

Another issue that loomed large at the time was discovering I had been a victim of incest on the part of my maternal grandfather when I was just an infant. Actually, by both my maternal grandparents, since I later remembered my grandmother looking on. I retrieved these memories over a period of a couple of years in sessions with a therapist I was seeing to help me with the transition home. Getting those memories back was important for my continued development, as a woman and human being. They explained the phobia of mushrooms I'd had for as long as I could remember. I've written about this in more detail in a previous chapter, but I mention it here in order to give a further sense of what my homecoming entailed.

And then there was my coming out as a lesbian. Not only to the world, but to myself. I've talked about how the Albuquerque women's community embraced me upon my return. That community was made up of both gay and straight women. Although my parents, brother, and—briefly—Floyce provided comfort, it was with those women that I found a solidarity that rivaled what I'd experienced in the revolutionary movements I'd left behind.

One evening a friend named Ann Nihlen and I drove an hour north to Santa Fe, New Mexico's smart, art-conscious capital. My memory tells me we'd been invited to dinner at the home of a friend of hers, though I can no longer recall the friend's name. I remember it as a pleasant evening, and our drive back down to Albuquerque as filled with easy conversation. In the midst of that conversation, Ann casually said, "When you come out as a lesbian . . ." I no longer remember the end of her sentence because its first seven words made such an impact. It was an offhand comment, but one issued with conviction. Ann simply assumed a future for me that had never crossed my conscious mind.

Strange as it may seem, it was as if that comment presented a possibility I hadn't previously considered. It felt right. Odd, because new and untried, but right. Over the next few days her words kept coming back, asking a question I felt compelled to answer. I'd had a number of close lesbian friends in New York, Mexico, Cuba, Nicaragua, and among those visitors from the United States who had kept me connected to my homeland all those years. If I allowed myself the luxury of looking at my own sexuality, I could even remember women who had physically attracted me. Once, in a fit of frustration after yet another bad experience with a man, I'd told myself "if only I were a lesbian . . ." But until I heard the words uttered by my friend in that darkened car between Santa Fe and Albuquerque, the idea that I really might be an almost fifty-year-old woman-loving woman who needed to come out of some flimsy self-imposed closet hadn't presented itself.

Looking back, I believe the demands of unequal revolutionary struggle were what prevented me from questioning my sexual identity. When one is involved in years of all-consuming battle, and perhaps especially when one is part of a group of Davids fighting a much more powerful Goliath, spending time on self-examination isn't really an option. No one I knew during my years in Cuba and Nicaragua had much time for exploring personal need. We all prioritized the collective, while engaging familiar forms of loving and allowing ourselves to be loved.

But now I was back in my country of origin. Although much was new, the deeper aspects of life were familiar. Landscape. Language. Humor and other cultural cues. The ways people relate to one another. It was as if I was suddenly free to look at myself more clearly. Within a week or so, I had my first lesbian experience. It was with a woman with whom I was miserably mismatched. Looking back, I can't imagine why I dated her on and off for several months. She was an artist, and we had some things in common, but she was troubled in ways that were impossible for me to deal with, and I later realized I'd put up with attitudes and even mistreatment from her that I never would have accepted from a man at that point in my life. I finally put an end to the unfortunate relationship. Its only virtue turned out to have been that of helping me make the move into territory that was new. Sexually, but more important emotionally, I knew I was home.

It was 1986. I was approaching fifty. I wasn't burdened by the stigma and lack of acceptance so many young girls struggling with their sexual identities are forced to face. Even if I had been, it wouldn't have fazed me; I'd rarely allowed society to make decisions about my life. I was fortunate in that my children and parents embraced my change.

Was the identity really new? Who can say? I had loved the men in my life and was grateful for the children they'd given me. Now, when I took my mother to lunch and came out to her, her first response was "You're lucky you were born thirty years later than I was." I'm still pondering exactly what she meant by that. She followed her initial comment with "Well, your father and I have always known." That too seemed a confusing statement. But then, my mother was known for saying what she believed her listeners wanted to hear. In any case, both she and Dad were accepting of my transition. They loved my longtime partner, Barbara, like they had never loved any of my previous husbands or lovers.

My children were supportive as well. Gregory and his family were living in Paris at the time, a city rich in diversity. He and his wife began taking their children to yearly gay pride marches involving tens of thousands. Sarah visited me in Albuquerque and asked to visit some of the gay bars and go to a softball game or two. Although these were places where lesbian social life happened,

Gregory (photo by Margaret Randall).

they weren't my places. A nonsmoker and only occasional drinker by now, I didn't frequent bars. And I'd never been into softball. I took her to those venues because I knew that she too was trying to understand a culture new to her.

Ximena was a bit more resistant to my transition. She asked me to accompany her to see a psychologist and insisted he be male, heterosexual, and a Spanish speaker. Ximena is my only child who has never been able to learn enough English to converse. We found such a professional on one of her visits to Albuquerque, and the session was satisfying. Ximena seemed relieved when we left the psychologist's office. For her, as well as for all those who loved me, my integrity and happiness were the most important considerations. My youngest, Ana, had been living in New York for a couple of years by then. As in Gregory's case, a more open-minded milieu enabled her to take my new identity in stride.

Sarah (photo by
Margaret Randall).

I had another consideration, however. My immigration case wasn't yet
resolved, and I knew that one of McCarran-Walter's clauses covered what the
law defined as sexual deviancy. I was being prosecuted under its ideological
exclusion clause. The Center for Constitutional Rights' whole strategy revolved around educating people about freedom of expression. If it were to
come out that I was a lesbian, what would that mean for my case? I spoke with
my lawyers. They were unanimous in hoping I might be able to keep my new
sexual identity under wraps. If it became known, they said, they would defend
me with the same energy and creativity they'd demonstrated to that point.
But it would require a major change in strategy.

For the next several years, until I won my case, my sexual identity may have
been the best-kept secret in the lesbian community nationwide. Because I was
something of a public figure, many people undoubtedly knew. I have to imagine

Ximena (photo by Margaret Randall).

the government knew as well. For whatever reason, it never became an issue. Perhaps social mores were changing even within the more conservative sectors.

....

I knew as I began writing about coming home that portraying Barbara would be challenging. I have never met anyone remotely like her. She is an artist with an artist's spirit: brilliant, innovative, creative. Having survived a criminal father and extremely repressive childhood, she is also troubled, prone to insecurities and depression. She can be observant and quiet, or overflowing with observations and ideas. She sometimes talks about how these "leak from [her] head." Through our years together I've watched her struggle, gaining ground in fits and starts. She possesses a deep wisdom and crackling wit, that particular watchfulness common to those who have grown up wary of that moment in which apparent normalcy always threatens to explode into violence.

One of the things I first noticed about Barbara was her integrity, and I have never seen it falter. She is eminently authentic, an ongoing lesson in honesty. We connect deeply, both culturally and politically. And yet we value silliness. Through the darkest times, whether personal or public, we tend to relieve unbearable tension with dark jokes or inappropriate comments repeatable only to each other.

Barbara chooses kindness every day. Not only in her relationship with me, our family, and friends, but also with those she meets on the street or in any

Ana (family snapshot, attribution unknown).

other venue. She sees people and lets them know she sees them. I used to get impatient, even irritated, when she would interrupt an outing by crouching beside someone in a wheelchair or striking up a genuine conversation with a person who has a mental or physical impairment. Now I watch the exchange with delight.

Observing the arc of Barbara's artistic expression continues to be thrilling. She has had to struggle simply to take herself seriously as an artist, not an identity anyone in her family of origin respected or even considered legitimate. When we got together, she was painting provocative cartoonlike landscapes in raw acrylics, often with purple earth and orange skies. She titled one drawing in which items of underwear flew through the air "Northern Bra Warning."

Those landscapes morphed into a series called "Personal Cartography," large multimedia maps on which the internal and external meet. I've seen her study the rock art found all over the Southwest, teaching herself the secrets of its deceptively simple language. Kachina dolls have been an inspiration, but she's taken care not to copy them exactly, out of respect for the secrets of their still-living tradition. We love visiting museums together, and both of us also dispense with them quickly. We are excited by the same artistic expression and become saturated at around the same time.

In recent years, Barbara has begun to make artist books and has learned the skills necessary to producing some of their infinite varieties. She's discovered asemic writing—writing devoid of semantic meaning—and begun combining it with images. She's been exploring print-making and has gravitated toward a small format in which tiny pieces are gems. She produces hundreds of these, each an original, and gives them away to friends and also to people she hardly knows.

Process is front and center in Barbara's work. Over the past couple of years, she's had exhibitions—here in Albuquerque and also in Matanzas, Cuba—in which she's mounted her open workbooks on the wall, inviting viewers to page through them, accompany her on her journey. It's exciting to live with an artist such as Barbara, whose work continually changes yet retains a profound continuity.

....

WHERE THEY LEFT YOU FOR DEAD

3
You say you are
leaving yourself behind. A sort of death (you watch
my face) but not in this dimension, a different recipe
for dying. Pay attention now. Watch your back,
both sides and everyone between: early family
requirements.

Forced to choose between this unnamed illness
and the labyrinth out, you must relax your gaze.
I cannot get close enough, cannot climb inside
your pummeled skin though I would barter
my years.

Helpless I follow your desperate gait, the streaks
of pain you trail. Climbing a debris field
of shifting boulders you despair, defy, break
running towards your infant self. Where they
left you for dead.

Now you pick life up and carry it. Life pokes
at this illness without name, crowds you, presses
for signature, forces a retake. You say you are
leaving yourself behind. I stand beside you,
waving.

SHE BECOMES TIME
FOR BARBARA

As she touches the boundary of time
she becomes time.
What is required of us at any moment,
unannounced, beyond pain or question.

As she settles against the mirror surface
she becomes a thousand versions
of herself,
every imprint she contains.

As she notices what grows between words
she moves from discomfort to terror
and back,
from breakdown to anticipation.

Her artist's hand pushes pathways
across the paper's surface,
creates spaces of silence
and spaces where secrets scream.

We grip hands so the knowing can flow
unobstructed through one to the other,
folding time and waiting
in braided fingers:

precisely here, precisely now.

I also knew that Barbara's and my relationship would be one of the most difficult subjects with which I'd have to deal. How can words do it justice? Yet words are what I have. It's hard for me to imagine being able to convey the heft or texture of our life together. After thirty-three years, describing the strong union we've made—its all-encompassing solidity and ongoing magic— remains a challenge.

We met in the fall of 1986, when she took my Women and Creativity course at UNM. Not a traditional student and older than most of those in the class, she was working in a sign shop at the time but enrolled in one university course each semester as a way of keeping herself engaged with a more stimulating environment. I remember her purple overalls, yellow sneakers, and incisive comments. She seemed to notice everything. One day she brought a single rose to my office, hidden in a gym bag. She said she saw my sadness—I think I was going through a particularly rough patch in my case—and wanted to cheer me up. After I'd turned my grades in, I invited her to dinner. She never left.

Barbara was thirty-five. I was just about to celebrate my fiftieth birthday. We came from very different backgrounds. She from a brutal, ultra-conservative father who belonged to a racist cult, tortured her with electrical current, and attempted to control her in many other ways until she managed to escape; her mother was utterly submissive to him. I was the oldest child of liberal parents who, despite their idiosyncrasies and an unhappy marriage, managed to provide a loving home.

Talking loud scared Barbara; in her childhood it was invariably a precursor to violence. Shouting was endemic to the New York culture of my early years and the Latin American cultures in which I'd spent so much of my adulthood. She thought long and hard before saying anything. I blurted out whatever came into my mind, believing I could always take it back later. At times it seemed we spoke different languages. During our relationship's first couple of years, we sought several sessions with a therapist in order to learn how to live with one another.

Yet we knew, from those first moments, that living together was what we would do. For the duration. Almost wordlessly, we fulfilled one another's need. I fell in love with Barbara's brilliance, her humanity, and her art. I still remember a particular painting of a New Mexico hillside dotted with pinyon trees, each with its small slanted shadow. I think I fell for that painting as I had fallen for the landscape that inspired it.

Each of us also brought big challenges to the relationship. Barbara had physical problems that often required she walk with a cane and occasionally put her in a wheelchair. During our first few years she barely had the energy to work more than six consecutive hours a day. She's suffered from chronic pain most of her life, long trivialized by doctors who told her it was "all in her head." When we met, her physical condition hadn't yet been diagnosed, even by her. I brought with me the problems of my as-yet-unresolved immigration status. If I lost the case, which seemed probable, I would have to leave the country. Where would I go? Mexico? Cuba? Both were places where Barbara didn't speak the language. Would she be able to adjust, find work, survive?

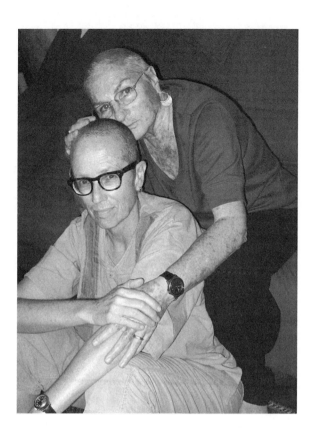

Barbara and Margaret (family snapshot by Mark Behr).

We didn't shy away from discussing these liabilities, but they made no difference to how we felt. We simply had to be together. As we built trust, there was an openness and gentleness neither of us had known before. We sometimes said we wished we'd met earlier in our lives, but the truth is we probably wouldn't be together now if we had. Each of us had made our way through many relationships. We knew what we didn't want, which may be as good a point of departure as any for building what we did.

When we'd been together a couple of weeks, Barbara received a late-night phone call from an ex-lover saying she had a problem only my new partner could solve. We both went to the woman's home, concerned. That incident was a lesson. We vowed never again to allow ourselves to be cornered by people who thrive on fabricated drama. There's a difference between the legitimate issues—war, poverty, illness, racism, misogyny, and others to which we must always respond—and those which certain people create in an effort to suck all the air from human interaction. That vow put us on a road that helped keep our own relationship sane.

Soon after Barbara moved in, we both admitted we wanted rings. In that pre–marriage equality time, such symbols of a relationship acquired special importance. One night I had a dream, in which Mary Elizabeth Jane Colter visited me.[3] She said we would find our rings at Grand Canyon, a seven-hour drive from Albuquerque. A week or so later we made the trip. It was January, and cold. We found our first rings at Hopi House, a curio shop on the Canyon's south rim, designed by Colter. They were simple silver bands with a line of bear claw impressions circling them. We wore them until the soft metal cracked and they fell from our fingers. Since then we've had a series of rings, finally settling on plain gold bands we bought when we were able to marry legally.

On that visit to Grand Canyon, huddled in our parked car, we placed those first rings on one another and spoke about what love meant to each of us. Many years later, when the United States finally recognized marriage equality, we repeated those vows at a wonderful ceremony surrounded by family and friends and hosted by my daughter Ana in Brooklyn. Ana's father, Robert, generously paid for Sarah and Ximena to come from Mexico for the event. Gregory and his family, in Uruguay, were present via Skype.

A couple of months before our Brooklyn marriage, a group of county clerks in New Mexico suddenly decided they were going to perform same-sex marriage ceremonies; their consciences no longer allowed them to discriminate. When we heard about their mutiny, Barbara and I went down to Albuquerque's City Hall. We were the sixth couple in line to obtain our New Mexico license. I remember most of the couples there that day were as old if not older than we were. They had been together for years and leapt at the chance to legalize their unions.

I couldn't have imagined that state-sanctioned marriage would make an emotional difference to me. I don't agree with my government about much and, besides, I'd gone through a number of legal marriages already, all of them ending badly. Barbara and I both thought we were engaging in a political act more than anything else, and one that also might bring advantages in terms of legal responsibility if one of us developed a serious medical condition or with regard to our yearly tax bill. We were astonished at how moved we were by the ceremony itself, especially the one in Brooklyn. It reflected the life we'd built together, one that had sustained us by then for almost three decades. We felt deeply supported by family and friends.

Soon after we got together, Barbara decided to go back to school and get her teacher's license. She was tired of the sign business and wanted to be doing something that gave back to the community. For twenty years she taught special education students in one of the poorest and most violent parts of Albuquerque, mostly at a public middle school. She retired in 2010 to devote herself to her art. I won my case, continued teaching at a series of universities, and retired in 1994. Retirement, for me, meant finally being able to write full-time. It still feels like a luxury I find hard to believe.

Our relationship fulfills me in ways I find difficult to describe. We are artists who respect and support each other's work. There's never been a moment of jealousy when one of us has had some creative success. We are easy and kind with one another, yet also our most honest critics. Early in our relationship I gave her a novel I had just finished; she told me it couldn't leave the house. These days, I rarely send anything out without her having read it. There is nothing like sharing a home in which she is at work in her studio, I in mine, and we come together to show or read to one another, share a meal, discuss some complex aesthetic or political issue, and then retire together at the end of a day that's been both stimulating and harmonious.

What needs to be done to keep our household running smoothly has never required a verbal division of labor, lists about who should do what or when. All such struggles are memories from my distant past. When I retired, and Barbara was still working, I took major responsibility for our home. As I age, she has largely taken over. I've always gravitated toward cooking, she toward cleaning, but we both wordlessly notice what needs to be done and do it.

For a while I made more money, then she was the one earning more. Contrary to my previous relationships, in which I was almost always the primary earner, finances have been easy for us. Early in our relationship, on a weekend trip to Mesa Verde, I was sitting out on our room's small balcony watching the evening light play on the shapes of far-off buttes. A robin perched on the railing and began to sing. I listened and heard words, instructions for how Barbara and I might manage our money.

That robin told me we should have a joint bank account into which we put our salaries; if possible, it should underwrite all household expenses. Additionally, each of us should maintain a personal account. The proceeds of every painting she sold or royalty I earned would be divided equally between those. This would allow us funds with which to buy something we didn't really want to discuss with the other. None of those issues that had been so problematic in my previous relationships and that seem complicated for so many couples—gay or straight—have been important to us. We share easily and generously.

Retirement has definitely been the most fulfilling time of my creative life. No longer working at a wage-earning job, no longer involved with making revolution (although I still believe in the same things and do what I can to support social change), no longer with the responsibility of raising young children, I can devote myself fully to my writing. It's a situation that never fails to amaze and inspire my gratitude. And it's freed me up to go deeper into my work than I'd thought possible.

....

BEING THEIR DAUGHTER

It was the question without an answer.
Sometimes her silence
was gunmetal gray,
sometimes rimmed in orchid pink.

He didn't know and didn't want to know.
Like most couples, they had their problems.
Being their daughter
didn't provide a clue.

DNA isn't part of this story.
Each year I ask
in the voice of a younger me
and reap an answer of rainbows.

People always told me I had big bones
like him. My resemblance to her
stared back in every mirror.
They're both gone now,

leaving me a story winding down,
repeating echoes
and resignation
transparent as morning sky.

My parents hoped to die in the house they'd built for themselves in the Sandia foothills, but it wasn't meant to be. After some forty years, the last seven of which we lived next door, it became too difficult for them to navigate daily life so far from the city. First Dad and then Mother was forced to give up driving. As the 1990s dawned, Dad's dementia became increasingly noticeable. He devised coping mechanisms and the rest of us clung to our denial, but one day he told Barbara he'd forgotten how to subtract and asked if she would teach him. When that wasn't possible, he gave management of his finances over to us. Mother, who'd always deferred to her Wharton School of Business husband, was only too happy to let us take responsibility. Like so many women of her class and generation, she could do little more than write a check and had no interest in learning much else.

Dad's problem managing money wasn't the only clue that something was wrong. His internal clock seemed off; he began getting up at one or two in the morning, demanding Mother make him breakfast. Small confusions were impossible to mask. Safety became an issue. They had never wanted to impose a suburban garden on their land, and the terrain leading up to their front door was rugged, hard for a man with erratic balance to navigate. Yet as my father's dementia progressed, he also became sweeter. We were spared the aggression that so often accompanies Alzheimer's. It may be true that as we age, no matter what our condition we become more fully who we have always been.

It was obvious that they needed to move. Mom was eager, Dad more reluctant, but after some convincing we managed to get them into a complex where they would have access to the help they needed. After a few false starts—one establishment careened toward bankruptcy, another soon showed itself to be corrupt—we got them settled in a pleasant apartment at an Evangelical Lutheran place with a wing for those with more serious healthcare needs. We all recoiled at the staff's routine suggestion that we begin meetings with prayer but appreciated their genuine devotion to the residents. By this time my father was confined to the care unit and Mother had their apartment to herself.

My parents had adopted Barbara as their own, and she'd developed deep relationships with them both. She finally had the parents she needed and a family that respected and loved her unreservedly. She and Dad had a wordless communication, especially important as he lost his ability to speak. With Mother she also had a special bond. Lacking the considerable baggage Mom and I carried in our relationship, Barbara was able to get her to relax. She wasn't affected by her self-serving veneer and accepted her on her terms. Seeing the way Mother let go in Barbara's arms was a revelation. As each of my parents fell into the neediness of age, Barbara joined my brother and me in caring for them. My sister, living in Northern California, made occasional visits to Albuquerque but wasn't interested in becoming too involved.

Dad went first, in 1994. He'd just turned eighty-eight. He seemed to recognize us all until almost the end, but often called me Elinor, my mother's name. As conversation became more difficult, I'd sit by his bed and tell him I loved him. He would answer "Ditto" until even that word eluded him. My father had long made it clear that he wanted no heroic measures at the end, but the nurses at the care unit made it equally clear they believed their duty was to prolong life no matter what. When they began forcing his mouth open to spoon-feed him and he clamped his lips shut and turned his face away but couldn't get them to stop, we brought him to Mother's apartment where we felt we could be more respectful of his wishes and make his final days more comfortable. Mother couldn't face such close proximity to the husband of sixty-two years with whom she had never felt that easy. She moved out of the apartment and in with a friend for the duration.

It was May. I was finishing up my semester at Trinity and flew home for the weekend. My brother, Barbara, and I took turns spending the night with Dad, who was completely comatose by then. He died the night after I returned to Hartford to hand in my grades. Ann asked us to wait a couple of months to hold the memorial, until it was convenient for her to come to town. A few months later we hosted it at Johnny's bookstore: a joyous community event with dozens of multigenerational friends. We celebrated a man well loved, a life well lived. Albuquerque was still a small town in many ways. One of Dad's nurses at the care unit had been a music student of his in fourth grade.

Mother wanted to divest herself of all Dad's things. Even his favorite armchair. Barbara, afraid she might have second thoughts, saved his wristwatch. Mom wore it for a while. Barbara had been wise about this as about so much else. Gradually Mother rewrote the script of her long marriage: in her emerging narrative they'd been happy, and she missed him terribly. I watched as her new state of mind replaced the old. There was some truth in it all. Loneliness took up residence along with an unfamiliar freedom—acquired when it was too late to take advantage of its possibilities. Mom had a number of good friends who took her to lunch, concerts, the occasional party. In her last couple of decades, she'd lost interest in attending weddings. "I just know they'll end in divorce," she would say.

I have known death many times in my life: the deaths of mentors, close friends, the constant presence of death during the war in Nicaragua. But the death of a parent is different. It takes with it a piece of oneself, a connection to one's own story. Except in those rare cases in which separating from cruel or criminal parents is necessary to survival, a parent's death always creates a rupture.

After Dad was gone, translating José Martí continued to be a passion for my mother and she spent hours each day going over previous translations, often rendering them less smooth, burdened with latter-day convolutions and unnecessary weight. The only thing I remember Mom asking of me was that I care for those translations, see to it that they were published. I have kept that promise to the best of my ability. When we could no longer acquire ribbons for her old typewriter, we introduced her to a computer. It was always an uneasy relationship. She treated it as a typewriter with a screen. This difficulty in embracing modernity must have been shared by many others where she lived; a kind man on the premises made the rounds of their apartments every few days, helping them save documents and do other functions they resisted learning.

Johnny had invited our mother to a concert on a Sunday. She'd seemed fine, said she really enjoyed it. The next morning—a Monday at the beginning of December 2006—I called, and Mom told me she didn't feel well. I was accustomed to calling her every day and we'd go to lunch once or twice a week. I said I'd come by and take her to her doctor, but she said no, she'd rather wait. By Tuesday she felt worse. That morning the emergency room doctor said he wanted to hospitalize her. All her organs were in failure mode.

Mother's agony lasted five days, although it wasn't an agony in any obvious sense. She was very clear that she didn't want heroic measures, and in contrast with the people who had cared for Dad, Mom's caregivers were responsive to her wishes. She asked me if she was dying. I said yes. I asked if she was afraid. She said no. All she wanted, she told me, was not to experience pain and that Johnny, Barbara, and I be with her at the end. Those first days in the hospital, Mother entertained a steady stream of friends who came to say goodbye. Her grandchildren called from various points around the globe. Ann thought about coming from California but ultimately didn't make the trip.

I was stunned as I watched my mother—a woman who had seemed so fearful and deceptive—face death with such equanimity. By Wednesday she said she'd had enough visitors. The hospital's cooperative floor doctor arranged for hospice, and that fine service stepped in to keep Mother comfortable. Plenty of morphine to ease anxiety and pain. On Thursday she fell into a peaceful sleep. She died late on Friday afternoon, with Johnny, Barbara, Joanna, and me at her side. In that small hospital room Joanna had been playing her cello and Barbara one of her Indian flutes. Common belief holds that hearing is the last sense to go. We hoped the music had reached her, along with our declarations of love. My seventieth birthday was the next day, and Barbara and I had invited a few friends to a local restaurant. Barbara would have canceled, but I decided to go ahead with the celebration.

With both my parents gone, I became the matriarch in my family of origin. It's a strange sensation, difficult to describe. There's missing those people who bore and raised me, gave me bedrock love, and shaped my early identity. In time the missing obliterates disagreements, disappointments, petty annoyances. With the passing years, the missing too rises and fades, then rises again. And then there are the secrets. Mother especially took hers with her. It wasn't vindictive. She couldn't have understood how much I would have loved having answers. As I myself have aged and experienced memory's unexpected contours, I also know that people often create such an indelible narrative that what really happened may fade, what they've invented takes its place.

In 2017 my sister, who suffered from many years of poor health, chose death over dialysis. She had always seemed extraordinarily anxiety-ridden, yet she too faced her decline with fearlessness and grace. Now it's just my brother and me at the waning end of our family line. Plenty of children, grandchildren, and great-grandchildren to carry on. My biggest fear is that we are leaving them an earth that cannot sustain them.

....

It's been extraordinary to see my children grow and have children and grandchildren of their own. It's deeply satisfying to me that each has carved a place for him- or herself in a field that gives them joy—and in which they give so much back. My relationship with my children hasn't always been smooth. My three daughters, to different degrees, feel I spent too much time making revolution and not enough attending to them. With some we've been able to deal with the tensions more successfully; with others, less so. I know those tensions are typical for the revolutionary women of my generation; for obvious reasons the children have blamed their mothers more than their fathers for what has felt like abandonment or neglect. In my own case it remains to be seen if there will be time enough to heal those wounds. I also know that having to send my children away during the Mexican repression scarred them all, probably more my daughters than my son.

After years in Paris, Gregory; his wife, Laura; and their three children, Lía Margarita, Martín, and Daniel, returned to Latin America. They went to live in Uruguay, Laura's home. Gregory got a professorship in electrical engineering at the University of the Republic, the nation's only public institution of higher education. His field is image processing and computer vision. He had a seven-year stint as university vice president, during which he spent a lot of time on the social values that the university embodies, adjusting the vision of the 1918 University Reform movement of Córdoba, Argentina, to the demands of the twenty-first century. He was also involved in creating additional college campuses throughout the country. Now, for the first time in Uruguay's history, provincial students don't have to travel to the capital to obtain a public university education.

Sarah and her husband, Javier, live in Cholula, Mexico, with their sons, Sebastián and Juan. Richi, a son by a previous marriage, lives in the capital. It took a while for Sarah to find her life's calling, but when she did it fit her like a glove. She teaches classes of Kundalini yoga at the Ibero-American University in Puebla and also has groups of private students. Her students say she is an authentic healer.

Ximena also lives in Mexico. She had a son, Luis Rodrigo, and daughter, Mariana, with her first partner. She left him and now lives with economist Cassio Luiselli. Their first few years together he was Mexico's ambassador to Uruguay, where sister and brother and their families had the rare opportunity of sharing everyday life. There Cassio encouraged Ximena to study gastronomy. She became a skilled and innovative chef, and now that they are back in Mexico City she has established a cultural/culinary venue where she hosts invitation-only evenings. They may feature a poetry reading, concert, or lecture, and Ximena accompanies the offering with a dinner tailored to the occasion.

Ana is the only one of my offspring who ended up in the United States. She lives in Brooklyn. She and her ex-husband, Louis, have two sons, Eli and Bartolomeo, or Tolo. Ana has been working in television for more than two decades. She started out with Diane Sawyer, spent many satisfying years with Bill Moyers, and is currently a senior producer for Christiane Amanpour. Her specialty is booking, and she seems to have acquired contact information for everyone of note in the international worlds of politics, the arts, entertainment, and sports. Her job is complex and requires finesse, long days, and constant attention to news cycles and the deeper issues underlying them. When I stay at her home and have occasion to watch her work, I am always astonished at how a young woman who came to the United States at the age of fourteen speaking almost no English has been able to make herself into the brilliant professional she is today.

My ten grandchildren include a biochemist, an electrical engineer, a visual artist who works with disadvantaged children, a chef, and an expert in international affairs with a specialty in environmental issues. The biochemist, who with her husband runs a university lab, teaches, has two small children, and is also in her fourth year of medical school. Among those still studying are a couple who may become photographers, two who will probably go into music, and one who has interned in the field of human rights. Each has been encouraged to find his or her unique contribution and, more importantly, each seems to have inherited the values and concerns that have been important in our family.

As I have been with a number of men and my children consequently have three different fathers, they also have what many call half-brothers and half-sisters in a variety of places. We've never used the terms "half" or "step" when describing these relationships. Although most haven't lived together, they all consider one another siblings and nurture relationships that allow their children to know one another as well. In our family, ties are based on curiosity, shared values, mutual interest, and love.

As I've aged, I've suffered some of the physical changes that come with the territory. My memory isn't as sharp as it once was, and I can sit at the computer long moments these days searching for a wayward word. What I've lost in physical and memory health, though, I've gained in a knowledge that can only come from longtime experience. I'm able to make connections I once only intuited. I feel I am at the height of my game, intellectually and creatively.

Barbara's work is also enjoying a particularly vibrant moment. Her art excites me as mine does her. She has made her own relationship with each of my children, and that has made both of us happy. She never had children of her own, and although mine are friends rather than offspring, having them in her life is important. With some of our grandchildren we have deep relationships; with others, it's been more difficult. I don't lose hope that I may achieve a closeness with them all before I die. We have two great-grandchildren whose presence has brought joy to everyone in our very dispersed family. With its members living in Uruguay, Mexico, New York, France, and Australia, seeing one another isn't as easy as any of us would like, but we try to keep connected.

....

One of the big changes Barbara brought into my life was physical activity: the sharing of a few sports such as hiking, biking, and even for a brief time working out at a rock-climbing gym. This enhanced my love of the New Mexican landscape that involved venturing into it as I hadn't done since my secret adolescent forays. For this I had to lose weight. I'd become sedentary as only writers can. Friends used to joke about me: "Yeah, Margaret loves walking . . . from the front door to the car." When I said I wanted to get fit, Barbara suggested we spend a couple of hours at a local gym each morning before she went to work. In a few months I'd lost enough weight and gotten sufficiently strong that I enjoyed accompanying her on twenty-five- and forty-mile bike rides.

I had other obstacles to overcome, though. What really attracted me was hiking, exploring desert and mountains as only one can on the ground. But I suffered from severe vertigo and a fear of heights.

For twenty years Barbara and I took some extraordinary trips: managing to travel first when she had vacations from teaching and then, after we were both retired, at other times of the year.

We retraced my 1974 visit to Vietnam, where our thirty-two-year-old guide, who was two when the war ended, told our small group, "We welcome Americans to our country. But we want you to know it wasn't alright for you to bomb us." In Turkey our guide turned out to be a literary person who helped me collect $2,000 from a pirated edition of one of my books that was still in print and being sold in Istanbul bookstores. Two African safaris—one in Kenya and Tanzania; the other in Botswana, Zimbabwe, and Namibia— were thrilling beyond words. It's powerful to visit terrain owned by animals.

I took Barbara to the countries that had helped shape my life: Mexico, Cuba, Nicaragua. Sometimes I'd be doing field work in one of them, so she would meet me there when my work was finished, and we'd visit my favorite places, meet my friends, make new memories together. In recent years she's accompanied me a half dozen times to Cuba, where she has shown her art while I've launched Cuban editions of my books.

In South Africa we met a dear friend, Mark Behr, and spent a week hiking in his homeland, the foothills of the Drakensberg Mountains. Our goals were San rock-art sites, but the beauty of the countryside was equally captivating. Mark also accompanied me on one of the great hikes of my life, in northern Arizona. He carried seventy pounds to my twenty so we could visit Keet Seel, an Anasazi ruin that requires hiking eighteen miles and includes forging a river riddled with quicksand and navigating heights and drops to challenge the toughest outdoorsperson. Mark died of a heart attack at the age of fifty-two, suddenly and tragically in 2015. He left several novels, one of which, *Embrace*, is one of the great books of our generation. I think of him almost every day.

Barbara and I have traveled extensively in Mexico, to Copper Canyon in the north and the Mayan world in the south. We took seven of our grandchildren, all those old enough to accompany us at the time, to the Galápagos Islands. We visited the astonishing south-central Pacific island of Rapa Nui, with its mysterious stone figures looking out to sea, and were surprised to discover we were in the same time zone as Albuquerque.

We've gone to Jordan where we spent four days exploring Petra. We've visited Egypt, Tunisia, Greece, Croatia, Albania, Montenegro, Cambodia, Laos, Burma, Argentina, Chile, Honduras, El Salvador, Costa Rica, Ecuador, Peru, Guatemala, Uruguay, and also extraordinary parts of the United States. In this latter category, three Colorado River trips through Grand Canyon were special in all sorts of ways. Two guides on those trips helped me overcome my vertigo and fear of heights, at least to the point where for a decade or so I was able to make mountain hiking an important part of my life. Two trips into Utah's Escalante Canyons gave us a sense of what it's like to explore wild areas before they are changed by tourism.

One of my proudest accomplishments was climbing Sandia Mountain to the east of Albuquerque. I tackled its ten thousand feet (four thousand of them rising above the trailhead) after I'd been diagnosed with emphysema and exercise became more of a challenge. It took me a year to make it a bit farther each time. When I reached the top, I was exhilarated. I repeated the feat for several years, sometimes with Barbara, sometimes alone.

Abundant travel has given us experiences we won't forget. Now that we are no longer able to travel for pleasure—we save our energy for visits to family, and I still fly here and there to give readings or present a new book—we often reminisce about those trips we shared. Making them together, whether a month in some far-off country or a few days' road trip on our beloved Colorado Plateau, was what made them so rich. As a photographer, I've loved the images they provided. Photography is also something I've had to give up since a tremor in my hands began blurring the focus in too many of my pictures.

A biking accident put an end to my riding in 1992. Just as I mounted the bike and before taking off, I turned on my seat to catch something Barbara was saying and my right foot got caught in the toe clip. I could hear the bones splintering as I went down. As a result, I now have a long metal plate and eleven screws in my right leg. Age put an end to my hiking. Crippled by arthritis and just plain tired, I don't even walk much anymore. But I'm grateful for those years of wandering known trails and even exploring a bit of wilderness. One of the hikes of which I'm proudest was making it down Grand Canyon's Bright Angel Trail as far as Plateau Point: twelve miles there and back. I did that one several times.

LIGHT

Light fills me now, spills from my mouth:
wave train
before a rapid.

Crystal darts across this canyon floor
wiping shadow from red rock cleft,
spitting questions.

Desert light sounds Grandmother flute,
her dancing mirror
of blown glass.

Dawn's transparent metal, passionate by noon,
paints sand and stone
leaps through falling water.

Sky full of stars spits silver
through dark foliage
of gamble oak.

Centuries reach forward
from those whose footsteps
whisper grass.

Light disguised as pain, faster than dream,
pulls me across this broken bridge
into its waiting arms.

The only teaching I do these days is a one-week stint each year at Naropa University's Summer Writing Program (SWP) in Boulder, Colorado. It's an eight-hour drive from our home. I was invited to Naropa for the first time in the mid-1980s, shortly after returning to the United States. The school dedicated that summer program to Latin American literature. I've been invited back for the past fifteen years. Naropa is a Buddhist university, and its Jack Kerouac School of Disembodied Poetics was founded by Allen Ginsberg, Diane di Prima, and Anne Waldman. Anne is still its artistic director and does a brilliant job of opening it to many different poetic traditions as she tries to diversify the staff and student body. I love teaching there.

I've also developed relationships with other cutting-edge cultural and art institutions. One is SITE-Santa Fe, a large gallery that hosts biannual exhibitions. A recent show there featured *El Corno Emplumado*. Brazilian curator Pablo León de la Barra included the journal in the exhibition and was responsible for the provocative display. One large wall and a glass showcase displayed page blowups. Visitors could also thumb through several original copies.

The magazine has received a lot of attention of late. Harris Feinsod at Chicago's Northwestern University established an open-access website on which every one of its thirty-one issues can be read in facsimile. He periodically adds ephemera and related articles of interest. In his excellent book, *The Poetry of the Americas: From Good Neighbors to Countercultures*, Feinsod describes *El Corno* as an "expression of geopolitical desire, a vision of an alternate world order."[4]

Lost & Found, Ammiel Alcalay's valuable project at City College of New York's Graduate Center, devoted one of its research pamphlets to *El Corno* and Edric Mesmer's *Among the Neighbors* focused on it in its issue #5, *Remembering El Corno Emplumado / The Plumed Horn*. Sergio and I both contributed new texts to the latter.

Several years back the journal was celebrated with a week of events in Mexico City. The hosts were professors Julio García Murillo and Regina Tattersfield and their graduate students at the National Autonomous University of Mexico, and some sessions were held at the university's cultural affairs building, which had formerly been Relaciones Exteriores at Tlatelolco.

In October 2018, the Nasher Museum of Art at Duke University held an exhibition called *Pop America 1965–1975*. The exhibition catalog included an essay by Roberto Tejada called "Printed Matters," in which *El Corno* figures prominently. Tejada argues that we were part of an aesthetic that was emerging simultaneously in different parts of the world and that carried political/cultural undertones not sufficiently acknowledged by art historians at the time. In an email received as I was writing this memoir, Tejada remarked, "*El Corno* in the historic view serves as a model for what it will take of the imagination to get us out of the current malaise in the Americas and beyond."

Master's theses and doctoral dissertations, as well as a documentary film, also continue to explore and preserve the journal's history. One particularly brilliant thesis is "Texto, contexto e índices de *El Corno Emplumado* (1962–1969)" by Mexican literary critic Gabriela Silva Ibargüen.

Occasionally I've been fortunate to be invited to poetry events that re-edit our literary history. One was Beat & Beyond, a weeklong remembrance of the Beat movement held in New York City in 2016. Bob Holman and Jane Friedman organized the gathering that took place at his Bowery Poetry & Science and her Howl Gallery, both in Lower Manhattan. There weren't many Beat poets left alive or healthy enough to travel to the event. Michael McClure, Hettie Jones, and I were the exceptions. Lawrence Ferlinghetti, approaching one hundred years of age, couldn't make the trip, nor could Diane di Prima who was struggling with health issues at the time. A number of younger poets provided important connections with the present. Steven Taylor re-created "The Fugs," an iconic musical group of the era. Our hosts housed the aging poets at the Hotel Standard, just a few blocks north on the Bowery. We could walk—or totter—to readings, panels, films, and a re-creation of the 1956 Six Gallery reading where "Howl" was read for the first time. Hettie Jones, small in stature but immense in energy, played Ginsberg's part to perfection.

....

Writers write books, and that's what I've done over my long life as a poet, essayist, oral historian, and translator. My generation may be the last to think of books, beyond only their contents, as beautiful physical objects. Over the past couple of decades, digital publishing has taken off. At first it was Kindle, then other e-book platforms were added. Now most publishing houses launch their titles electronically as well as on paper. Many literary magazines publish only online. Beginning authors, who once sent manuscripts to agents and publishers hoping for acceptance, now simply produce their own titles digitally. A number of self-publication systems exist for this purpose; the modality is called print on demand.

Although I don't read books that way myself, I have nothing against the new technology. Barbara favors the digital model because she can travel with a hundred or more books in a device that weighs ounces. Being able to make the typeface larger or change the page background from white to gray or black with white letters is helpful since a strange attack that caused one of her optic nerves to demyelinate has altered her vision. I'm pleased that most of my publishers put my books out electronically as well as in traditional editions.

Still, I thrill to the heft, feel, and design of an old-fashioned book. I've always loved curling up in the corner of a couch with a good read. I'm old enough that I think of books this way: as comfortable objects as well as valuable texts.

I can remember the pristine elegance of letterpress printing, the slow joy of setting a page of type by hand.

None but a few famous poets make money from their books. Rarely have I received an advance for a poetry manuscript. So, holding a newly published book of mine in hand, looking at its attractive cover, turning its pages, is one of life's satisfactions. Without taking the comparison to unreasonable lengths, each new book's publication feels like the birth of a child.

My own books now number more than 150. When I lived in Latin America, I published with Siglo XXI and a few other Mexican houses. Many of the United States' publishers back then were uneasy about taking on work by those like myself who were writing favorably about Latin American revolutions, and English editions of my books were most often put out by New Star, an independent publisher in Vancouver, and Women's Press in Toronto. After my return to the United States, though, I began acquiring publishers here.

Alex "Sandy" Taylor at Curbstone in Willimantic, Connecticut, and John Crawford at Albuquerque's West End Press brought out several of my poetry titles. Taylor published Roque Dalton, Claribel Alegría, and Daisy Zamora in English, among others. When he died suddenly, the press fell apart. Crawford also had a long and impressive list, although it included more working-class and authors of color from inside the United States than foreign writers. He started his press in New York when I was still living south of the border, then moved it to Minneapolis (where he rediscovered the great Midwest writer Meridel Le Sueur) and finally to Albuquerque. He died in 2019.

Several of the vibrant feminist presses of the era brought out books of mine, among them *This Is about Incest* (Firebrand, 1988) and *The Shape of Red: Insider/Outsider Reflections* (with Ruth Hubbard; Cleis Press, in the same year). A Boston collective called South End Press, Common Courage of Maine, and the University of Nebraska Press published collections of my essays. Karin Aguilar-San Juan, my brilliant editor at South End, became a good friend.

Various publishers produce my books these days. A stalwart is Duke University Press, where Gisela Fosado has been an exceptional editor and friend. She's published several of my recent books on Cuba.[5] I've done a couple of book-length translations for Duke as well.[6] Lynne DeSilva-Johnson, who runs the experimental Brooklyn press, the Operating System, is someone whose conceptual framework resonates with me. The Operating System has published a number of my translations, including a brief but exciting chapbook introducing the forgotten texts of Bolivian poet and guerrilla fighter Rita Valdivia.[7]

TRANSLATION AFTER ALL

We trip over language, revel in the spoken word
and wonder about origins, who is distinguished
by its use and who less human
lacking its finesse.

The *big brain small brain* thing serves as explanation.
But isn't it ironic we of the tiniest computer chips
insist large brains are needed
for cognition?

Suddenly a linguist informs us it's not language but grammar
raises humankind above the other mammals,
combining words the skill
that sets us apart.

I wonder then how we might hear the silence between barks,
bugle calls, growls, whistles, trills and grunts,
how many discrete phrases a whale sends
through its darkness of singing seas.

Imprisoned within an image of self that admits no rival,
we measure sound with our own poor ears,
spend billions on gaping receptor dishes
listening to the universe.

Unable to fathom others' language except through ours,
we may be polished in our speech
but arrogance and failed imagination
keep us from translation.

I began translating poetry from the Spanish back when Sergio and I had *El Corno*. We often worked together bringing work from one language into another. Over the years I continued to hone my translating skills. But recently I've found so many powerful works, most of them by Cuban authors, that I've labored excitedly and feverishly to make them available to an English readership. Unexpectedly, I've found myself producing as many translations as books of my own.

A half dozen of these bilingual editions were produced by the Operating System.[8] Red Mountain Press in Santa Fe, New Mexico, brought out four of my translations, all by Cuban authors.[9] As I've approached and passed my eightieth year, I've worked with an intensity I hadn't known to this point in my life, with regard to translation but also my own work. I almost seem to be flying. My mind is constantly in motion, making connections and opening itself to new possibilities. Barbara's encouragement and support have been vital, as well as the fact that this end of life has given me so much more time than earlier decades. The receptivity of editors such as Fosado, DeSilva-Johnson, and Bryce Milligan has been important.

The press to which I owe the most is Wings in San Antonio, Texas. Its longtime owner and editor, Bryce Milligan, has curated almost all my poetry collections since 2009.[10] He's done eleven of my books so far, plus one translation of an anthology of stories by thirty-five Cuban women, *The Oval Portrait* (2017), edited by Soleida Ríos. He's made four handbound, gemlike chapbooks of single poems, two of them including art by Barbara, the other two with my photographs. Bryce is a skilled and caring editor, designer, and promoter of books, who keeps publishing many of his authors as a way of curating journeys rather than only single titles.

A Wings book that is extraordinarily special to me is *As If the Empty Chair / Como si la silla vacía* (2011), a bilingual, handbound, limited edition of four hundred that is a suite of twelve poems for Latin America's disappeared. I'd always felt a debt to those men and women, several of whom were friends. Leandro Katz and Diego Guerra did the Spanish translations. That book has also had editions in Mexico and Uruguay. I presented the latter at Montevideo's Museum of Memory, a tremendously moving experience. Many in the large audience had a disappeared person in their family.

Time's Language: Selected Poems (1959–2018) is without doubt the most beautiful and meaningful edition of my poetry. Katherine M. Hedeen and Víctor Rodríguez Núñez read thirty collections of my poems, made the selection, and wrote an insightful introduction. I provided a lengthy chronology and lots of photos. Bryce curated and designed the 450-page elegantly produced hardback through personally difficult times, then released it in 2018. I launched this anthology, sixty years of my life in poetry, at City Lights Books in San Francisco. City Lights, like Bellas Artes in Mexico City, Naropa in Boulder, and Poet's House in New York, is one of those venues filled with literary history and artistic energy where reading embraces one in tradition.

Having a *Selected Poems* edition is a humbling experience. Having such a beautiful one is a gift. I reread the earliest poems and am embarrassed by their derivative nature and naivete. Then I remind myself how important it is to reveal process. Publication of this book has changed my life in poetry. Barbara says I read with more conviction and power since it appeared.

A few other publishers have produced books of mine over the years. In 2007 the University of Arizona Press did a beautiful job with *Stones Witness*, a collection of my poetry, prose, and thirty full-color photographs. In 2011 the University of New Mexico Press brought out *Ruins*, a collection of my poems with black and white images. Rutgers University Press published what I consider to be my best oral history work, *When I Look into the Mirror and See You: Women, Terror, and Resistance* (2002). Rutgers also published my Cuban memoir, *To Change the World: My Years in Cuba* (2009); brought out *Sandino's Daughters Revisited*; and reissued *Sandino's Daughters* in 1996. I could go on, but the list is a long one.

I must mention two Cuban publishers. One is Vigía, a three-decade-old independent collective in the city of Matanzas that produces two hundred copies of handmade limited-edition books that are works of art. Vigía has no printing press. All its books are fashioned using an old mimeograph machine, with individual coloring for each copy, found objects, and hand binding. Poets inside and outside Cuba dream of publishing a book with Vigía. I have been fortunate to have two: *La Llorona / The Llorona* (2015, a Spanish translation by María Vázquez Valdez, with a design by Elizabeth Valero Molina, edited by Laura Ruiz Montes) and *When Justice Felt at Home / Cuando la justicia se sentía en casa* (2018, a translation by Katherine M. Hedeen and Víctor Rodríguez Núñez, with a design by Elizabeth Valero Molina, edited by Laura Ruiz Montes).

In addition to Vigía's exquisite artistry—its books are in public and private collections throughout the world, including that of New York's Museum of Modern Art—the collective is noteworthy for having published writers who were ignored in Cuba during that country's repressive periods. This makes its founders and other workers real revolutionaries in my eyes.

One of those founders, poet and cultural critic Alfredo Zaldívar, eventually parted ways with the collective and launched a commercial publisher in Matanzas. It is called Ediciones Matanzas and has produced several of my books for Cuba's insatiable reading public. Ediciones Matanzas also demands the right to produce titles that don't fit safely into acceptable categories. When other Cuban publishers were reluctant to do so, it brought out my memoir,

Para cambiar el mundo: Mis años en Cuba (2017). In 2018 it produced *Del pequeño Charlie Lindbergh y otros poemas*, translated by Israel Domínguez. And in 2019 I put together a large anthology of Beat poetry for the house, some four-hundred-plus pages translated by Edelmis Anoceto.

I'm also immensely grateful to those who have translated my poetry into other languages, especially Spanish, for which I feel I have a natural audience. Víctor Rodríguez Núñez, Katherine Hedeen, Israel Domínguez, and Edelmis Anoceto have all spent time rendering my poems in that language. I am currently working with Sandra Toro in Buenos Aires, who is translating a forthcoming collection of my poetry for a publisher there. Her renditions are profoundly sensitive to my voice and style. But Mexican poet and translator María Vázquez Valdez has done more to reproduce my work in Spanish than anyone. She has translated five of my collections, all of which have been published in Mexico. We've shared many a lectern, and I've also had the pleasure of translating a book of her poetry into English.[11] She and Víctor and Kate have also accompanied me to important book launches, readings, and award ceremonies in recent years; they are family.

With translation occasionally there have been special considerations as well. When I was looking for someone to translate my suite of poems about the disappeared into Spanish, I didn't just want a poet with a profound command of that language but someone of my generation whose life, like mine, had been affected by the tragic phenomenon. I asked Argentine poet, visual artist, and filmmaker Leandro Katz and was moved when he accepted. My book about Che Guevara was translated into Bengali, a language with very different conventions than English. The translator contacted me often with questions. He would ask me to give him the phonetics of a word because its sound would determine how it was written in his language. He also asked if a passage describing Che's favorite aunt referred to his maternal or paternal relative; the distinction would lead him to use an entirely different word in each case. In my own translating I've had interesting challenges as well: how to approach a woman writing in the voice of another, monologues by drunken Dominican peasants, and Spanish prose written by a man of the Peruvian Andes whose first language was Quechua.

There's one more thing I'd like to say about books. I want to mention some written by others that have been especially influential in my own development and thinking. The list is far from exhaustive. The earliest book that made a lasting impression may have been *Daughter of Earth* by Agnes Smedley. I've read it dozens of times, beginning when I was quite young. I am always freshly moved by Smedley's search for identity in a hostile misogynistic world, and by the ways she sought out experiences on the front lines of social change.

Michael Coe's *Breaking the Maya Code* is another book I go back to often. Its density makes it necessary for me to return periodically in order to try to understand certain mathematical and/or linguistic relationships. I also return to *God's Bankers* by Gerald Posner; his history of deceit and corruption in the Vatican is good to keep in mind when thinking about powerful institutions in general, secular as well as religious. Well-documented nonfiction is a genre I love.

From South African novelist Mark Behr, narrative power combines with intuitive brilliance to have given us books that rise above others. My favorite of his is *Embrace*. I also love Minrose Gwin's *The Queen of Palmyra*. Both these novels are by white authors but deal with race in profound ways. Barbara Kingsolver's *The Poisonwood Bible* and *The Lacuna*, and Sandra Cisneros's *Caramelo* are other novels that have made an impact on me.

There are poets whose work thrills me, among them César Vallejo, William Carlos Williams, Allen Ginsberg, Juan Gelman, Adrienne Rich, Audre Lorde, Roque Dalton, Joy Harjo, Susan Sherman, Anne Waldman, Laura Ruiz Montes, Renato Rosaldo, and V. B. Price. I love, read, and reread poems by many poets, but these writers' bodies of work lift them above others in my experience. They reenergize and excite my consciousness in ways difficult to describe. You have to read them yourself to know.

....

Over the years, before going to Latin America and after my return, I've applied for my share of grants and prizes. These are among the few sources of income for poets in the United States. I've almost never received one, especially those involving stipends that allow a writer to live for a while. The Bunting Fellowship once offered me its second-level fellowship, an unfunded year that would have meant an office and library access only. I declined. I felt I was better off working at home, and in fact have never sought stays at writer's retreats or refuges. I love my own "room of my own."

On the other hand, I've appreciated attending poetry festivals and other gatherings where a few days mingling with poets from other cultures and languages is always exciting. I especially remember those in Bisbee, Arizona; Medellín, Colombia; Granada, Nicaragua; Quito, Ecuador; and Bogotá, Colombia. One of the most seductive of these has been the University of Mexico's

Festival de Lenguas de America. It brings together a dozen poets every two years, four representing the continent's European tongues and the rest some of its many indigenous languages. I was fortunate to have been included in 2006 and 2018.

In 1990 I was awarded a Lillian Hellman and Dashiell Hammett grant for writers victimized by political repression. In 2004 the New Mexico chapter of PEN International gave me a Dorothy Doyle Lifetime Achievement Award for Writing and Human Rights Activism. In 2017 KPFA, a radio station in Berkeley, California, celebrated my life and work. And in the same year Literatura El Bravo, in Ciudad Juárez, Mexico, awarded me its prestigious Medalla al Mérito Literario, a silver medal too heavy to wear. I was proud to have been the second woman and second non–Latin American poet to have earned that award. The other woman was Mexican poet Amparo Dávila, now in her nineties. The other non–Latin American was my old friend Jerome Rothenberg, who received the medal in 2009. In 2019, Poesía en Paralelo Cero (Ecuador) awarded me its "Poet of Two Hemispheres" prize; Cuba's Casa de las Américas gave me its Haydée Santamaría medal on the occasion of the Revolution's sixtieth anniversary; and the University of New Mexico granted me its Doctor Honoris Causa in Letters.

....

EVERYONE LIED

We wanted to make the world a better place
but everyone lied,
fought power with humble flesh,
blood, brilliance,
and the luck of the innocent.

The enemy's lies assaulted us, their language
diminished our numbers,
turned us against one another,
touched lovers, confused our sense
of who we were and why.

And we lied about them, claimed they were
drug dealers and murderers,
all their food poisoned,
all their streets unsafe.

Then we lied about our own,
sowed serious doubt, set fatal traps.

Of course we lied to the CIA
and others who tortured us,
but also to our parents, children,
and those who came to us
for truth.

We lied by omission, convinced we must
reveal no contradiction.
The real story could only benefit
those who would destroy the dream,
who wanted us dead.
Accounts to be settled later.

We lied to protect our own and then
to justify not protecting our own.
We lied on a need to know basis,
parroted our leaders
even when they pretended genocide away.

We failed to question his disappearance,
100 knife-wounds in her body,
followed our leaders who lied to us,
then lied to ourselves:
the pain that changed our molecules.

Until later turned out to be the promise
we could not keep, a tired ghost
destined to wander hollow-eyed:
the lie that would come back to haunt
a sacrifice too big to name.

These are brutal and dangerous times. Times we couldn't have imagined even a few years back. Neofascism is on the rise throughout much of the world. In history's relentless shift between ultra-nationalist authoritarianism and a more open and embracing politics, today's panorama is cruel. Here in the United States we suffer a president who is a self-serving isolationist, who has withdrawn from every multinational effort to improve life on the planet, who mocks women and minorities, who encourages abuse of all but rich white men, who constantly provokes social division and hate crimes, and who systematically rolls back every hard-won protection of the environment and social justice.

How did we get here? Undoubtedly by failing to engage in the national conversations we needed to have. By allowing the erosion of public education and replacing critical thought with rote memorization and an absurd emphasis on multiple-choice testing. By blaming the poor for our social inequalities. By allowing racism, misogyny, and homophobia to corrode our social fabric. By replacing basic moral values with false patriotism. And by making greed a virtue. The gulf between rich and poor is now so wide and deep it doesn't seem bridgeable. And none of the above will matter if we continue to disregard global warming and allow our oceans to rise, mammoth storms to kill and maim, and drought and fire to overwhelm our land.

Those of us who spent so much of our lives working for a healthier society continue to do what we can. Young people take our place. Too old and tired now to remain on the front lines, I use my writing to exemplify, convince, encourage change. Yet art is much more than persuasion; it has a life of its own, is necessary in and of itself. Today I am consumed with writing the culmination of my imagination, experience, and vision; my time and the places I have lived and worked. People who have come into my life, some fleetingly, others more enduringly, accompany me now. Some are ghosts. Others live. I converse with them all and they with me.

I wish my generation could have left a better world to those coming up. Our victories were scant and so much less lasting than we dreamed. Perhaps our greatest gift has been our integrity. It's up to the new generations now to build upon our wins and failures, making use of their own creativity.

I am a natural optimist. I believe in a world I will not live to see. And I feel an intimate pride in having given what I could.

....

MADE RICH BY ART AND REVOLUTION

When I am gone, and August comes
to my desert,
rain will soak sand,
its rich scent rising

Downtown Albuquerque, 1990s (photo by Margaret Randall).

to enter the lungs of another mother or walker,
someone whose intention and desire
I cannot know.

When I am gone this painting of little islands
miniature trees and birds
floating in a magical sea of blue
will hang in someone else's house.
Will that person tell the story
of poor Nicaraguan peasants
made rich by art and revolution?

A granddaughter may inherit
my turquoise earrings.
The clay pans I've used for years,
their pungency filling the house,
will offer up a new generation
of bread.
Someone not yet born may read this poem.

But who will ask the questions
born of the answers
I juggle today.
Who will know the heat
of this great love,
or catch fragments of my memory
reassembling just before dawn?

PUBLISHED BOOKS

POETRY AND PROSE

Giant of Tears. New York City, self-published, 1959 (with drawings by US artists Ronald Bladen, Elaine de Kooning, Al Held, Robert Mallary, and George Sugarman).

Ecstasy Is a Number. New York City, self-published, 1961 (with cover, frontispiece portrait of author, and drawings by Elaine de Kooning).

Poems of the Glass. Cleveland, OH: Renegade Press, 1964.

Small Sounds from the Bass Fiddle. Albuquerque, NM: Duende Press, 1964 (with cover and interior prints by Bobbie Louise Hawkins).

October. Mexico City: El Corno Emplumado Press, 1965 (with photographs of sculptural collages by Shinkichi Tajiri).

Getting Rid of Blue Plastic. Bombay, India: Dialogue Press, 1967.

So Many Rooms Has a House but One Roof. Minneapolis, MN: New Rivers Press, 1967 (with cover by Felipe Ehrenberg).

Twenty-Five Stages of My Spine. New Rochelle, NY: Elizabeth Press, 1967.

Water I Slip into at Night. Mexico City: El Corno Emplumado Press, 1967 (with cover and drawings by Felipe Ehrenberg).

Part of the Solution. New York: New Directions, 1972.

Day's Coming! Los Angeles, privately printed by friends, 1973.

Parte de la solución. Lima, Peru: Editorial Causachún / Colección Poesía, 1973 (translations by Antonio Benítez, Víctor Casaus, Oscar de los Ríos, Roberto Díaz, Roberto Fernández Retamar, Ambrosio Fornet, Carlos María Gutiérrez, Edwin Reyes, and Exilia Saldaña).

With These Hands. Vancouver: New Star Books, 1974.

All My Used Parts, Shackles, Fuel, Tenderness, and Stars. Kansas City, MO: New Letters, 1977.

Carlota: Poems and Prose from Havana. Vancouver: New Star Books, 1978 (cover by Sylvia de Swaan).

We. New York: Smyrna Press, 1978 (cover by Judy Janda).

A Poetry of Resistance. Toronto: Participatory Research Group, 1983 (texts by Latin American activists; photographs by the author).

Albuquerque: Coming Back to the USA. Vancouver: New Star Books, 1986 (photographs by the author).

The Coming Home Poems. East Haven, CT: Long River Books, 1986 (published to benefit the Margaret Randall Legal Defense Fund).

This Is about Incest. Ithaca, NY: Firebrand Books, 1987 (photographs by the author).

Memory Says Yes. Willimantic, CT: Curbstone Press, 1988 (cover photograph by Colleen McKay; cover design by Barbara Byers).

Dancing with the Doe. Albuquerque, NM: West End Press, 1992 (cover reproduction of tapestry by Coca Millan).

The Old Cedar Bar. Nevada City, CA: Gateways, 1992 (with drawings by E. J. Gold).

Hunger's Table: Women, Food & Politics. Watsonville, CA: Papier-Maché Press, 1997 (cover art by Dianne Sacchetti).

Esto sucede cuando el corazón de una mujer se rompe: Poemas, 1985–1995. Madrid, Spain: Hiperión, 1999 (translations by Víctor Rodríguez Núñez).

Coming Up for Air. Santa Fe, NM: Pennywhistle Press, 2001 (photographs by the author).

Where They Left You for Dead / Halfway Home. Berkeley, CA: EdgeWork Books, 2001 (cover photograph by the author; interior photograph by Barbara Byers).

Dentro de otro tiempo: Reflejos del Gran Cañón. Mexico City: Alforja, 2004 (translations by María Vázquez Valdez).

Into Another Time: Grand Canyon Reflections. Albuquerque, NM: West End Press, 2004 (cover and drawings by Barbara Byers).

Stones Witness. Tucson: University of Arizona Press, 2007 (full-page color photographs by the author).

Their Backs to the Sea. San Antonio, TX: Wings Press, 2009 (cover art by Jane Norling; photographs by the author).

My Town. San Antonio, TX: Wings Press, 2010 (cover and interior photographs by the author and from Albuquerque Museum archives).

As If the Empty Chair / Como si la silla vacía. San Antonio, TX: Wings Press, 2011 (Spanish translations by Leandro Katz and Diego Guerra; limited numbered and signed edition).

Como si la silla vacía. Montevideo, Uruguay: Rumbo Editorial, 2011 (photographs by Annabella Balduvino).

Como si la silla vacía / As If the Empty Chair. Mexico City: La Cabra Ediciones, 2011.

Ruins. Albuquerque: University of New Mexico Press, 2011 (cover and interior photographs by the author).

Something's Wrong with the Cornfields. Boulder, CO: Skylight Press, 2011 (cover art by Barbara Byers).

Testigo de piedra. Zacatecas, Mexico: Taberna Librería Editores / Ediciones de Medianoche, Universidad Autónima de Zacatecas, 2011 (translations by María Vázquez Valdez).

Where Do We Go from Here? San Antonio, TX: Wings Press, 2012 (chapbook with a single long poem and eighteen full-color photographs by the author).

Daughter of Lady Jaguar Shark. San Antonio, TX: Wings Press, 2013 (with photographs by the author).

The Rhizome as a Field of Empty Bones. San Antonio, TX: Wings Press, 2013 (cover art by Rini Price).

About Little Charlie Lindbergh and Other Poems. San Antonio, TX: Wings Press, 2014 (cover photograph by the author).

Beneath a Trespass of Sorrow. San Antonio, TX: Wings Press, 2014 (with art by Barbara Byers).

Bodies / Shields. San Antonio, TX: Wings Press, 2015 (with art by Barbara Byers).

La Llorona. Matanzas, Cuba: Ediciones Vigía, 2015 (translation by María Vázquez Valdez; edited by Laura Ruiz Montes; design by Elizabeth Valero).

When Justice Felt at Home / Cuando la justicia se sentía en casa. Matanzas, Cuba: Ediciones Vigía, 2015 (translations by Katherine M. Hedeen and Víctor Rodríguez Núñez; edited by Laura Ruiz Montes; design by Elizabeth Valero).

She Becomes Time. San Antonio, TX: Wings Press, 2016 (cover photograph by the author).

The Morning After: Poetry and Prose in a Post-Truth World. San Antonio, TX: Wings Press, 2017 (cover art by Barbara Byers).

Del pequeño Charlie Lindbergh y otros poemas. Matanzas, Cuba: Editorial Matanzas, 2018 (translation by Israel Domínguez; cover art by Barbara Byers).

El rizoma como un campo de huesos rotos. Mexico City: Editorial Mar Es Cierto y Secretaría de Cultura, 2018 (translations by María Vázquez Valdez; cover art by Mauricio Gómez Morín).

Margaret Randall and Dennis Brutus Tribute. Philadelphia: Moonstone Arts, 2018.

Time's Language: Selected Poems (1959–2018). San Antonio, TX: Wings Press, 2018 (edited by Katherine M. Hedeen and Víctor Rodríguez Núñez; cover art by Liliana Wilson; frontispiece by Elaine de Kooning; vignettes by Barbara Byers; photographs from the author's archive; introduction by anthologizers; chronology by the author).

Against Atrocity: New Poems. San Antonio, TX: Wings Press, 2019 (cover photograph by the author).

Contra la atrocidad. Buenos Aires, Argentina: Aguacero Editorial, 2019 (translations by Sandra Toro).

El lenguaje del tiempo: poemas 1985–2017. Quito, Ecuador: El Angel Editores, 2019 (edited and translated by Katherine M. Hedeen and Víctor Rodríguez Núñez).

Espejos cortados a la medida: poemas 1985–2019. Las Líneas de su Mano, Bogotá, Colombia, 2019 (edited and translated by Katherine M. Hedeen and Víctor Rodríguez Núñez).

ORAL HISTORY

La mujer cubana ahora. Havana, Cuba: Editorial Ciencias Sociales, 1972.

Mujeres en la revolución. Mexico City: Siglo XXI, 1972.

La mujer cubana. Bogota, Colombia: Ediciones Populares, 1973.

¿Como vive la mujer trabajadora en el Perú? Lima, Peru: Sinamos, 1974.

Cuban Women Now. Toronto: Women's Press, 1974 (photographs by Mayra Martinez).

La mujer cubana—revolución en la revolución and *La mujer cubana ahora—tomos I y II*. Caracas, Venezuela: Salvador de la Plaza, 1974.

"Afterword," addendum to *Cuban Women Now*. Toronto: Women's Press, 1975.

Cubaanse Vrouwen Aan Het Woord. Utrecht, Holland: Venceremos Publishers, 1975.

El espíritu de un pueblo: A dos años de los acuerdos de París. Mexico City: Siglo XXI, 1975.

Spirit of the People: Vietnamese Women Two Years from the Geneva Accords. Vancouver: New Star Books, 1975.

Somos millones. Mexico City: Extemporaneos, S.A., 1976.

Inside the Nicaraguan Revolution: The Story of Doris Tijerino. Vancouver: New Star Books, 1978.

Nicaragua Een Vrou in De Revolutie. Amsterdam, Holland: Venceremos Publishers, 1978.

No se puede hacer la revolución sin nosotras. Havana, Cuba: Casa de las Américas, 1978.

El pueblo no sólo es testigo: La historia de Dominga. Rio Piedras, Puerto Rico: Huracán Publishers, 1978 (photographs by Grandal).

Sueños y realidades de un guajiricantor. Mexico City: Siglo XXI, 1979 (in collaboration with Angel Antonio Moreno; photographs by Grandal).

Sandino's Daughters. Vancouver: New Star Books, 1981 (photographs by the author).

Todas estamos despiertas. Mexico City: Siglo XXI, 1981.

Christians in the Nicaraguan Revolution. Vancouver: New Star Books, 1983 (cover photograph and interior photographs by the author).

Estamos todas despertas, as mulheres da Nicaragua. São Paulo, Brazil: Global Editora, 1983.

No se puede hacer la revolución sin nosotras. Caracas, Venezuela, 1983.

Y también digo mujer. Santo Domingo, Dominican Republic: Ediciones Populares Feministas, 1983.

Cristianos en la revolución nicaragüense. Managua, Nicaragua: Editorial Nueva Nicaragua, 1984 (cover photograph by the author).

Cristianos en la revolución nicaragüense. Caracas, Venezuela: Editorial Poseidon, 1984.

Risking a Somersault in the Air: Conversations with Nicaraguan Writers. San Francisco: Solidarity Publications, 1984 (cover by Jane Norling; photographs by the author).

Sandino'nun Kizlari. Istanbul, Turkey: Metis Yayinlari, 1985.

Fakten Argumente, Cristen in der Revolution Gespräche in Nikaragua. Berlin: Union Verlag, 1987.

Sandino's Daughters Revisited. New Brunswick, NJ: Rutgers University Press, 1994.

Sandino's Daughters. New Brunswick, NJ: Rutgers University Press, 1996 (revised edition).

Las hijas de Sandino: Una historia abierta. Managua, Nicaragua: ANAMA, 1999.

When I Look into the Mirror and See You: Women, Terror, and Resistance. New Brunswick, NJ: Rutgers University Press, 2002 (cover art by Rini Templeton).

ESSAYS

Los hippies; análisis de una crisis. Mexico City: Siglo XXI, 1968.

La mujer y la revolución. Lima, Peru: Editorial Causachun, 1972.

La situación de la mujer. Lima, Peru: Centro de Estudios de Participación Popular, 1974.

Childcare in Cuba. Toronto: Women's Press, 1975.

Testimonios. San José, Costa Rica: Alforja Centro de Estudios de Participación Popular, 1983.

Testimonios. Toronto: Participatory Research Group, 1985.

Cuban Women Twenty Years Later. New York: Smyrna Press, 1980 (cover and photographs by Judy Janda).

We Have the Capacity, the Imagination, and the Will: Milú Vargas Speaks about Nicaraguan Women. Toronto: Participatory Research Group, 1983.

The Shape of Red: Insider/Outsider Reflections (with Ruth Hubbard). Pittsburgh, PA: Cleis Press, 1988.

Coming Home: Peace Without Complacency. Albuquerque, NM: West End Press, 1990.

The Shape of Red: Insider/Outsider Reflections (with Ruth Hubbard). Tokyo: Misuzu, 1990.

Walking to the Edge: Essays of Resistance. Boston: South End Press, 1991 (cover art by Barbara Byers).

Gathering Rage: The Failure of Twentieth Century Revolutions to Develop a Feminist Agenda. New York: Monthly Review Press, 1992 (cover by Barbara Byers).

Our Voices / Our Lives: Stories of Women from Central America and the Caribbean. Monroe, ME: Common Courage Press, 1995.

The Price You Pay: The Hidden Cost of Women's Relationship to Money. New York: Routledge, 1996.

Narrative of Power: Essays for an Endangered Century. Monroe, ME: Common Courage Press, 2004 (cover photograph by the author).

To Change the World: My Years in Cuba. New Brunswick, NJ: Rutgers University Press, 2009 (cover photograph by Gilda Pérez; interior photographs by the author).

First Laugh: Essays 2000–2009. Lincoln: University of Nebraska Press, 2011.

Selections from El Corno Emplumado / The Plumed Horn 1962–1964. New York: City College of New York Graduate Center, Lost and Found, Series 2, no. 1, 2011.

More Than Things. Lincoln: University of Nebraska Press, 2013 (cover photograph and interior photographs by the author).

Che on My Mind. Durham: Duke University Press, 2013 (photographs from several archives and by the author).

Haydée Santamaría, Cuban Revolutionary: She Lived by Transgression. Durham: Duke University Press, 2015 (photographs from Cuban archives and by the author).

Aklimdaki Che. Istanbul, Turkey: Iletisim, 2016.

Che on My Mind. New Delhi, India: Monfakira Books, 2016.

Talking Stick. Miami: Igneo, 2016 (cover photograph by the author).

Cambiar el mundo: Mis años en Cuba. Matanzas, Cuba: Editorial Matanzas, 2017 (translation by Barbara Maseda; cover by Johan Trujillo; interior photographs by the author).

Exporting Revolution: Cuba's Global Solidarity. Durham: Duke University Press, 2017.

Remembering El Corno Emplumado / The Plumed Horn (with Sergio Mondragón). Buffalo: State University of New York, 2018.

ANTHOLOGIES

Las mujeres. Mexico City: Siglo XXI, 1970.
Poesía Beat. Madrid, Spain: Visor, 1977.
Breaking the Silences: 20th Century Poetry by Cuban Women. Vancouver: Pulp Press, 1982 (introduction, notes, translations, and photographs by the author).
12 poetas. Mexico City: Editorial Mar Es Cierto y Secretaría de Cultura, 2018 (translations by María Vázquez Valdez; cover art by Quetzatl León Calixto).
Poesía Beat. Matanzas, Cuba: Ediciones Matanzas, 2019.

PHOTOGRAPHY

Nicaragua libre! Boston; and *Gritaré!*, Sisters of Notre Dame, 1985 (with texts from statistical surveys and Nicaraguan poets).
"Women and Photography: How and Why I Make Pictures in *IKON*." New York: Spotlight on Photography, second Series, #4, 1985.
Women Brave in the Face of Danger. Freedom, CA: Crossing Press, 1985 (with texts by Latin and North American women).
Photographs by Margaret Randall: Image and Content in Differing Cultural Contexts. Scranton, PA: Everhart Museum, 1988.
The Rebellion on the Walls, unpublished (a history of the Nicaraguan Revolution shown through the writing on that country's walls; photographs and introduction by Margaret Randall; interview with Dora María Téllez and others).

TRANSLATIONS

Let's Go! London: Cape-Golliard, 1970 (a selection of poems by Guatemalan poet Otto-René Castillo).
This Great People Has Said Enough and Has Begun to Move: Poems from the Struggle in Latin America. San Francisco: Peoples Press, 1972 (introduction and translations by the author; cover by Jane Norling).
Estos cantos habitados / These Living Songs, Fifteen New Cuban Poets. Colorado State Review 6, no. 1, Spring 1978 (translated and with an introduction by Margaret Randall).
Breaking the Silences—Poems by 25 Cuban Women Poets. Vancouver: Pulp Press, 1982 (introduction, notes, and photographs by the author).
Carlos, the Dawn Is No Longer beyond Our Reach. Vancouver: New Star Books, 1984 (a long prose poem by Tomas Borge Martínez).
Let's Go! Willimantic, CT: Curbstone Press, 1984.
Clean Slate (with Elinor Randall) by Daisy Zamora. Willimantic, CT: Curbstone Press, 1994.

Let's Go! Washington, DC: Azul Editions, 2006.

When Rains Become Floods by Lurgio Gavilán Sánchez. Durham: Duke University Press, 2015.

Al pie del río amado / At the Foot of the Beloved River: Cinco poetas cubanos / Five Cuban Poets. Matanzas, Cuba: Editorial Matanzas, 2016.

Only the Road / Sólo el camino: Eight Decades of Cuban Poetry. Durham: Duke University Press, 2016 (selection, translations, introduction, and notes by Margaret Randall).

The Comandante Maya: Rita Valdivia. Brooklyn, NY: Operating System, 2017.

Diapositivas / transparencias by Laura Ruiz Montes. Santa Fe, NM: Red Mountain Press, 2017 (cover art by Susan Gardner).

Lo que les dijo el licántropo / What the Werewolf Told Them by Chely Lima. Brooklyn, NY: Operating System, 2017 (cover photograph by the author).

To Have Been There Then: My Life in Cuba by Gregory Randall. Brooklyn, NY: Operating System, 2017 (cover art by Lynne DeSilva-Johnson).

Trillos precipicios concurrencias / Pathways Precipices Spectators by Alfredo Zaldívar. Santa Fe, NM: Red Mountain Press, 2017 (cover art by Susan Gardner).

Viaje de regreso / Return Trip by Israel Domínguez. Brooklyn, NY: Operating System, 2017 (cover art by JR and José Parlá).

Contemplación vs. acto / Contemplation vs. Act by Yanira Marimón. Santa Fe, NM: Red Mountain Press, 2018 (cover art by Susan Gardner).

Kawsay: The Flame of the Jungle / Kawsay: La llama de la selva by María Vázquez Valdez. Brooklyn, NY: Operating System, 2018 (cover art and interior drawings by Cizuko Osato).

Otros campos de belleza armada / Other Fields of Armed Beauty by Reynaldo García Blanco. Santa Fe, NM: Red Mountain Press, 2018 (cover art by Susan Gardner).

The Oval Portrait: Contemporary Cuban Women Writers and Artists. San Antonio, TX: Wings Press, 2018 (edited by Soleida Ríos; cover art by Amalia Iduate).

The National Economy / La economía nacional by Gaudencio Rodríguez Santana. San Antonio, TX: Wings Press, 2019 (cover photograph by Grandal; interior photograph by Gilda Pérez).

You Can Cross the Massacre on Foot by Freddy Prestol Castillo. Durham: Duke University Press, 2019.

Zugunruhe by Kelly Martínez. Brooklyn, NY: The Operating System, 2020.

Voices from the Center of the World: Poetry from Ecuador. San Antonio, TX: Wings Press, 2020 (selection, prologue, translation, and notes by Margaret Randall).

NOTES

CHAPTER ONE HOW THIS BOOK CAME TO BE

1. In September 2018 congressional confirmation hearings were held for Trump's Supreme Court nominee, Brett Kavanaugh. Although Kavanaugh was accused of sexual assault by several women and one of them, Dr. Christine Blasey Ford, gave eloquent testimony to that effect, a Republican-controlled Congress confirmed Kavanaugh.

CHAPTER TWO WHERE IT ALL STARTED

1. *This Is about Incest* (Ithaca, NY: Firebrand Books, 1988).
2. This hugely popular syndicated column was written by Eleanor Roosevelt almost every day from 1936 to 1962.
3. From 1979 to 1999, Salt of the Earth Books moved from one location to another, all around the University of New Mexico in Albuquerque. It was known throughout the country for readings and lectures, protests against the banning of books, and other contributions to the community. It and many other independent bookstores were forced out of business when the chains took over. Later Amazon closed some of the chains. Today, despite the increase in digital publishing, a few literary bookstores are making a comeback.

CHAPTER THREE LANDSCAPE OF DESIRE

1. Although Jews were by far the greatest number of Nazi victims, Communists, socialists, and homosexuals were also sent to the death camps. Their victimization wasn't publicized until much later.
2. An example was Anne Revere (1903–1990), who won an Academy Award for her portrayal of Elizabeth Taylor's mother in *National Velvet*, resigned from the Screen Actors Guild in 1951 (she was a member of the US Communist Party at the time), and refused to testify before HUAC. She would be blacklisted for the next twenty years, and never again play an important role. This gender aspect of the blacklists was brought to my attention by my friend V. B. Price, who observed its effects in his own family.

3. In 2018 women still earn only 81 cents to every dollar earned by men, and pregnant women continue to be discriminated against in the workforce.

4. In 1991, President George H. W. Bush nominated Clarence Thomas, a federal circuit judge, to succeed retiring Associate Supreme Court Justice Thurgood Marshall. A young lawyer named Anita Hill accused Thomas of having sexually harassed her when he was her supervisor at the Department of Education and Equal Employment Opportunity Commission. Congressional hearings were held, at which Hill testified before a panel of dismissive white men. Thomas won his lifelong seat on the High Court.

5. Chicano rebels often get Virgin of Guadalupe tattoos on their backs as a deterrent to beatings by the police. It is unusual to get such a tattoo on one's chest. I owe later bits of information about Clarence's life to my friends Elizabeth Kennedy and Jim Faris.

6. My sister, Ann, graduated from the University of New Mexico with a degree in education, moved to California, and had a career as a remedial teacher at a community college. My brother John did his undergraduate and doctoral work in anthropology at UNM as well but was prevented from receiving his final degree when his political awakening caused him to question the motives of the Fulbright that took him to Ecuador. In 2019, UNM awarded me an honorary doctorate in letters, bringing my relationship with the school to an unexpectedly positive conclusion.

CHAPTER FOUR THE PICTURE PLANE

I thank my friend Greg Smith for suggesting I write this chapter on a key location and important time in our collective lives and in mine personally. I'd long wanted to do so, but his encouragement convinced me to begin. This piece was the impetus for the entire memoir and the first part of it that I finished.

1. The Stonewall riots were a series of spontaneous demonstrations by members of the gay community against a police raid that took place in the early morning hours of June 28, 1969, at the Stonewall Inn in the Greenwich Village neighborhood of Manhattan. The police violently repressed them. The events, spearheaded by Puerto Ricans, initiated the modern-day movement for gay rights.

2. Franz Kline (1910–1962) was a member of the first wave of abstract expressionists.

3. *Ecstasy Is a Number* (New York, self-published, 1961); *Time's Language: Selected Poems (1959–2018)*, edited and with an introduction by Katherine M. Hedeen and Víctor Rodríguez Núñez (San Antonio, TX: Wings Press, 2018).

4. The exhibit was *Elaine de Kooning: Portraits* (2015).

5. The protests began in earnest in the 1970s. *Openings: A Memoir from the Women's Art Movement, New York City 1970–1992*, by Sabra Moore (New York: New Village Press, 2016), gives an excellent history.

6. For an exceptionally well-done biography of five of the women in the abstract expressionist movement, albeit in the decade before the one about which I write, see Mary Gabriel's *Ninth Street Women* (New York: Little, Brown, 2018).

7. This event occurred on January 1, 1961.

8. In the mid-1980s, when I returned from Latin America to the United States, Becky Bosch was the psychotherapist who helped me retrieve my incest memories. She followed one of the several psychotherapeutic schools that grew out of Reich's work.

9. I interacted with painters Willem and Elaine de Kooning, Franz Kline, Mark Rothko, Ad Reinhardt, Helen Frankenthaler, and Larry Rivers; sculptors Alexander Calder, Mary Frank, Mark di Suvero, Ibram Lassaw, David Hare, John Chamberlain, and George Segal; writers William Carlos Williams, Allen Ginsberg, Frank O'Hara, Jerome Rothenberg, Denise Levertov, LeRoi Jones (later to be known as Amiri Baraka), Diane di Prima, Hettie Jones, Robert Creeley, and Joel Oppenheimer; dancers Merce Cunningham and Martha Graham; jazz musicians Thelonious Monk, Charlie Parker, John Coltrane, and Miles Davis; folk singer Odetta and gospel singer Mahalia Jackson; photographers Rudy Burckhardt and Robert Frank; architect Buckminster Fuller; filmmaker Jonas Mekas; actor Roberts Blossom; cartoonists Saul Steinberg and Jules Feiffer; art historians Harold Rosenberg, Tom Hess, and Lucy Lippard; and Julian Beck and Judith Malina of the Living Theater, among others.

10. Biological determinism is the belief that human behavior is controlled by an individual's genes or some component of their physiology, generally at the expense of the role of the environment, whether in embryonic development or in learning.

11. After a long fight, abortion became legal in the United States in 1973 with the Supreme Court's landmark *Roe v. Wade* decision. Today it is being targeted once again.

12. Although abortion was made legal in 1973, its opponents have never stopped whittling away at a woman's right to control her body. Even as I write, the otherwise progressive 2018 midterm election gave wins to legislators determined to curtail that right.

13. The first of these was *Giant of Tears* (1959), the second the already-mentioned *Ecstasy Is a Number* (1961), both self-published and both with artwork from some of the artists I knew.

14. Williams introduced what he called the variable foot into American poetry. He argued that "our poems are not subtly enough made, the structure, the staid manner of the poem cannot let our feelings through." Citing "the rigidity of the poetic foot" as an obstacle to contemporary poetry, he proposed turning to speech as a new form of measure, shifting American dialects in order to listen to the language.

CHAPTER FIVE WHERE STONES WEEP

1. *The Shape of Red: Insider/Outsider Reflections* (San Francisco: Cleis Press, 1988).
2. *For Love of Ray* (London: London Magazine Press, 1971).
3. I'm thinking of the tradition that includes Julio Antonio Mella, Leon Trotsky, Victor Serge, Laurette Séjourné, Leonora Carrington, León Felipe, Edward Weston, Tina Modotti, Anita Brenner, Cedric Belfrage, Mathias Goeritz, Agustí Bartra, and Erich Fromm.
4. Translations of this and all subsequent Spanish texts are by the author.

5. Among these were writers Bella Akhmadulina, Yevgeny Yevtushenko, Pablo Armando Fernández, Leandro Katz, Edward Dorn, Roberto Fernández Retamar, Otto-René Castillo, Anselm Hollo, Besmilr Brigham, Roque Dalton, Yannis Ritsos, Hans Magnus Enzensberger, Alejandra Pizarnik, Nancy Morejón, Cecilia Vicuña, Gary Snyder, George Bowering, Lawrence Ferlinghetti, Diane Wakoski, Susan Sherman, Denise Levertov, Mario Benedetti, and Charles Bukowski. We also featured the work of many great visual artists, among them Leonora Carrington, Posada, Clyfford Still, David Alfaro Siqueiros, Franz Kline, Nuez, Bruce Connor, Halvario Barrios, Eddie Johnson, José Luis Cuevas, Alberto Gironella, Connie Fox, Antonio Seguí, Sylvia de Swaan, Judith Gutiérrez, Mariano, Argeliers León, Antonia Eiríz, Mathias Goeritz (Werner Bruenner's pseudonym), Arnold Belkin, and Pedro Alcántara; and great photographers such as Nacho López, Mayito, George Cohen, and Lawrence Siegel.

6. Elinor Randall (1910–2006) did a lot of translating for us. Her translations of the work of Cuban patriot and poet José Martí were widely published.

7. Among these were *Tropic of Cancer* by Henry Miller and *Howl* by Allen Ginsberg. Both were writers we published in *El Corno*.

8. Although the term existed for several decades, it was the explosive literary Boom of the late 1960s and early 1970s that made the category familiar in other parts of the world.

9. These included *Los Hippies: Expresión de una crisis* (1968), *Las mujeres* (1970), *Mujeres en la revolución* (1972), *El espíritu de un pueblo* (1975), *Sueños y realidades de un guajiricantor* (with Ángel Antonio Moreno, 1979), and *Todas estamos despiertas* (1981).

10. *The Mexican Night* (New York: New Directions, 1970).

11. Paz did renounce his diplomatic post in India, but very soon accepted a more coveted one in Paris. I have never believed his protest was as sincere as others did.

12. "*Eco contemporáneo*" is a pun because it is also the name of a prominent Argentinian magazine of the era.

13. The story of this fascinating endeavor is best told in *Breaking the Mayan Code* by Michael D. Coe (New York: Thames & Hudson, 2012).

14. After two previous attempts, left candidate Andrés Manuel López Obrador was victorious by a large margin of votes. He began his six-year term in December 2018. His challenges are great, but one breathes new air and renewed hope in the country.

CHAPTER SIX INTERLUDE

1. I sent word to them, explaining our situation and asking for their help. I received a letter from my mother in which she told me I "should have thought about my politics before having children or my children before engaging in such radical politics." Her response hurt and angered me at the time, but I've come to understand that taking in four young children, including an infant, wouldn't have been easy for my parents. They didn't even speak the same language.

2. Armstrong's words were first quoted as "That's one small step for man, one giant leap for mankind," but he insisted he had used the added article, which

makes sense. Of course, back then "mankind" was supposed to represent women as well as men.

CHAPTER SEVEN FIRST FREE TERRITORY

1. *To Change the World: My Years in Cuba* (New Brunswick, NJ: Rutgers University Press, 2009).

2. These astonishing figures are backed by the United Nations and other independent observers. Follow-up programs encouraged beneficiaries to move beyond being able to write their names and a few additional paragraphs to achieve a basic education.

3. In the early 1970s the Revolution began addressing a serious housing shortage by establishing micro brigades, groups of approximately twenty-five workers who left their place of employment to build apartment blocks consisting of twenty or so apartments in each. These workers continued to earn their salaries, and their coworkers had to commit to assuming responsibility for keeping production levels up. From each micro brigade, several workers were assigned to construct common buildings such as schools, clinics, shops, and cultural centers. When a building was finished, a workplace assembly was held at which the neediest were given new homes, but not necessarily those who had participated in the building. An early example of micro-brigade success was Alamar, a seaside community east of Havana with 130,000 apartments.

4. Especially in the Revolution's early years, many people named their children after Soviet heroes and heroines. I knew a few Lenins, some Vladimirs, and even one Bladimir (with a B).

5. Arnaldo T. Ochoa Sánchez (1930–1989) was a Cuban general who fought at the Bay of Pigs in 1961 and went on to assume leadership roles in Cuban internationalist or advisory efforts in Venezuela, Congo, Angola, Ethiopia, and Nicaragua. In 1984 Fidel Castro awarded him the title of "Hero of the Revolution." In the summer of 1989, Ochoa, Tony de la Guardia, and several other high-ranking military men were charged with crimes including drug smuggling and treason. Their trials were sudden and swift. Four of the defendants, including Ochoa and de la Guardia, were given death sentences, which were carried out on July 13. Although the official version was widely publicized, with sessions from the trials televised to the Cuban people, there are some (myself included) who find the explanation too partial and the punishment too severe. Facts and figures didn't add up. We may never know the whole truth about this shameful page in Cuban revolutionary history.

6. *Cambiar el mundo: Mis años en Cuba* (Cuba: Editorial Matanzas, 2015).

7. Lada is a brand of car manufactured by AvtoVAZ, a Russian company. The rugged model was popular in the Soviet Union and became popular in Cuba beginning in the 1970s. Many of them, battered by their years, are still being driven there.

8. Celia Sánchez Manduley (1920–1980) was a Cuban revolutionary who organized rebel forces in the eastern part of the country and became Fidel Castro's right-hand aide during the insurgency in the mountains. After the war she was an important

presence, especially as a researcher and archivist. For a good biography, see Nancy Stout's *One Day in December: Celia Sánchez and the Cuban Revolution* (New York: Monthly Review Press, 2013).

9. Alfredo Guevara (1925–2013) studied Letters at the University of Havana where he met Fidel Castro and began his revolutionary activism. After the victory of the Revolution, he founded ICAIC, Cuba's Institute of Film Art and Industry. There, for many decades he oversaw the creation of outstanding films and a provided a space for creative openness and diversity.

10. Fidel is credited with the Revolution's principal concepts of justice, Che with an unequaled personal and political integrity, Celia with preserving the memory of the process and creating projects of lasting value, and Haydée and Alfredo with establishing cultural institutions as open and embracing as they are important to the country's cultural life. These were not the only exceptional revolutionaries, of course; honest and innovative people can be found in all walks of life.

11. In May 1980, 125,000 Cubans left the island. A political incident involving the Peruvian embassy led to hundreds taking refuge there, and the Cuban government finally announced that anyone who wanted to leave could. Permission was given for boats to come from Miami to pick up relatives and friends.

12. The attack on Moncada Barracks in Santiago de Cuba on July 26, 1953, was the first engagement of Fidel Castro's revolutionary force with the Batista dictatorship. It was a military failure but political success, giving name to the movement that would prove victorious on January 1, 1959.

13. Among them were Jean-Paul Sartre, Simone de Beauvoir, Gabriel García Márquez, Mario Benedetti, Ernesto Cardenal, José María Arguedas, Violeta Parra, Julio Cortázar, Rodolfo Walsh, Roberto Matta, Laurette Séjourné, Roque Dalton, Idea Vilariño, René Depestre, Angela Davis, Claribel Alegría, Eduardo Galeano, Gioconda Belli, and hundreds of others.

14. Felix Rubén García Sarmiento, known as Rubén Darío (1867–1916), was a poet who initiated the literary movement known as modernism, which became popular in Latin America at the end of the nineteenth century.

15. *Haydée Santamaría, Cuban Revolutionary: She Led by Transgression* (Durham: Duke University Press, 2015).

16. In 2019, just before this book went to press and on the occasion of the Cuban Revolution's sixtieth anniversary, I was awarded Casa de las Américas's Haydée Santamaría Medal. It is among my most treasured possessions.

17. Juan Velasco Alvarado (1910–1977) was president of Peru from 1968 until 1975. Formerly a commander-in-chief of the Army, Velasco came to power in a bloodless coup against President Fernando Belaúnde Terry. His revolutionary military government was unique among modern Latin American military regimes for its reformist and popular character. It was responsible for sweeping changes in Peruvian society. The government limited US economic influence; nationalized utilities, transportation, and communications; and converted millions of acres of privately owned farms into worker-managed cooperatives. It also made Quechua an official national language.

18. Ricardo Morales Avilés, a member of the national leadership of the FSLN, was assassinated by Somoza's National Guard on September 17, 1973.

19. *Somos millones* (Mexico City: Extemporáneos, S.A., 1976). A later English edition is *Inside the Nicaraguan Revolution: The Story of Doris Tijerino* (Vancouver: New Star Books, 1978).

20. In April 2018 massive protests against the Ortega/Murillo regime began to spread across Nicaragua. Repression has been ferocious, and several hundred civilians have been killed, imprisoned, or forced to leave the country. The struggle continues, and some authentic Sandinistas refer to the revolutions of 1979 and 2018.

21. The other judges were Ernesto Cardenal, Cintio Vitier, and Washington Delgado. We awarded the prize to Uruguayan Carlos María Gutiérrez for his splendid book *Diario del cuartel*. Later I translated that book into English, but it never found a publisher. The manuscript has been lost.

22. The Venezuelan MIR was an armed-struggle group inspired, like so many others in Latin America, by the Cuban Revolution, in this case by Fidel Castro's 1959 trip to Caracas. It was primarily active from 1961 to 1962 and had been defeated by the middle of that decade.

23. The Chilean MIR was an armed-struggle political organization founded in 1965. At its height in 1973, it numbered about ten thousand members. Miguel Enríquez was its general secretary from 1967 until his assassination by the country's repressive forces in 1974. The MIR was not a part of the popular front that took power in 1970 but supported its goals.

24. *Exporting Revolution: Cuba's Global Solidarity* (Durham: Duke University Press, 2017).

25. Padilla entered a poetry collection titled *Fuera del juego* (Outside the Game) in an important literary contest. The national and international judging panel awarded it first prize, but Cuba's Union of Writers and Artists (UNEAC), the institution publishing the book, did so with a disclaimer. Padilla was also accused of maintaining negative relationships with foreign journalists and giving them erroneous ideas about the Revolution.

26. *To Change the World*, 171–190.

27. During the writing of this narrative, I asked both Víctor and Arturo if they could provide a more detailed account of that warning they'd been given when they were at the university. Neither of them could. But Arturo told me that allusions to my person, or to the influence of foreigners in general, took place on several occasions—at the University in Havana and later in Matanzas, where he moved after graduation. Cuba's retrograde minds of the era also tried to dissuade him from friendships with homosexuals or those perceived as such. Arturo vehemently defended his independence and suffered no lasting consequences.

CHAPTER EIGHT VOLCANO

1. When she ran for president in 1990, Violeta Barrios de Chamorro (1929–) wore pale blue and white, the colors of the Virgin, throughout her candidacy. This identified her with the deepest feelings of the electorate. She was president from 1990 through 1996.

2. Carlos Mejía Godoy (1942–) is a much beloved Nicaraguan singer/songwriter. In addition to the *Misa Campesina,* he wrote "Nicaragua, Nicaraguita," a beautiful song that has become something of an anthem for the FSLN. Carlos's younger brother, Luis Enrique, is also a well-known musician.

3. This book eventually became my best seller, with editions in Spanish (Mexico, Venezuela, and the Dominican Republic), English, Portuguese, Dutch, Bulgarian, Turkish, and other languages (some of them legitimate, others pirated). The English edition was first published by New Star Books in Vancouver and later picked up by Rutgers University Press. Over the years hundreds of readers have told me that reading it encouraged them to go to Nicaragua to see for themselves a revolution that the US press routinely ignored or about which it lied.

4. The speed rating of film. It may be called ASA or ISO, and describes how quickly the film reacts to light.

5. The second twentieth-century Latin American revolution was actually in Chile, when Salvador Allende took power in 1970. It had been achieved through the electoral process, though, and was destroyed by Augusto Pinochet's bloody coup three years later. When the Sandinistas came to power, the Latin American left welcomed a second "free territory."

6. *Testimonios* (San José, Costa Rica: Alforja Centro de Estudios de Participación Popular, 1983). The English-language edition of this pamphlet was also called *Testimonios.* It was published by the Participatory Research Group of Toronto in Canada in 1985.

7. Ana Herrera had been a close friend during my last years in Cuba. She was a Uruguayan political refugee who worked for the news agency Prensa Latina. Ana was the first Latin American feminist I knew, and brilliant in her thinking. Soon after they left Cuba, she and her husband had a child, and soon after that suffered a serious automobile accident. Ana was holding her baby on her lap and automatically bent over the infant to protect it. Her husband and child were unhurt, but she lived out the rest of her days in a vegetative state. In Nicaragua I wrote under her name in tribute.

8. *Carlos, the Dawn Is No Longer beyond Our Reach* (Vancouver: New Star Books, 1984).

9. Puntos de Encuentro is one of a number of Nicaraguan organizations and institutions that emerged out of the Sandinista movement. It has outlived the Revolution and remains among its most impressive products. It describes itself as "non-governmental and non-profit, integrated by a multicultural and multidisciplinary collective of women and men who want to contribute to their country's development by promoting the social autonomy, participation, equality and decision-making of women and young people in all areas of life." The organization was founded in the late 1980s and became a legal entity in 1991. Among its many successful initiatives have been a couple of weekly TV sitcoms that present complex social issues and have attracted immense audiences.

10. The Iran-Contra affair, or Contragate, was a US political scandal that took place during Ronald Reagan's second term. Senior administration officials secretly facilitated the sale of arms to Iran, hoping to fund the Contras in Nicaragua while at the same time negotiating the release of several US hostages being held in Lebanon

by Hezbollah. In 1985, when it was revealed that Lieutenant Colonel Oliver North of the National Security Council had diverted a portion of the proceeds from the Iranian weapon sales to fund the anti-Sandinista fighters known as the Contras, the plan was exposed, but continued undercover.

11. *Sandino's Daughters Revisited* was published first in English by Rutgers University Press in 1994. A Spanish-language edition eventually came out in Nicaragua, but it was plagued by so many typographical errors I didn't consider it worth recommending. That edition, though, had an impact among the women I'd interviewed for it; having their stories appear in Spanish was meaningful to their families and friends.

12. In February 2019, as an ailing Ernesto lay in a hospital bed, he received news that Pope Francis had reinstated his right to say mass and all other priestly duties, thus reversing the wrong committed against him so many years before by Pope John Paul II.

13. See *Christians in the Nicaraguan Revolution* (Vancouver: New Star Books, 1983). This title also had a Nicaraguan edition published by Editorial Nueva in 1984 and a Venezuelan edition published by Editorial Poseidon in the same year. *Risking a Somersault in the Air: Conversations with Nicaraguan Writers* was published in 1984 by Solidarity Publications in San Francisco. When Solidarity Publications folded, the title was reissued by Curbstone Press in Willimantic, Connecticut.

CHAPTER NINE HOME

1. Born in 1943, Kathy Boudin joined the Weather Underground in the 1970s and was involved in the failed robbery of a Brinks truck in 1981. Although she did not herself have a gun, two Nyack, New York, policemen and a state officer were killed in the attack. Boudin received a sentence of twenty years to life. While in prison she worked on behalf of incarcerated mothers and their children, developed an HIV/AIDS program, promoted adult education, and obtained a master's degree. Surprisingly, and despite opposition from the New York Police Association, at her third parole hearing in 2003 she was released from prison. She went on to earn a doctorate and is currently an adjunct professor of social work at Columbia University in New York, where she has established a program for prison reform.

2. Readers can find a detailed history of my case in *Coming Home: Peace without Complacency* (Albuquerque, NM: West End Press, 1990). I later expanded that small book into a longer piece included in *Walking to the Edge: Essays of Resistance* (Boston: South End Press, 1991).

3. Colter (1869–1958) was an American architect and designer, largely self-taught, who became the chief architect for Fred Harvey, who ran the hotel and restaurant concessions along the railway lines that opened the western United States to tourism. She designed many of the buildings on Grand Canyon's south rim, and others at important depots. I have long been inspired by her life and work.

4. *The Poetry of the Americas: From Good Neighbors to Countercultures* (Oxford: Oxford University Press, 2017), 2.

5. *Che on My Mind* (2013); *Haydée Santamaría, Cuban Revolutionary: She Led by Transgression* (2015); *Only the Road / Solo el Camino* (2016); and *Exporting Revolution: Cuba's Global Solidarity* (2017). *Che on My Mind*, interestingly enough, has had Indian (Bengali) and Turkish editions. My book about Haydée will be published in Cuba in 2019.

6. *When Rains Become Floods* by Lurgio Gavilán Sánchez (2015) and *You Can Cross the Masacre on Foot* by Freddy Prestol Castillo (2019).

7. *La Comandante Maya: Rita Valdivia* (2017).

8. *Lo que les dijo el licántropo / What the Werewolf Told Them* by Chely Lima (2017); *To Have Been There Then: My Life in Cuba* by Gregory Randall (2017); *Viaje de regreso / Return Trip* by Israel Domínguez (2018); and *Kawsay* by María Vázquez Valdez (2018).

9. *Trillos precipicios concurrencias / Pathways Precipices Spectators* by Alfredo Zaldívar (2017); *Diapositivas / Transparencies* by Laura Ruiz Montes (2017); *Contemplación vs. acto / Contemplation vs. Act* by Yanira Marimón (2018); and *Otros campos de belleza armada / Other Fields of Armed Beauty* by Reynaldo García Blanco (2018).

10. These titles include *Their Backs to the Sea* (2009); *My Town* (2010); *The Rhizome as a Field of Broken Bones* (2013); *About Little Charlie Lindbergh and Other Poems* (2014); *She Becomes Time* (2016); *The Morning After: Poetry and Prose in a Post-Truth World* (2017); and *Against Atrocity* (2019).

11. *Kawsay: Flame of the Jungle / Kawsay: llama de la selva* (Brooklyn, NY: Operating System, 2018).

INDEX

class: and art in New York, 79, 82; the
author's background and, 9–15, 19, 23,
27–28, 39, 46–48, 73; in Cuba, 185–86,
194; gender and sexuality and, 48–50, 63,
115, 136, 275; in Mexico, 139–41, 149–51,
172; and revolution, 186, 225, 239. *See also*
gender; racism; sexism; sexuality
Clay, Cassius, 130
Clinton, Bill, 260
A Clockwork Orange (film), 249
The Closing of the American Mind (Bloom),
259
Codina, Norberto, 213
Coe, Michael, 291
Coffeen Serpas, Carlos, 126
Cohen, Robert, 135, 141–42, 168–69,
176–77, 182, 186, 206, 246, 272
COINTELPRO, 75
Cole, David, 254
Coleman, Ornette, 85–86
colonialism. *See* imperialism
Colter, Mary Elizabeth Jane, 272, 313n3
Committee for the Defense of the Revolu-
tion (CDR), 186–87, 193
Communism, 75, 107, 201, 256–61, 305n1.
See also anti-Communism; Cuba; Marx-
ism; socialism
Communist Party, Cuba, 183–92, 209, 214,
241–42
Communist Party, Spanish, 106
Communist Party, US, 6, 22, 98, 305n2
concentration camps, 24, 42, 305n1. *See also*
Holocaust
Constitution, Cuban, 191
Constitution, Nicaraguan, 242
consumerism, 41, 87, 153, 249, 252, 261.
See also capitalism
Contragate scandal, 241, 312n10. *See also*
Nicaragua
Contra war, 2, 218, 228, 238, 245–48, 312n10.
See also Nicaragua
Cormorán y Delfín (magazine), 161
"Corner of Latin America" (Randall),
118–19
El Corno Emplumado (documentary),
158–60

El Corno Emplumado, The Plumed Horn
(Davison), 159
El Corno Emplumado/The Plumed Horn
(magazine), 113, 127–44, 151–68, 171, 206,
257, 284, 287, 308n7
Corrales, Raul, 210
Corrington, John William, 131
Corrington, Leonora, 122
Cortázar, Julio, 129, 213, 228
Cortés, Hernan, 164
Cortés, Martín, 164
Countess of Pareda, 165–66
Crane, Hart, 92
Crawford, John, 286
Creeley, Robert, 102, 129
Cuando la justicia se sentía en casa
(Randall), 289
Cuba: author's move to, 170–80; author's
time in, 181–214; blockade of, 153, 161,
187–89; comparisons between the revo-
lutions of Nicaragua and, 223–26, 229,
238–43; early influence on the author
of, 104, 107; exchange between Mexico
and, 133, 141–44, 149, 153, 161–63; gender
and sexuality and, 184, 187–88, 196, 211,
239, 311n27; immigration away from, 195,
310n11; revolution of, 104, 181–203, 208–
14, 309n8, 309nn2–5, 310n10, 310n12
El Cuento (magazine), 152
Cuevas, José Luis, 153
Cunningham, Myrna, 238

Dalton, Roque, 136, 142–43, 205–6, 213–14,
286, 291
Darío, Rubén, 143, 226, 257, 310n14
Dash, Robert, 89
Daughter of Earth (Smedley), 290
Davidson, Aaron, 7
Davidson, DeWitt A., 13–19, 59–61, 73, 116,
261–62
Davidson, DeWitt S., 16–18
Davidson, Harry, 21
Dávila, Amparo, 292
Davison, Alan R., 159
Day, Dorothy, 87
de Allende, Hortensia, 256

Freinet, Celestino, 149
Freud, Sigmund, 48, 68
"Friday Night at the Community Center" (Randall), 51–52
Friedman, Jane, 285
Fromm, Erich, 120
FSLN. *See* Nicaragua; Sandinista National Liberation Front (FSLN)
Fuentes, Carlos, 256
Fuera del juego (Padilla), 311n25
The Fugs, 285
The Function of the Orgasm (Reich), 87

Gabeira, Fernando, 205
Gadea, Hilda, 137, 201
Galeano, Eduardo, 213, 256
García Sarmiento, Felix Rubén. *See* Darío, Rubén
Garver, Alice, 253
gay rights movement: Cuba and the, 191, 211, 311n27; Nicaragua and the, 203, 239, 242; in the US, 74, 77, 272, 306n1. *See also* sexuality
Gelman, Juan, 213, 291
gender: abortion and, 95–97, 307nn11–12; the author's early experiences of, 2–3, 12, 15, 23, 29–31, 38–39; the author's high school years and, 41–43, 47–50, 53–58; and the author's time in Mexico, 125, 134–36, 140–41, 151–53, 166; and the author's time in New York, 77, 84–85, 89, 93, 98–99, 104–5, 306n5; blacklisting and, 43, 305n2; and the Cuban Revolution, 184, 187–88, 196, 242; Mexican history and, 164–66; and the Nicaraguan Revolution, 223–24, 231–44; US immigration policy and, 257, 261; in the US today, 3, 294, 306n3. *See also* class; racism; sexism; sexual abuse; sexuality
genocide, 32, 76, 120, 189–90
Gerhardt, Rainer, 129
Giant of Tears (Randall), 307n13
Gil, Silvia, 162, 193
Gilbert, Ronnie, 256
Ginsberg, Allen, 72–73, 101, 117, 132, 143, 154, 228, 283–85, 291, 308n7

Giugni, Alfred, 255
Glantz, Jacob, 93
Gleeson, Matt, 163–64
"The Gloves" (Randall), 107–8
God's Bankers (Posner), 291
Goldman, Herbie, 70f
Goldman, Jane, 70f
Golub, Leon, 88
González, Guadalupe, 257–59
Goodman, Paul, 87
Gorky, Arshile, 86, 91–92
The Gorky Poems (Rothenberg), 134, 160
Gorostiza, José, 129, 171
Goulart, João, 107
Goytisolo, José Agustín, 163
Grandal, Ramón Martínez, 209–11, 221, 224
Granera, Aminta, 242
Grass, Günter, 228
"The Green Clothes Hamper" (Randall), 59–60
Greene, Graham, 228
El grillo de papel (magazine), 162
Grinberg, Miguel, 142
Grooms, Red, 102
Guatemala, 77
Guernica (Picasso), 106
Guerra, Diego, 288
Guevara, Alfredo, 194, 310nn9–10
Guevara, Che, 137, 141, 153–54, 192–95, 290, 310n10
Guido, Lea, 223, 242
Guillén, Nicolás, 129
Gutiérrez, Carlos María, 136, 311n21
Gutiérrez, Judith, 154
Gwin, Minrose, 291

Hampton, Fred, 75
Harjo, Joy, 291
Hart, Armando, 212
Hartigan, Grace, 85
Hartman, Mary, 244
Harvey, Fred, 313n3
Harvey, Jason, 105
The Hasty Papers (newspaper), 84
Haydée Santamaría medal, 292, 310n16
H.D., 127

Revere, Anne, 305n2
Revista Casa (magazine), 198
Revista de América (magazine), 126
revolution: Cuban, 104, 181–203, 208–14, 309n8, 309nn2–5, 310n10, 310n12; Nicaraguan, 125, 201–3, 218–19, 223–45, 310n18, 312n2, 312n5, 312n9
Rich, Adrienne, 256, 291
Ríos, Soleida, 288
Rivera, Diego, 85
Rodman, Selden, 120
Rodríguez, Rigoberto, 210
Rodríguez, Rolando, 175
Rodríguez Nuñez, Víctor, 213–14, 240, 288–90, 311n27
Rodríguez Prampolini, Ida, 140
Roe v. Wade, 97, 307n11
Roosevelt, Eleanor, 19, 305n2
Roosevelt, Franklin, 24, 219
La rosa blindada (magazine), 162
Rosaldo, Renato, 291
Rosenberg, Ethel, 42–43
Rosenberg, Harold, 86
Rosenberg, Julius, 42–43
Rossi, Matti, 132
Rothenberg, Jerome, 101, 134, 160, 292
Rothko, Mark, 91
Rouault, Georges, 86
Roy Choudhury, Malay, 132
Rugama, Leonel, 136
Ruins (Randall), 289
Ruiz Montes, Laura, 289, 291
Rulfo, Juan, 153
Rushdie, Salman, 228

Sabina, María, 170
"A Sadness of Plywood" (Randall), 43–45
Sánchez, Celia, 194, 310n10
Sanchez, Sonia, 256
Sánchez Manduley, Celia, 309n8
Sanders, Joop, 109
Sandinista National Liberation Front (FSLN), 125, 201–3, 218–19, 223–45, 310n18, 312n2, 312n5, 312n9. *See also* Nicaragua
Sandino, Agusto César, 226

Sandino's Daughters (Randall), 221, 240, 243, 289, 312n3
Sandino's Daughters Revisited (Randall), 240, 243, 289, 313n11
Sanger family, 14–15
Santamaría, Haydée, 143, 194–98, 310n10
Santiago (magazine), 152
Sawyer, Diane, 279
Schleifer, Abdallah, 104
Schleifer, Marc, 104
Schlesinger, Arthur, Jr., 103
Schröder, Gustav, 42
Schweitzer, Robert, 3, 158–59
Science and Health with Key to the Scriptures (Eddy), 17
segregation, 23, 61, 142, 208–9. *See also* racism
Séjourne, Laurette, 120–21, 129, 140, 144, 148, 153, 169, 175, 213
Selby, Hubert, Jr., 111
Selected Poems (Randall), 83, 108–9, 289
Sender, Ramón, 62
Serge, Victor, 121
Serrano, Nina, 169
sexism: abortion and, 95–97, 307n12; art and New York and, 85, 89, 93, 98–100; author's family background and, 3, 15, 23, 31, 39–43; author's high school years and, 41–43, 47–50, 53–54, 58; author's return to the US and, 257, 261; author's second marriage and, 140–41; Cuban revolution and, 184, 187–88; domesticity and, 41, 77, 89, 115; Hollywood blacklists and, 43, 305n2; Mexican mythology and, 165–66; Nicaraguan revolution and, 231–38, 242–44; in present day, 294, 306n3, 307n12; writing and, 125, 135–36, 151–53. *See also* class; gender; patriarchy; racism
sexual abuse: of the author, 2, 16–17, 49–50, 54, 58–60, 73, 261–62, 307n8; author's high school years and, 48–50; author's years in New York and, 100, 104; by the Catholic Church, 194; within the Nicaraguan revolution, 205, 230, 234–35; rape and, 42, 50, 100, 194, 234–35; US politics and, 50, 305n1, 306n4. *See also* gender

sexuality: author's family background and, 11–12, 17–18, 23–24; author's introduction to sex and, 27–28, 39–40, 49, 53–56; author's later years and her, 262–64; author's time in Mexico and, 135–36; author's time in New York and, 99, 104–5; Cuba and, 191, 211, 311n27; Nazism and, 305n1; Nicaragua and, 203, 231, 239, 242; poetry and, 73, 228; US policy and, 256, 265. *See also* class; gay rights movement; gender; racism

The Sexual Revolution (Reich), 87

Shalako, Zuni, 74

The Shape of Red (Hubbard, Randall), 116, 286

"She Becomes Time" (Randall), 269

Sherman, Susan, 161–62, 256, 291

The Shining (film), 249

Siegel, Eli, 87

Siegel, Rita, 4, 175

Siglo XXI (publishing company), 149, 166, 286

Signos (magazine), 152

Silva Ibargüen, Gabriela, 284

single motherhood, 93–95, 103, 115

Siqueiros, David Alfaro, 126, 134

the sixties, 2, 74–77, 160

The Sixties (magazine), 152

Smedley, Agnes, 290–91

Smith, David, 106

Smith, Greg, 4

Smith, Tommie, 142

Snyder, Gary, 131

"So and So Paints a Picture" (de Kooning), 83

socialism, 66, 184, 187–89, 201, 237–39, 256, 305n1. *See also* Communism; Marxism

Sol cuello cortado (magazine), 161

Somoza García, Anastasio, 202, 219–21, 229, 310n18

Soriano, Juan, 153

Sor Juana Inés de la Cruz, 165–66

Sosa, Mercedes, 228

Spain, 64–66, 103, 106

Spanish Civil War, 120

Spanish Refugee Aid (SRA), 103–7, 116

Spender, Stephen, 103

Spiegel, Martin, 257–58

Sputnik, 49

Squirru, Rafael, 144

Stalin, Joseph, 107

Stavenhagen, Kurt, 122

Stavenhagen, Ruth, 122

Stones Witness (Randall), 289

Stonewall riots, 77, 306n1. *See also* gay rights movement

Stuart, Michelle, 90

Styron, William, 256

Suárez, Jacinto, 203

Sueños y realidades de un guajiricantor (Randall), 308n9

Sugarman, George, 101

Tajiri, Shinkichi, 135

Tamayo, Rufino, 154

Tattersfield, Regina, 284

Taus, Roger, 133

Taylor, Alex "Sandy," 286

Taylor, Elizabeth, 84, 305n2

Taylor, Steven, 285

Techo de la Ballena (group), 143

El techo de la ballena (magazine), 152, 161

Tejada, Roberto, 285

Téllez, Dora María, 223–24, 240–42

Templeton, Rini, 133

"Texto, contexto e índices de *El Corno Emplumado* (1962–1969)" (Silva Ibargüen), 284

Thelonius Monk, 85

This Is about Incest (Randall), 59, 286

Thomas, Clarence, 306n4

Thomas, John, 86

Thornburgh, Richard, 257

Tijerino, Doris, 201–2, 242

Time's Language (Randall), 83, 108–9, 288

The Tin Drum (Grass), 228

Tlatelolco massacre, 141, 158, 171. *See also* Mexican Student Movement

To Change the World (Randall), 289

Todas estamos despiertas (Randall), 308n9

El topo con gafas (magazine), 161

Topor (artist), 132
Toro, Sandra, 290
transgender people, 188, 239. *See also* gender
"Translation After All" (Randall), 287
Trinity College, 6, 257
Trobar (magazine), 84
Trojan (magazine), 152
Tropic of Cancer (Miller), 308n7
Truman, Harry, 24, 256
Trump, Donald, 75–76, 187, 261, 293–94, 305n1
26th of July Movement, 188

Uhthoff, Maru, 150, 173–75
United Nations, 200–201, 309n1
University of New Mexico (UNM), 60–61, 249–50, 292, 306n6
Urondo, Paco, 136
"Uxmal" (Randall), 147–48

Vacca, Fred W., 259
Valdivia, Rita, 286
Valero Molina, Elizabeth, 289
Valle, Francisco, 125
Vallejo, César, 127–29, 206, 291
Vallejo, René, 175
Vanni, Alba, 201
Varese, Stefano, 201
Vargas, Milú, 240–42
Vargas, Roberto, 228
variable foot, 102, 307n14
Vázquez Valdez, María, 128, 289–90
V'Cella, Carl, 49
Velasco Alvarado, Juan, 200, 310n17
Venezuelan Movement of the Revolutionary Left (MIR), 206–8, 311n22
Vicente, Esteban, 90
Vicuña, Cecilia, 160, 163
Vietnam war, 2, 74, 77, 98, 130, 134, 199–200, 257–58
Vigía, 289
Virgin Mary, 306n5, 311n1
Vitier, Cintio, 311n21
Voice of Vietnam (radio show), 199
Vonnegut, Kurt, 256

Wald, George, 256
Waldman, Anne, 283–84, 291
Walker, Alice, 256
Walker, William, 219
Wallach, Eli, 100
Ward, Bill, 102
Ward, Nancy, 85
Weather Underground, 77, 313n1
Wheelock, Jaime, 203, 240
When I Look into the Mirror and See You (Randall), 289
When Justice Felt at Home (Randall), 289
"When Justice Felt at Home" (Randall), 215–16
"Where They Left You For Dead" (Randall), 268
whiteness, 115–16, 150–51. *See also* racism
Whitman, Walt, 127
Willentz, Eli, 92
Willentz, Ted, 92
Williams, Flossie, 102
Williams, Tennessee, 100, 127
Williams, William Carlos, 102, 129, 160, 291, 307n14
Wilson, Dorothea, 238
Wings Press, 288
"With Gratitude to Vallejo" (Randall), 180
"Without Warning" (Randall), 70–71
Wobblies, 22
Wolin, Harvey, 125–27, 135
women's rights movement, 3, 151, 165–66, 223–26, 238–39, 242. *See also* feminism; gender; sexism
World War II, 24, 32–35, 41–42, 120, 305n1. *See also* Holocaust

"Yaqui Deer" (Brigham), 138
Yevtushenko, Yevgeny, 228

Zacharias, Anthe, 80, 91
Zalaquett, Gladys, 203
Zaldívar, Alfredo, 289
Zamora, Bladimir, 207f, 213
Zamora, Daisy, 136, 221, 242, 285
Zinn, Howard, 256
Zukofsky, Louis, 129